Oregon Coast

Oregon Coast

a Family Travel Adventure

David Bushnell

ABOOKS
Alive Book Publishing

Oregon Coast
A Family Travel Adventure
Copyright © 2025 by David Bushnell
Photography by David Bushnell

Additional copies may be ordered from the publisher for
educational, business, promotional or premium use.
For information, contact ALIVE Book Publishing at:
alivebookpublishing.com or call (925) 837-7303.

Book Design by Alex Johnson

ISBN 13
978-1-63132-246-4 Deluxe Color Paperback
978-1-63132-253-2 Standard Paperback

Library of Congress Control Number: 2024925123

Library of Congress Cataloging-in-Publication Data
is available upon request.

First Edition

Published in the United States of America by
ALIVE Book Publishing
an imprint of Advanced Publishing LLC
3200 A Danville Blvd., Suite 204, Alamo, California 94507
alivebookpublishing.com

PRINTED IN THE UNITED STATES OF AMERICA

10 9 8 7 6 5 4 3 2 1

For Linda, my Wife, Friend,
and Travel Companion

Acknowledgements

The author gratefully acknowledges the essential technical help provided by my son Brian, keeping my computer working, updated, and free of viruses during the writing of this book. Kudos to Alex Johnson, the Art Director at Alive Book Publishing for taking my dozens of disparate articles, rest stops, and photographs and creating a book. Also important, as well as enjoyable, has been the friendly support, always delivered with helpful literary criticism, by his friends with the Wesley Writers group at United Methodist Church, Alamo, California.

Table of Contents

Crissey Field State Park and Visitors Center: Rest Stop, beach hike, stroll
Oregon Redwood Trail: Side Trip, woodland hike, stroll
Future Marine Biologist: Tide Pools
Brookings Azalea Park: Rest stop, playground, stroll
Loeb State Park: Side trip, rest stop, woodland hike, stroll, Gardener Ridge: Side trip
Chetco River Harbor: Rest stop, beach hike, stroll, restaurants
Easter Lilies
Harris Beach State Park: Rest stop, beach hike, stroll
Future Geologist: Rainbow Rock
Lone Ranch Beach: Rest Stop, beach hike, stroll
Thomas Creek Bridge: Rest stop, scenic viewpoint
Arch Rock Viewpoint: Rest stop, woodland hike, stroll

Gold Beach
Gold Beach Waterfront: Rest stop, stroll, restaurants

Chapter 14 - Depoe Bay, World's Smallest Harbor   255

Introduction

Growing up in a rural part of the southern Oregon Coast in the 1950s, I was accustomed to beautiful unspoiled beaches and tide pools, creeks and rivers full of fish, and great unspoiled expanses of the Pacific Northwest rainforest. Only after traveling and working as an earth scientist in many parts of the world did I come to understand what a unique and wonderful natural environment it was. Few children were so lucky. Coming back to the Oregon Coast after more than half a century, I can see that it has changed only a little. The towns have grown, but not a lot; much of the rainforest has been logged, but new forests are being grown to replace them as they should be; and perhaps there aren't quite so many salmon and steelhead in the rivers. But the coast is just as beautiful as it ever was, and even more accessible with new roads, scenic viewpoints, and parks. I found myself able to love it again just as I did in my youth.

Now retired, I have found the time to study the Oregon Coast in its many aspects, and have come to appreciate it as a truly marvelous place, well worth its inclusion in lists of the places you must see in your life. I know and appreciate it much better now: it really is a natural science field trip, and the town histories make fascinating stories. I hope this book will help your family to enjoy the great travel adventure that is there waiting for you.

What You Will Find in This Book

A goal of this book is to introduce the readers to the fascinating natural and cultural history of our spectacular Oregon Coast. Many fine books have been written about the coast, each emphasizing a favorite subject or subjects of the authors. I have reviewed many of them for you in the late chapter entitled "Publications". You will find books on hiking, on geology, on the ocean and tide pools, on things to do, on plants and wildlife, and on places to stay and to dine – a book or two on practically anything you might be interested in, and most are readily available.

Town Histories

Because the Oregon Coast is the very last frontier in the lower 48 states, it was settled much later than most of the country, even the state of Oregon, mainly starting in the early 1850s. Many of the towns have fascinating beginnings, and I have included their early histories. Most are located on the estuaries of small to large rivers that influenced their origin and growth, from Brookings on the Chetco in the south to Astoria on the Columbia in the north. No histories about mayors and city elections, but facts about why the town is there, how it got started, what made it prosper, and why it is an interesting place to visit. I found some of the town beginnings quite surprising – even my hometown Brookings.

Explanations of Natural Phenomena

While traveling along the Oregon Coast you will observe a great variety of fascinating landscapes – beaches, seastacks, seacliffs, sand dunes, rivers, lakes, and forests. This book explains how they formed, how they are changing, and their importance in the natural environment.

Side Trips

As much as I enjoy recreation on the Oregon Coast, I must admit that the weather is not always as pleasant as one would like on a vacation trip – cold, foggy, and windy days sometimes happen. At least in the summertime, these conditions are usually restricted to the immediate coastline: a few miles inland, warm summer weather ordinarily prevails. For that reason I have outlined a few side trips that take you just a few miles inland to visit forests, rivers, mountain vistas, and fish hatcheries. The short drives up the rivers and into the mountains can be quite beautiful. Other side trips take you to interesting areas west of Hwy 101, where the highway has had to abandon the coastline for a distance.

Future Scientist Challenges

I would like to entice young visitors to follow in my footsteps as a natural scientist, as I believe this can lead to important and re-warding careers. The first element of science is observation. For the natural sciences, it is the observation of the natural environment we experience: the rivers and estuaries, the seashore, the geology, the plants and wildlife, the climate, the ocean in its many moods, and how they all interact. The Oregon Coast is the ultimate natural sci-ence field trip. Features that might be of interest to a future scientist are explained in some detail; those that might inspire further study or even careers are included with the heading "Future (science dis-cipline)". Natural sciences are also the essence of environmental sci-ence, a field of increasing importance in the United States and across the world.

Rest Stops with Stroller Walks

Another of my objectives has been to outline family-oriented rest stops for the coastal traveler. I have found many rest stops that the whole family can enjoy for a travel break – a stroller-accessible walk, a hike along a beach, a stream, or through a forest, and restroom fa-cilities. The stops are located every ten or twenty miles along the coast highway, from the California border to the Columbia River. As we all know that children have lots of energy to burn off, and perhaps less appreciation of the rugged and beautiful scenery we adults came to see, I have also located a playground with climbing equipment in each of the towns you will pass through.

About restrooms: Some have flush toilets and running water: I call these modern restrooms. Others, where the necessary infrastructure is unavailable, are basically outhouses, sometimes portable, with no running water: I call these primitive restrooms, but I have found them to be clean and well maintained. As there is no running water on site, you need to bring your own: a gallon jug of spring water from the grocery store will be useful to have along. Of course the traditional rest stop of yore is the gas station, but over the years many of these have become snack markets selling gasoline on the side. In my local major oil company service station, I counted more than 500 different sugary snacks and 100 sugary drinks between the front door and the restrooms – which are located, of course, in the rear of the shop. Herding a passel of kids through all of these temptations can be a daunting task which I want to help you to avoid.

You will notice that I locate the rest stops by distance north or south of prominent landmarks, many of them bridges that have signs denoting the river they cross. While there are mileage posts for this purpose, I have found them easy to miss.

Libraries

For days with inclement weather, I have located a library in each of the towns along the way.

Emergency Help

Each town has a hospital or emergency clinic. These are listed with open hours, phone numbers, and addresses.

One More Point

I encourage visitors to travel the Oregon Coast from south to north. The sun will be behind you most of the day, shining on the landscape and sea you came to see. Road glare you encounter while driving southward into the sunlight can be tiring.

A Note of Caution

Of course every vacation trip has its unique dangers, but a trip along the Oregon Coast may have more than most. Here are some to watch for, a few of which I myself have experienced:

Sneaker waves: On the Oregon Coast, one must always be on the watch for unusually large waves while hiking the beach, fishing, examining the tide pools, or enjoying the surf. Small children and pets are especially vulnerable, as they can easily be washed away by a big wave. Please be cautioned that walks along the beach are subject to tides and wave conditions; One should always be cognizant of possible escape routes from sneaker waves if needed. Be aware that collections of driftwood can be mobilized by a large wave and can be especially dangerous.

Stranding: Sneaker waves are not the only beach peril that might befall the unwary traveler. In this book I have suggested beach hikes at many of the rest stops, some of them quite long. Many pose little danger, but the longer hikes may span much of a tidal cycle. This is a coast with strong tides, ranging up to eight feet when the moon is full, and if you aren't watching, they can catch you unawares. If the beach has a 2% slope, or 2 feet per hundred, an average six-foot tide will advance the shoreline by a surprising 300 feet when the tide comes in. Most of the time, a stranded hiker simply has to scramble up a bank through the brush to reach safety. But occasionally the tide traps a hiker, even a whole family, backed up against an unscalable cliff, and help needs to be summoned. Every year, the Coast Guard is called to rescue someone who wasn't careful when starting a beach hike and became trapped along the way by the incoming tide.

So be aware of the rising tide: carry a tide table, available at all fishing tackle stores, or know how to access tide tables on your cell phone: simply key in tide table – closest town – Oregon. Plan your beach hikes accordingly, preferably when the tide is receding, always being watchful for potential escape routes from rising water. Pocket beaches can be particularly hazardous: one may walk around a rocky point to the beach, later finding the return awash with dangerous waves. Just remember, if the sand is wet and smooth, the ocean has been there and it will return.

Seacliffs: Many of the rest stops and scenic stops are located at the tops of dangerous cliffs. Some, but not all, are fenced off. But the fences are usually low split rail constructions that children or pets can easily climb through – the fences serve as warnings, not barriers. In many places, a fall over a seacliff can lead to injury or drowning, and rescue either by land or by sea is extremely difficult as well as long delayed. Visitors should also avoid climbing the cliffs located along the beaches.

Seastacks: Some of the tall seastacks along the Oregon Coast extend onto the beach; Haystack Rock at Cannon Beach is an example. One must not attempt to climb them – not only is it dangerous, but these seastacks are included in the Oregon Islands National Wildlife Refuge and climbing them is prohibited.

Rock jetties: The Army Corp of Engineers has constructed rock jetties to aid navigation at many of the estuaries along the Oregon Coast. They are dangerous to walk on, as there are no pathways atop them. A retreat from dangerous surf or sneaker waves is difficult – each year people are washed into the sea from these jetties and some do not survive. Fishing is just as good where the jetties meet the beach.

Rip Currents: Should you brave the cold water and go for a swim, you need to watch for rip currents that can quickly carry you out to sea. If you get caught in one, swim parallel to shore to get out of the current; they are not usually very wide.

Allergies: At many of the rest stops and side trips, you may find wild berries to eat. Allergies to berries are uncommon but can be serious. If you are susceptible to berry allergies, it is wise to carry appropriate medication.

Lyme Disease: Lyme disease is not common in Oregon but it does occur, particularly in the southwestern counties. It is something to watch out for, so I warn you early. A recent study in northern California found blacklegged ticks in the brush along the coast, and these can carry the disease. The host animals are squirrels and deer; both are occasionally seen in coastal forested or brushy areas. No ticks are found on the beach itself. One should be careful not to brush against the shrubs when walking to the beach, as ticks like to transfer hosts that way.

Clothing

Of course you will want to bring bathing suits and shorts for a summer vacation on the shore, but you might not be tempted to wear them. Blue jeans and a sweat shirt, perhaps a warm windbreaker, work better for most summer days. Even then the daily high temperature at the beach is seldom out of the sixties, and it is frequently windy, foggy, or both. Besides, the ocean is much too cold to enjoy swimming, unlike the coasts of the Atlantic and Gulf of Mexico. Because of oceanic upwelling, the water is even colder in the summer than in the winter – often in the low 50s or colder. Not good for playing in the surf for very long and even then one must always be on the watch for sneaker waves. You may see surfers, but they are all wearing wet suits – and even hoping for extra-large waves! You will find a useful chapter on appropriate clothing to pack in Tom Stienstra's excellent guide *Oregon Camping*.

Park Entry Permits

Park use permits are required for many of the coastal state parks. These can be purchased at the park offices or online at their website: Oregon State Parks day-use parking permit vendors. For the national seashores, permits can be purchased at the entry kiosk.

Free Newspaper Advertisers

Don't pass up the free local advertisers you see displayed in the motels and grocery stores! They were written for you and contain a lot of useful local information. For example, I picked up the *Insider of Southern Oregon,* a 32-page June 2022 issue published in Brookings. It covers the all coastal towns from Crescent City to Bandon, as well as the interior towns of Grants Pass and Cave Junction that you might pass through on the way. In it I found six well-written articles of local interest, along with advertisements for nine festivals, ten music events, three plays, three pubs, and an art show. Of course the paper is advertiser-supported, so there were 77 advertisements of everything else, broadly ranging from real estate to restaurants to radio stations.

Chapter 1

Favorite Strolls

As I traveled the coast northward from Brookings to Astoria, these are my 25 favorite short strolls, all no more than a mile or two in length. So you can locate them easily, I have listed them by the town they are closest to. Each has a stroller-appropriate trail, either hard-surface or packed earth, and restroom facilities located near the trailhead. Those with hard-surface trails are likely suitable for wheelchairs as well. Very young hikers may also enjoy them. In general, earthen trails in the forested areas are likely to have exposed roots, and there may be muddy patches in the wet season. These trails are excellent open-air exercise options for a young family with lessons to learn about the natural world. Each is worthy of inclusion in your trip itinerary. More details on each stroll can be found near the bold-print town descriptions in the following text and have the same underscored trail captions.

   1. California State Line: <u>Oregon Redwood Trail.</u> This ridge-top stroll on a well-maintained earthen trail starts you right out in the Pacific Northwest rainforest in a grove of large second-growth redwoods. Miles from roads, the ocean, and commercial flight paths, on a still day I have found the silence to be absolute. But first visit the Crissey Field Visitor Center as you enter the state.

   2. Brookings: <u>Loeb State Park</u>. This walk is a great rainforest experience, on an earthen trail through an ancient grove of red alder and Oregon myrtle trees along the *Wild and Scenic* Chetco River.

   3. Brookings: <u>Arch Rock</u>. A short hard-surface trail takes you through an ancient Sitka spruce grove shading a carpet of false lily-of-the-valley. Viewpoints introduce you to a cliff-lined coast with fascinating geological and botanical histories.

   4. Gold Beach: <u>Frances Shrader Old Growth Trail.</u> Here you have an earthen trail through a grove of enormous old-growth Douglas-fir and western redcedars. It is an isolated remnant of the Pacific Northwest rainforest that has been logged nearly to oblivion elsewhere along the Oregon Coast.

5. Gold Beach: <u>South Jetty Beach</u>. Just west of town you find a packed-sand trail running for half a mile just behind the beach and driftwood. It is perhaps your best opportunity on the Oregon Coast to drive a stroller along the ocean beach in full view and sound of the ocean.

6. Port Orford: <u>Cape Blanco</u>. A 20-minute hard-surface trail through a coastal meadow to the old lighthouse, nearly 300 feet above the Pacific, with grand views of the coastline to the north and south. Cape Blanco is the westernmost point in the lower forty-eight states, and as such it is famously windy. But there is also a longer and more protected stroll through the densely forested campground nearby on paved access roads. And lots of wild berries.

7. Bandon: <u>Oregon Islands National Wildlife Refuge</u>. A quarter mile of hard-surface trails traverse a coastal meadow perched a hundred feet above a sandy beach and close-to-shore seastacks with many seabirds.

8. Bandon: <u>Bullards Beach State Park</u>. A one-mile hard-surface trail runs through shore pine groves with huckleberry bushes and coastal meadows with wild strawberries. Most days it will be largely protected from the wind.

9. Coos Bay/Charleston: <u>South Slough National Estuarine Research Reserve</u>. A featured ten-minute walk on an earthen trail leads through a dense second-growth forest with abundant berry bushes of many varieties – something to pick all summer long. The visitor center is a worthy attraction in itself.

10. Winchester Bay: <u>Umpqua Lighthouse State Park</u>. A one-mile walk on an earthen trail takes you around Lake Marie, completely surrounded by a dense mixed forest of Sitka spruce, western hemlock, Douglas-fir, western redcedar, and shore pine. Undergrowth includes sword fern, deer fern, bracken, false lily-of-the-valley, and in marshy areas, expanses of skunk cabbage and horsetails.

11. Reedsport: Tugman State Park. A mile and a half one-way, earthen-trail walk through a 60-year old, second-growth rainforest above the shore of Eel Lake, with berry-bush and fern undergrowth.

12. Florence: Jesse M. Honeyman State Park. This park is one of the jewels of the Oregon state park system. The day use area has picnic tables, canoe and paddle boat rentals, sand dune access, modern restrooms, and a beach for swimming on tiny Cleawox Lake – but don't expect the water to be very warm. For strolling, take advantage of the extensive asphalt access road system winding through the forested day-use area and campground.

13. Florence: Darlingtonia State Natural Site. Only a short walk, but worth doing for the unusual botanical experience. This tiny park is dedicated to the protection of *Darlingtonia californica,* a pitcher plant commonly called "cobra lily" because of its strange hooded appearance. There is a boardwalk through a dense forest to a small fen crowded with these odd plants. Cobra lilies are not known to occur anywhere else along the Oregon Coast, as they generally prefer higher elevations.

14. Waldport: Heceta Head Lighthouse State Scenic Viewpoint. Heceta Head is one of the scenic stars along the Oregon Coast, featuring a lighthouse, a pocket beach, seacliffs, seastacks where seabirds are nesting, and a small river and estuary where steelhead run in the winter. A quarter-mile asphalt trail climbs 150 feet to the base of the lighthouse, recommended for a fine view and to watch for migrating whales in the spring and fall, perched as it is directly above relatively deep water. For those that prefer not to climb to the lighthouse, there is a 500ft paved trail along the beach side of the main parking lot with a view of the lighthouse, beach, ocean, and seastacks. Not to be missed is the close-up view of the unique Roman aqueduct-style Cape Creek Bridge.

15. Yachats: The earthen Giant Spruce Trail starts at the Cape Perpetua Visitors' Center and runs for more than a mile through the densely forested canyon of another Cape Creek – a true rainforest experience. The upper story of the forest is dominated by unusually tall red alders and Sitka spruce, sheltering a varied mid-story that includes salmonberry, thimbleberry, huckleberry, salal, red elderberry, and a variety of ferns.

16. Yachats: <u>Yachats State Recreation Area</u>. The "804" paved trail runs for 0.7 miles in a coastal meadow along the edge of the marine terrace, where it is isolated from highway traffic. The trail looks down on a long rocky shore with small pocket beaches with tide pools visible at low tide.

17. Newport: <u>South Beach State Park</u>. Here a hard-surface trail leads you a mile through meadows and open scrub conifer forest from the day-use parking lot to the south jetty of Yaquina Bay. There are huckleberry and salal berry bushes all along the way. At the south jetty you are likely to see commercial, recreational, and even research boat traffic. Yaquina Bay is a busy harbor, home to a NOAA fleet, a Coast Guard station, and Oregon State University ship operations.

18. Nehalem: <u>Nehalem Bay National Wildlife Refuge</u>. A hard-surface trail climbs gently 0.6 miles through a pristine meadow with an amazing assortment of wildflowers, to a viewing platform. On a June day, I counted 26 varieties of wildflowers, including expanses of blue lupines. Along the access road there is another viewing platform above a large marsh that attracts large numbers of Canada geese during their spring and fall migrations.

19. Netarts: <u>Cape Meares Lighthouse</u>. Not a long trail, but an interesting one. The paved 1800 foot loop trail from the parking lot takes you to an observation deck on the bluff just above the lighthouse, where you are on the same level as the huge, red-and-clear Fresnel lens only fifty feet away. There are close-up views of seabirds nesting on the vertical basalt cliffs of the cape, and information posters guiding you to the species you can see. There are longer earthen trails in the campground in the evergreen forest just to the east.

20. Rockaway: <u>Rockaway Cedar Tree</u>. A 1.2 mile boardwalk through a marshy rainforest to a truly giant western red-cedar, estimated to be between 500 and 900 years old. Skunk cabbages bloom along the way.

21. Cannon Beach: <u>Oswald West State Park</u>. A network of earthen trails wind through a magnificent old-growth forest, along a rushing stream, and down to Short Sand Beach. Huge western hemlocks, western redcedars, and Sitka spruce line the paths. This path is a little steeper but kept in good condition.

22. Seaside: <u>Cullaby Lake Wetlands Interpretive Trail</u>. A hard-surface trail running for a mile and a half through a fen, with viewing platforms, benches, and interpretive panels. You may see a beaver working there. In season you will find lots of edible berries along the trail – huckleberry, salmon berry, wild blackberry, and a few canes of evergreen blackberry.

23. Seaside: <u>Seaside Promenade</u>. This stroll is the famous mile-and-a-half walkway separating the hotels of Seaside from the broad beach and vegetated dunes. People-watching is the main activity here, not wilderness or wildlife. Along the promenade there are restaurants and a small aquarium featuring local marine life.

24. Warrenton: <u>Fort Stevens State Park</u>. A fine 2.2-mile earthen strolling trail runs all the way around Coffenbury Lake. You will find it quite secluded; most of the visitors stay around the meadow by the parking lot and dock. This is the best strolling trail in the park, staying just above the lake in a conifer forest most of the way. Other trails in the park tend to be too sandy for sidewalk strollers, but you might try them.

25. Astoria: <u>Astoria Riverwalk</u>. A railroad separates the Columbia River from the town, and a popular five-mile paved trail has been built alongside. For the full length you will have a view across the estuary to the Washington shore.

Conde McCullough Bridges: The magnificent Oregon Coast bridges, designed and built in the 1930s by Conde B. McCullough, have roadways 27 feet wide that include 3.5 foot walkways on either side. They can be accessed at either end, often from a small parking lot. Usually there are no restroom facilities. On sunny days when the wind is calm, the bridges offer interesting possibilities for strolls with magnificent views of the harbors, the towns, and out to sea - panoramas that are difficult to appreciate from a speeding car, especially if you are the driver. One doesn't need to go all the way across; some are quite long: part way out and back might suffice. Usually the more interesting highest part of the span is close to one end. Of course there is always car and truck traffic on the bridges, which you may find annoying. The bridge walkways are included as components of the Oregon Coast Trail, as there are no other options for crossing the broad estuaries. Watch for the warning lights, as a couple of them are drawbridges.

Chapter 2

A Birder's Paradise

Serious birders may want to skip this paragraph and go on to the sections below. For the rest of us casual birdwatchers, here are a few pointers I have picked up as a natural scientist working in the out of doors. First, the early bird really does get the worm. Particularly in farm and woodland settings, you will see more birds in the early morning out looking for breakfast than you will find in the fading evening light as they are looking for perches for the night. In addition, the males of the species often sing to re-establish their territories just around sunup, and you may be able to recognize them by their songs. So hit the trail before breakfast if you can, while you are fresh and the birds are actively singing and feeding. As an added bonus, you may spot mammals like rabbits and deer that are often most active around sunup. Second, you will see more bird species some distance away from the parking lot, as most really dislike our motorized civilization and will strive to avoid it. A quarter of a mile is usually enough. There you should be totally immersed in nature, not sharing the natural environment with the sounds, sights, and smells of civilization. Sea gulls and crows may frequent parking lots, but you can see them anywhere. Finally, you can let the birds come to you, especially in heavily vegetated areas where many of the birds are small, move very quickly when disturbed, or live high in the canopy. Find a comfortable log to sit on, ideally next to an open glade with a variety of broad-leaf or annual vegetation, pull out your binoculars, and wait a while. Motionless. The birds will be around and may come quite close to you. They have little fear of the human form: it is movement that alarms them. You may also have an opportunity to observe elk, deer, gray squirrels, chipmunks, garden snakes, and other shy creatures. You are unlikely to find rattlesnakes along the Oregon coast, as the weather is too cool and wet for them, but you could encounter a northern Pacific rattlesnake in the Coast Range or the Klamath Mountains.

More than twenty different wildlife habitats are found along the Oregon Coast

It can be no secret that the Oregon Coast is a birder's dream. Oregon has recorded the one of the highest bird species totals in the country. At least twenty distinct bird habitats can be found along the coast and in the nearby coastal mountains. A branch of the Pacific flyway runs right along the coast of British Columbia, Washington and Oregon. This flyway is particularly important for shorebirds; they can stop to rest and feed in the many river, estuary, and lake habitats you will be seeing. While reduced rainfall in the inland parts of the flyway is causing the "watering holes" there to dry up, the wetter areas along the coast are becoming even more valuable for aquatic species. An interesting bird you might encounter is the Hudsonian godwit, (*Limosa haemastic)* on its annual flights from northern Alaska to southern Chili and back. It is a long trip, so they need to occasionally stop for a meal, and may be seen feeding on the estuary mudflats. Arctic terns migrate even farther, from the North American arctic to Antarctica and back!

As you travel along Highway 101 and visit the scenic attractions, you will traverse a variety of these wildlife habitats. As each environment offers different feeding and sheltering opportunities, each has its own collection of birds and other wildlife attuned to that specific habitat. Each habitat is worth an article of its own, certainly already written somewhere else, so I shall merely introduce them in the paragraphs that follow, starting from the coastline and progressing inland to the Coast Range. As in much of our country, many of the birds are resident, others are seasonal, and still others just migrate through in the spring and fall. So birders can observe many different bird species at different seasons in many of the Oregon Coast habitats.

Most of the terrestrial habitats have been extensively modified or subdivided as the Oregon Coast was developed. New habitats have been created. One result is that in many areas two or more habitats are found juxtaposed. They blend into one another, allowing bird populations to benefit from more foraging environments and nesting sites.

You will find the books *Birds of Oregon* and *National Audubon Society Field Guide to the Pacific Northwest* will be particularly useful for bird identification. For shorebirds, the Audubon guide is the most complete. Neither is comprehensive. The Oregon Coast Birding Trail website at http://www.oregoncoastbirding.com/ lists the bird species that have been reported at each of its 150 recommended birding locations along the coast, and provides news on current birding activities. Some of these locations are the same as the rest stops covered in this book. Serious birders may want to print out a current copy of this 51 page document before leaving home, as internet access along the coast is spotty and it is a bit cumbersome for a cell phone. Photographic opportunities abound, but I shall leave that to the serious birders who have more patience and better cameras.

Open Ocean, Seastack and Seacliff Habitat

Just offshore from the coastline, the Oregon Islands National Wildlife Refuge was established in 1935 and continues to be managed by the United States Fish and Wildlife Service. It really is huge, extending more than 350 miles along the coast from near the Columbia River to the California border. Some 1800 of the larger offshore rocks and seastacks that you will see have been included: they are critically important components of the ocean habitat. The term "islands" is actually a misnomer - the largest of the islands, Bird Island just offshore Harris Beach State Park in Brookings, is barely a quarter mile long, but the large, sloping crest provides excellent nesting sites. Seabirds can also be seen clinging to inaccessible cliffs on the rocky headlands at Heceta Head and Cape Meares, some of them actually building nests. Some of the larger islands have a patch of soil with grass, brush, and even a few Sitka spruce trees. These appear to be remnants of an earlier time when the islands were part of the mainland, preserved as the ocean eroded its way inland.

More than a million sea birds nest in colonies on the offshore rocks and seacliffs, where they are inaccessible to land-based predators and feel safe. Boats are required to remain at least 500 feet away from the offshore rocks, which is a good idea anyway as many of the rocks have underwater extensions and barely submerged neighbors. Importantly, seabirds frightened off their nests by boats may not return.

Many of the seastacks can be readily viewed from the shore, so carry your binoculars. If a rock is white with guano, sea birds are living there, nesting there, or resting up between dives or feeding excursions. More than a dozen seabird species may be seen on the cliffs and offshore rocks. Nesting species include three species of cormorants, common murres, tufted puffins, pigeon guillemots, Leach's storm-petrels, Caspian terns, two species of auklets, and several species of gulls. Except for the gulls, these shorebirds are almost never seen on the shore, so the beach and coastal promontories can be ideal vantage points for observing them. Brown pelicans and some species of gulls that nest farther south are also present locally in the summertime.

Seabird diets and feeding habits are distinct. Some species, like auklets, are planktivores, feeding on krill, larval forms, and other tiny nektonic animals, just like baleen whales. They dive for these delicacies or scoop them up from the water surface. Common murres eat schooling foraging fish, and may travel tens of miles out to sea to find them and dive to catch them. Others, like gulls which are not built for diving, are primarily surface and beach feeders. There appears to be a place in the nearshore marine ecology for each of them. Harris Park, near Brookings, is an excellent example of this habitat.

Beach Habitat

The beaches offer a separate biome, although one with little food supply for shorebirds. Since 1913 the ocean beaches of Oregon have been protected, initially by a legislative bill declaring the beach to be a public highway. That is not as far-fetched as it at first seems, as the coastline in places is extremely mountainous and rugged. U.S. Highway 101 with its many bridges wasn't completed until the 1930s. The beaches needed to be used for travelling from town to town along the coast. In 1967 the act was modified to include that "all wet sand up to 16 vertical feet above the low tide line" belongs to the State of Oregon, with a public easement up to the vegetation line. Oregon is the only state that was able to accomplish that, as the Pacific shoreline in Oregon became populated quite late. As a result, almost the entire shoreline was saved from commercial development. The beach and tide pool environments were saved for all to enjoy. You will find that frequent beach access is available all along the coast, although much of the shoreline is very rugged and dangerous and, in those areas, few trails have been constructed for shore access. So be careful: rescue services may be far away.

Like sandy deserts, ocean beaches provide a meager food supply. But they have two advantages: Waves washing across the sand bring in plankton for any life forms that can catch it, like sand crabs and razor clams. High tides and storms may deposit piles of seaweed high on the beach where sand fleas live in it and slowly devour it, but only a few small birds take advantage of the meal. Consequently, the indigenous bird population is sparse. The species that takes best advantage is the sanderling. You may have seen them – small sandpipers that live on beaches all over the world, dashing up and down the beach in little flocks as the waves advance and retreat. They are feeding mainly on the abundant sand crabs on the Oregon beaches, but will also eat worms and small mollusks – whatever the waves uncover for them. Flocks of sanderlings are not seen in the Oregon summer, as they migrate to breed on the tundra of northern Canada. It is interesting that the sanderlings are harvesting the same fare as the silver perch that live in the breaking waves, just on the other side of the water's edge. It is these perch that the surf fishermen are seeking.

During the summer months, many beaches have shallow pools behind berms that the waves have built up. Sea gulls seem to like them. Some are filled by small creeks; others by sea water washed in at high tide. The pools are often warmed by the sun and make great splash pools for children, but check first to see that the feeder creek is clean. Normally the pools are no more than two or three feet deep, but small deeper zones may have been scoured out near beach rocks, so beware.

It is gulls that patrol the beach, dining on whatever the waves wash up or got left behind by picnickers. There are several species of gull in Oregon, present in different seasons. As they all look somewhat alike, it can be a challenge to determine who you are watching. But gulls make it easier by not being particularly wary of people. At a large motel on the beach at the Chetco River harbor, I have seen gulls fly by to snatch tidbits from people standing on the balconies. You will find this habitat at most of the coastal rest stops.

Rocky Shoreline Habitat

You may find rocky shorelines more varied and interesting than beaches, particularly when the tide is out and tide pools are exposed. Various species of gulls, sandpipers, oystercatchers, and other shorebirds are often seen foraging there: there is more food to be had. Rocky shore and tide pool environments offer a wealth of marine food species. *Between Pacific Tides* devotes 180 pages to that subject alone. However, one must be careful, as the rocks are wet and slippery at low tide, and may be encrusted with delicate marine plants and animals you don't want to tread on and damage. Birdlife in this habitat is wary and is often best observed with binoculars from the adjacent beach or overlook. You will find this habitat at many of the rest stops along the southern Oregon coastline.

Rock Jetty Habitat

This habitat seems at first like an artificial subdivision, as rock jetties are manmade and are superficially similar to the rocky shore habitat. But below the water surface, rock jetties with their abundant secure hiding places provide a distinct habitat for marine life, both sessile and free-swimming. Seabirds recognize this. Cormorants and other diving birds often frequent jetties, particular on the estuary side, finding prey that rocky shorelines do not offer. Human anglers recognize this as well; they can catch both jetty-resident species and fish that are just swimming by. But be warned: jetty tops are normally only a little above sea level and have poor or no walkways on top. There is no escaping freak waves, so I recommend you stay off them. Many of the estuary mouths have such jetties.

Coastal Conifer Forest Habitat

Sandy terrains near the coastline are frequently covered by a dense-to-open forest of shore pines (a variety of the more familiar lodgepole pine that grows in all the western states), Sitka spruce, and various broadleaf trees and shrubs – many bearing nuts, berries or seeds. Salal, salmonberry, and huckleberry are typical shrubs. Generally these areas have never been logged or cleared: the trees are too small to be of commercial value. This habitat provides shade for many of the coastal state park campgrounds. The terrain has its own unique assortment of bird and animal species. It is a good place to see mourning doves and flocks of wild band-tailed pigeons. Bullards Beach State Park north of Bandon is an excellent example, with a long paved trail.

Brushy Bluff Habitat

Often the trail down the bluff to the beach will traverse brushy landscape, where the conifer forest perhaps never grew. These areas are usually covered with a wide variety of broadleaf shrubs and vines, grasses, and a few stunted conifers. A wide variety of berries is usually present, especially salal, huckleberries, and blackberries, both wild and the introduced Himalayan kind. You may find tiny but sweet wild strawberries in grassy areas. Wild hazelnuts also grow there – smaller, but just as tasty as the commercial variety widely grown in the Willamette Valley. With such varied food, this environment has its own unique collection of bird species, none of them related to the seacoast itself. But they are mostly small, quick to hide, and often difficult to spot in the brush. Wrens and sparrows are common residents. Beware of poison oak, as it is common there. The bluff at Harris Beach State Park is an excellent example; you will see many along the coast.

Sand Dune Habitat

On the central Oregon Coast there is an extensive coastal sand dune field, the largest of its kind in the United States. Some dunes are more than 300 feet tall. Little wildlife lives in the dunes, as they are largely barren and there is nothing for them to eat there. However, a few vegetated "islands" within the dune field offer small protected habitats.

Shore Dune Habitat

On the landward edge of many of the sandy beaches at the rest stops you will find a line of low sand dunes, usually only a few feet high. As they are normally largely covered by dune grasses and little else, they offer little food for wildlife, so little lives there. However, snowy plovers may be nesting in the low dunes close to the beach, especially where they have been stabilized by dune grasses. It is important to watch for their nesting areas so as not to disturb them. When frightened, they may leave the nest and never return. Some, but certainly not all, of their nesting sites have been located and taped off for their protection.

Dune-Trapped Lake Habitat

Along the central Oregon Coast, many small streams have been dammed up by the coastal sand dunes and a collection of some forty beautiful lakes has formed as a result. They lie on either side of the Highway 101 between Coos Bay and Florence, some right next to the highway. The lakes have surface elevations only a few feet above sea level; ancient stream channels visible on the lake floors often extend well below sea level. The larger lakes, like Siltcoos Lake and Tahkenitch Lake, still have small rivers emptying to the sea, but most do not. They drain to the sea through the porous and permeable sand dunes. These lakes offer a unique birding opportunity with abundant fresh-water ducks, geese, and loons, some resident and others migratory. Boat launches and boat and canoe rentals are available at the some of the larger lakes. A few are far enough inland to avoid the sometimes unpleasant foggy and windy coastal weather.

Coastal Meadow Habitat

In a few coastal areas just behind the row of beach-facing sand dunes or on the bluffs you will occasionally find meadows with varieties of grasses and wild flowers that are attuned to the sandy soil. Because of the mild coastal climate, wildflowers bloom well into the fall season. Often this habitat is bordered by the scrub conifer, shore dune, or other coastal habitats, and wildlife can take advantage of the mix of feed and shelter offered. Cottontail rabbits are common there. Crissey Field south of Brookings is a good example of this habitat.

Estuary Habitat

These protected tidal inlets with their sloughs, mud flats, and salt marshes constitute a shorebird environment quite in contrast with the open shoreline. It is also the richest in bird species, both resident varieties and large numbers of migrating shorebirds. Estuary and bay species harvest most of their food from mud flats, salt marshes, and shallow brackish water as the tide ebbs and flows. Some Oregon estuaries have been protected from development, although fishing and duck hunting may be allowed in them. Others have not been protected but still offer fine waterfowl viewing. Bandon Marsh National Wildlife Preserve currently protects some 889 acres of tidal marsh on the Coquille River estuary, just upstream from the coastal town of Bandon. Varieties of sandpipers and plovers are commonly seen there, and several rare shorebirds occasionally visit. Near Reedsport, the north spit at the mouth of the Umpqua estuary has been designated as a western snowy plover critical habitat. Remarkably, in an Audubon Society bird count in January, 1991, nearly 8000 waterfowl were counted in the Coos Bay estuary – and coots were excluded! Farther up the coast, Siletz Bay National Wildlife Refuge near Lincoln City protects over 500 acres of salt marsh, mostly reclaimed from pastureland.

Estuaries and their associated tidal flats harbor a wealth of life forms, a real smorgasbord for the birds that live or visit there. My edition of Ricketts' and Calvin's *Between Pacific Tides* devotes 115 pages to this habitat alone. Crabs, mollusks, and worms are common food items for the estuarine bird population, harvested from the mud flats during low tide. Four areas in particular can be recommended: the national wildlife refuges at Nestucca Bay, Siletz Bay, and Bandon Marsh on the Coquille River, and the South Slough of Coos Bay. You may encounter bald eagles, ospreys, and peregrine falcons in addition to many varieties of waterfowl and wading shorebirds. The largest estuaries are in the lowlands of the central and northern coast and these often have convenient roads alongside them.

Harbor Habitat

The harbor habitat is a special part of the estuary habitat. In the constructed boat harbors in the estuaries there is a unique aqueous environment created by wooden pilings, jetties, and docks – all in one place. They provide a combination of food and shelter not usually present in the open estuary. Fish-cleaning stations add to the food bounty. Above the water there are roosting points on railings, posts, boats, and the docks themselves. Waterfowl seem to like it there, seemingly unafraid of people. You may see harbor seals sleeping on unused floating docks. At the Bandon harbor I saw a great blue heron perching on a post at the public dock waiting for me to take his picture. At the Crab Pier in lower Winchester Bay, abandoned rotting pilings just past the end had been taken over by double-crested cormorants and pigeon guillemots.

Conifer Forest Habitat

All the time you are travelling along the Oregon Coast, you are on the seaward edge of the world's greatest temperate rainforest, although most of it in Oregon was cut down over the last century and a half. Once stretching almost unbroken along the Pacific coast and coastal mountain ranges from the redwoods groves of northern California to the Kenai Peninsula in Alaska, the Pacific temperate rainforest is a truly unique and enchanting environment. An article by Jonathan Lambert in a recent issue of *Science News* identifies this rainforest as one of the last great repositories of "irrecoverable carbon" that should remain uncut to combat global warming. Of course there are battles between the conservationists, who want few or no trees cut at all, and people still working in the forest products industry whose ancestors have made their living from the forest for many generations. At present, different federal government agencies see the situation differently and policies are in flux.

A current focus is on the vast Sitka spruce forests in Tongass National Forest on the mainland and islands of southeast Alaska, which contain billions of tons of carbon that are perhaps better off left in the forest than released to the atmosphere. Logging is wasteful by its very nature: a large portion of a felled conifer tree is burned as slash or left on the ground to rot, and the understory shrubs are decimated. Even the harvested logs have thick bark that may be discarded or bagged for landscaping use. A lot of sawdust, shavings, and trimmings are produced in the lumber mills; these are often burned but may be cycled into chipboard or paper pulp.

From south to north, the rainforest is made up of different trees. In northern California, the principle conifer species is redwood, but Douglas-fir is commonly present as well. Redwoods are mostly absent in Oregon, with only a couple of groves near the Chetco and Winchuck rivers. A panoply of conifers takes their place in the rainy forest farther north. Douglas-fir is the most abundant in the Coast Range, but Sitka spruce, western hemlock, western redcedar, and Port Orford cedar are often mixed in. Farther north in Washington and British Columbia, Port Orford cedar drops out of the mix and Sitka spruce becomes dominant species in the lower elevations. Even farther north as the climate becomes boreal, western hemlock is replaced by mountain hemlock, which in Oregon it is more commonly found in the Cascades. At the north end of the rainforest on Kodiak Island, Sitka spruce and mountain hemlock have become the dominant evergreens. Shore pine (a variety of lodgepole pine) is common along the coast but doesn't compete well in the rainforest. Pacific yew, the smallest conifer of the group, is commonly found in the understory, with its poisonous red berry-like seeds.

Broadleaf trees are much less common – the rainforest is basically a conifer regime. Red alder is present all along the belt, especially along streams. Along the Oregon coast, the tall bigleaf maple grows along streams: this species is being investigated with some success for maple sugar production. Spindly vine maples, with their beautiful fall leaf colors, are found in the understory. Of course I must mention Oregon myrtle of the south coast, which south of the border is called California laurel. This is the source of the beautiful wood carvings and bowls you will find in shops in the towns – we still use a salad set given as a wedding present more than fifty years ago. Many varieties of berries are also present in the understory, especially where some sunlight peeks through.

An old-growth conifer forest provides many foraging opportunities for birds and other wildlife, but much of it is in the treetops. These forests are fundamentally different from the tree farms, which are basically monocultures of Douglas-fir trees. Tree farms have little or no understory of shrubs; the only open glades tend to be along the access roads. Few annual plants thrive in the total-shade environment. In contrast, old-growth conifer forests have generally reached a point in their long life where some of the original trees have succumbed to disease or insect invasion. Unlike the redwoods and sequoias of northern California, these trees don't live forever. Some have been felled by the wind or struck by lightning; others have died but still stand as decaying snags. The resulting forest has openings in the canopy where sunlight can reach the ground and allow shrubs and annuals to flourish. Deciduous foliage in the understory and in forest clearings provides different food resources than coniferous foliage above, and those resources may be available at different times of the year. Throughout the year in the mild coastal climate, deciduous trees and shrubs support a diverse assemblage of insects, creating an abundant food supply for resident birds. This vegetation mix is an essential part of the old-growth forest ecology. Each of the many plant species contributes something important to the food chain: nuts, fruit, berries, seeds, or just forage for insects and caterpillars. Caterpillars and grubs, in particular, provide a high-energy resource for breeding forest birds, as they are nearly one hundred percent food – no wings, legs, and indigestible exoskeletons. Berries are also important, and there is a huge variety: salal, huckleberry, red huckleberry, thimbleberry, salmonberry, blackberry, Oregon grape, red elderberry, and currant are varieties frequently found in forest clearings or in open old-growth forests. All but the Oregon grape and elderberry are edible and delicious, but some birds even feed on those.

As Ann Sverdrup-Thygeson points out in *Buzz, Sting, Bite*, litter and rotting logs on the forest floor provide food and cover for insects and other creepy-crawlies, who also aid in the decomposition and recycling. Raccoons and skunks partake of these, but you may not see them as they tend to be nocturnal. Watch for their small hand-like tracks in the mud. Dead tree snags, normally absent from young forests, supply their own contribution of beetles and insects to the food chain as well as protection for birds that like to nest in them – particularly woodpeckers and the freeloaders that nest in abandoned woodpecker nests. If you are really lucky, you may spot a pileated woodpecker, a handsome bird with a flaming crest. With the demise of the ivory-billed woodpecker, it is now the largest woodpecker in North America and the fourth largest in the world. On cold, foggy, or windy days, you might want to escape the severe coastal weather, and the inland rainforests can be your refuge. Steller's jays, downy woodpeckers, and flocks of band-tail pigeons are typical residents. If you are stealthy you may see a ruffed grouse. It is the also the home of the infamous spotted owl, for whom preservation campaigns led to the cessation of logging in old-growth forests managed by the United States Forest Service. But their numbers have been declining and they are well camouflaged in their brown and white flecked plumage. You may see instead the similar barred owl, as they have been encroaching on the conifer forest habitat.

There are a few patches along the Oregon and Washington coasts where the original old-growth forest has been preserved. For the casual hiker as well as the birder, a few easy rainforest hikes are described in the *Coast Explorer Magazine* at the following link: https://www.coastexplorermagazine.com/features/best-oregon-coast-old-growth-forest-hikes. These hiking trails are located near the Chetco River, the Rogue River, Yachats, Heceta Head, Cape Perpetua, Cape Lookout, and Cape Falcon. Some of the trails are a little strenuous although well maintained, with 300 to 600 feet of elevation gain, but you don't need to go all the way to appreciate the habitat. Francis Schrader Old Growth Trail near Gold Beach is an excellent example; another is Oswald West State Park south of Cannon Beach. The walks feature huge Sitka spruce, Douglas-fir, western redcedar, western hemlock and, along the Chetco River, Oregon myrtle and a grove of redwoods. Both bigleaf maple and vine maple are common. If your travels take you farther north into Washington, you can see well-preserved old-growth forests in the river valleys and lower slopes in Olympic National Park.

Logged Forest Habitat

In the coastal mountains you may notice extensive areas in which the Douglas-fir forest has been harvested, leaving a very messy environment. But the logging operation leaves the forest understory to thrive in the sunshine and it often does quite well in the interim before the conifer forest becomes re-established or replanted. The resulting panoply of mixed forest environments can be particularly rich in wildlife. An assortment of young conifer and broadleaf trees often coexists with a variety of shrubs and annuals, providing a rich variety of foraging and nesting sites. These habitats will be found in any stage from bare logged or burned land to a dense forest that may soon be targeted for logging once again. Huckleberry bushes are a main beneficiary, as are wild mountain blackberries and salal. Native grasses may become established, but are soon out-competed. It can be a rich habitat for wildlife for many years with the wide variety of annuals, grasses, and brushy plants. Blacktail deer and cottontail rabbits, which don't find much to eat in a dense conifer forest, thrive in the logged lands during their years of recovery. You will see a wide variety of birds. Gardener Ridge near Brookings is a good example. A long stretch of logged land can be seen along W. Beaver Hill Road south of Charleston.

Second Growth Forest Habitats

Tree farms have created monocultures of Douglas-fir that can cover very large areas. As the original forest is clear-cut and the new young trees are closely-spaced, little sunlight filters to the forest floor. There is very little undergrowth of shrubs and annuals so the food supply is meager. Usually the tree crop is harvested and re-planted before the natural openings that characterize mature forests have developed. Dead trees and rotting logs on the forest floor are almost always absent. Consequently, the sparse bird life is largely limited to the forest canopy overhead and is difficult to observe. However, as in the mature forest habitat, the needles and branches that fall from the growing trees do not decompose by themselves. The process is aided by insects, worms, and other small inverte-brates that feed on rotting organic material, providing food for any birds and animals that want to scratch for them. Wrens and other insectivores can thrive there. You can find second growth forests at various stages of maturity on the side trip to Gardener Ridge.

River Valley and Pasture Habitat

As soon as settlers arrived on the Oregon Coast in the 1850s, they began to clear the richest land on the river floodplains for new farms and ranches. A new bird habitat was created. Along the river valleys, if you are lucky you may see kingfishers, ospreys, and bald eagles. In the verdant pastures on the floodplains, I have seen robins, varied thrushes, crows, doves, flickers, hawks, and many other non-aquatic birds. Nearly all of the coastal rivers have scenic paved roads along-side, some extending far into the Coast Range, even to the interior valleys. They are recommended for side trips into sunny weather when the coast is cold, windy, or fogged in. Most of the paved roads running up the rivers from the coast pass through rich pastureland; the road to Morgan Creek Fish Hatchery east of Coos Bay is an excellent example.

Brushy Wetland Habitat

Some of the coastal rivers and their estuarine deltas are still bordered by fresh water wetlands in floodplains that have not been reclaimed. The rivers and wetlands themselves are usually lined with riparian trees such as maples, willows, and alders and are not readily visible from the roads. Float trips may be the best way to see some of these. Small creeks may flow through such wetlands; there are many along the coast. Good examples may be seen near the mouth of the Winchuck River and where Lone Ranch Creek reaches the beach. On streams where anadromous salmon, steelhead, and cutthroat trout return to spawn, these wooded wetlands are critically important. Not only do they shade the stream, keeping the water temperature comfortable for the young fish, but they also drop insects and larvae into the water for them to eat. This stream-edge riparian vegetation is now being legally protected in logging operations. As the climate warms and the number of sunny days increases, fish need all the protection we can give them if they are to survive and migrate to the sea. Steller's blue jays and bandtail pigeons may frequent this environment.

Mountain Meadow Habitat

Montane meadows in the Coast Range and Klamath Mountains are not extensive, mainly scars from ancient forest fires that have not yet regrown. As they may be snow-covered for extended periods during the winter, the bird populations are mostly seasonal. Nevertheless, they provide a rich habitat during the spring and summer.

By their nature, they are surrounded by forest and scrub brush habitats. There is a great mountain meadow at Saddle Mountain State Park and another near the crest of Mary's Peak. Both display a great variety of grasses and wildflowers.

Mountain Scrub Brush Habitat

This is another habitat with relatively few birds representing only a few species, but for different reasons. First, there is only a small variety of plants with edible seeds, as the soil is often thin and poor and growing conditions harsh. Most of the berries that are so abundant in the coastal forests and brushlands do not do well in the higher elevation in full sun. Second, because the mountains experience more distinct seasons than the temperate coastal belt, the seed-bearing plants tend to mature around the same time in the summer, limiting the time range of edibles. Finally, the coastal mountains may be covered with thick snow for part of the winter, making it difficult to harvest what food there is. Fortunately, this habitat is often intermingled with mountain meadow and various forest habitats, and the birds can take advantage of the variety. However, the open terrain makes the birds easier to spot. The side trip to Vulcan Lake and Snow Camp Lookout passes through this habitat.

Town Habitat

Finally, the town habitat, a rich bird habitat with which we are all familiar. Why so rich? It is the great variety of both native and foreign ornamental plants we have planted and maintain year round. Flowers, seeds, and berries from all over the world can be found in residential yards, often maturing at different seasons throughout the year. They may not be the traditional diet of the Oregon Coast bird population, but by the end of winter you will note that little of this avian smorgasbord remains on the bush. As I write this section in mid-December a flock of lesser goldfinches is harvesting our crepe myrtle seeds. Crepe myrtle is native to China and Korea, and lesser goldfinches live mainly in the southwestern United States and Mexico. A plethora of trees and shrubs, even bird houses, provide secure nesting sites. Predation is mainly limited to domestic cats. Consequently, birds of many species thrive in the town habitat. But they may be different species than you are used to in a similar habitat where you live, as the mild Oregon Coast climate is unique. An additional factor is that towns usually lie next to one or more natural habitats or include parkland or stream courses. Birds that live in the country may come to town for a meal.

Chapter 3

Brookings and the Southern Coast

Crissey Field State Park and Visitors Center: Rest stop, beach hike, and stroll. Located off Hwy 101 just north of the California border, immediately south of Winchuck River Bridge.

Welcome to Oregon! Crissey Field was once a grass landing strip, but there is little sign of that now – all that remains is a flowery coastal meadow being slowly overtaken by shrubs. In its place, the state has built a first-class visitor's center to welcome travelers to Oregon. The facility has educational nature displays, an extensive selection of Oregon travel books and pamphlets, knowledgeable attendants on site with information about the state, and modern restrooms. It is a good place to start your trip. Perhaps you can purchase my book there!

There are no camping facilities or picnic tables, but one can picnic on the nearby beach. Crissey Field serves as the southern terminus of the Oregon Coast Trail, a splendid work in progress. The 362-mile trail runs from the California state line to the Columbia River – right along the coast where the highway doesn't interfere, a little ways farther inland where the highway hugs the beach, and straight through the coastal towns on designated streets where the towns take up all the room on the coastal plain, like in Brookings and Yachats. It is mainly on bridges across the many rivers and creeks that the trail and Hwy 101 share space. You can find details in the splendid book *100 Hikes / Travel Guide Oregon Coast & Coast Range* by William L. Sullivan.

Behind the visitors center there is a short trail through the low dunes and driftwood to the beach, where a four mile beach hike to the south leads to mouth of the Smith River in California. I have found nicely rounded pebbles of low-quality black nephrite jade along this hike. However, the beach is narrow and rocky in some areas. A high tide can come right up to the driftwood, but you can escape up the bank if the waves get too high. Most of the year, the outlet of the Winchuck River blocks beach hikes to the north; in the late summer when the river mouth is sanded in, you can trek about a mile in that direction. If you can get there on a low tide, especially a minus tide (usually around daybreak), you will find excellent tide-pools in either direction.

I have found pebbles of low-quality
black nephrite jade along this hike

The Winchuck is a very small river. It usually doesn't flow into the ocean all summer. Like at many small rivers and creeks along the coast, the summer waves build up a sandy berm on the beach and the rivers drain through it. It takes only a few feet of raised water level in the estuary to provide the necessary hydraulic head to instigate flow through the permeable sand berm into the sea. There is no commerce here; you will need to go into Brookings-Harbor to find motels and restaurants.

Immediately south of the visitor center there is an easy trail for strollers through a coastal meadow for 0.3 miles along the old landing field. Wildflowers bloom there all summer and into the fall, and it is somewhat protected from the wind. Near the visitors' center you will see a large patch of wild yarrow, a spring and fall bloomer. Strollers can also follow the trail from the visitors' center part way to the beach, then branch off to the right into a Sitka spruce and red alder forest. The trail continues through the forest all the way to the northeast end of the parking lot, with a couple of short branches to the edge of the Winchuck estuary where a canoes or kayaks could be launched. Watch out for exposed Sitka spruce roots crossing the trail.

An unusual feature of the beach at the Winchuck River outlet: a varied collection of colorful boulders. They are mostly metamorphic rocks, created by high temperatures and pressures deep within the earth, now exposed in the Klamath Mountains upstream. The boulders are all very hard and have been well rounded by the surf and beach sand. But the Winchuck estuary seems too placid to carry boulders, even in a winter flood – how did the boulders get to where we find them? It is possible that the boulders may be remnant from the Pleistocene Era, more than ten thousand years ago. When sea level was lower, what is now a calm estuary was the lower Winchuck River canyon, and the river running in it was then quite capable of moving rocks downstream to where we find them. They were left stranded where the river reached the ocean, then polished and moved around by storm waves to the gravel patches we see today. However, it is conceivable that they were carried down the Winchuck by a more recent "thousand-year flood" and deposited on the beach. A good question to ponder. Are there any future geologists in the family?

The boulders provide an interesting project for youngsters – how many different kinds can they find and put in a row? How many colors? When we were there, we found a diverse selection of pebbles that were gray, white, black, red, yellow, orange, purple, green, spotted, and striped. The beach boulders are the best clue to the rock types present in the Winchuck River drainage, which is heavily vegetated and difficult for geologists to map. On the northern Oregon Coast, the beach rocks are mostly black basalt, derived from the basalt sea-cliffs, and far less interesting. For the more sophisticated visitor, how many different rock types can you find, and can you identify any of them? Some are granitic, some volcanic, some metamorphic, many quartz veined, but none are the softer sedimentary rocks. There is also a good selection of seashells along the beach, including crab shells, various clam shells, mussel shells, and a few limpet shells. These are the shellfish that live on a rocky coast and in the tide pools.

Wildlife habitats: Open ocean, sandy beach, rocky coast, estuary, shore dune, coastal meadow, scrub conifer forest, forested fresh water wetland.

Mouth of the Winchuck River during Ebbing Tide. *During most of the year, the short Winchuck estuary is open to the tides, alternately filling and draining with the tidal flow twice daily. However, during late summer, a sand berm is built up by the waves, and the small flow of the Winchuck is unable to keep a passage open. The sand is highly permeable so the fresh river water seeps through it to the ocean. Salmon and steelhead must wait for stronger river flow with the fall and winter rains to clear a passage through the berm before they can enter the river and swim upstream to spawn.*

Beach Gravel Bar at the Mouth of the Winchuck River. Many different varieties of rocks have washed down the Winchuck River from its nearby head-waters in the Klamath Mountains. Young future geologists can have a contest here, seeing who can find the most different kinds of rocks. Can you identify any of them? Most are metamorphic rocks from rock formations that were deeply buried before becoming uplifted and eroded.

Oregon Redwood Trail: Side trip, rest stop, woodland stroll. Exit Hwy 101 on Winchuck River Road just north of Winchuck River Bridge. Drive 1.6 miles east up the verdant Winchuck River valley to Peavine Ridge Road and turn right, crossing the river, and continue another 3.9 miles up Peavine Ridge to a parking lot in

the forest. There may be no sign for Peavine Ridge Road; just watch for the narrow bridge. Some of the road is poorly maintained but still passable. Two road branches are both private driveways; stay to the right. I don't recommend RVs, as passing could be a problem on the narrow road.

Oregon Redwood Trail starts by the posts near the entrance to the parking lot and runs through an older secondary forest of Douglas-fir, Sitka spruce, red alder, a couple of bigleaf maples, and eventually redwoods, some quite large. A few of the original redwoods remain, with trunks six to eight feet in diameter, but nothing like the giants you may have seen in California. The canopy is so high above the trail, perhaps 150 feet, that you can recognize the trees mainly by the bark. Midlevel vegetation consists mainly of berry bushes - red elderberry, thimbleberry, salmonberry, red huckleberry,

The canopy is so high above the trail, perhaps 150 feet, that you recognize the trees mainly by the bark

wild blackberry, and currant - but in the deep shade they are unlikely to produce many berries. A few rhododendron and cascara bushes are mixed in. At the ground level you will see sword ferns, wood sorrel, and various forbs, including trilliums, in a blanket of needles. The trail is in good shape for strollers with only a little up and down, 1.6 miles out and back. As the area is far from roads, away from the sound of the surf, and not beneath any commercial airline paths, the silence in the forest can be absolute on a still day. Most days it should also be high enough and far enough inland to avoid coastal fog. At the parking lot there is only a primitive restroom, but there are modern restrooms in the visitors' center off Highway 101 just across Winchuck River Bridge. On the way up I saw a pair of bobwhite quail dashing up the road – watch for them. The location is quite isolated: be sure to lock your car.

Wildlife habitats: Conifer forest.

Future Marine Biologist: Tide Pools

One of the delights of the rocky Oregon Coast is the expanse of tide pools that become exposed during low tides. Minus tides – the lowest tides of any given lunar month – provide the best opportunities, but any lowest of the two daily low tides will do. You can find tide tables for any location online at *tide tables (city)* and at fishing tackle stores. Unfortunately, the lowest tides on the Pacific coast tend to be in the early morning, usually before breakfast, when the full moon and the sun are working together. This results in the water being drawn offshore and the tide pools exposed.

But watch out! Tide pools are located only on rocky shores, and should not be visited when a high surf is running. Rocks enclosing the tide pools are often covered by slippery algae, as they are submerged most of the time. It is easy to slip and fall even if you are sure-footed, and there are no soft landing places. Trekking poles are useful. I have found that grabbing a tall pole from the driftwood pile can be helpful, serving as a third leg to aid stability. One also needs to be watchful of sneaker waves, as it is difficult to move quickly to avoid them. Plan on getting your feet wet.

There are seven protected tide pool areas, designated as marine gardens, along the Oregon Coast: Harris Beach State Park, Cape Perpetua, Yachats State Park, Yaquina Head, Otter Rock, Cape Kiwanda, and Haystack Rock. Maps to these areas can be found online. But as the entire Oregon shore has long been protected for public use, most other rocky shorelines have good tide pools that are readily accessible.

A wide variety of sea life is visible in the
tide pools, with a magical array of colors

A wide variety of sea life is visible in the tide pools, with a magical array of colors. Most prominent are starfish (formally called sea stars, as they are not fish), hermit crabs, sea anemones, nudibranchs, purple sea urchins, chitons, and sea cucumbers. Barnacles, mussels, and limpets that live farther up the shore are less common in the tide pools. Clams can be dug in sandy or muddy areas between the tide pools. They make tasty chowder, but I have found them to be very sandy. You will often see sculpins, a finger-sized fish, scurrying about. On the exposed rocks you can find a wide variety of sea-weeds, some of which are edible. You may even recognize some as ingredients of sushi and other Japanese delicacies.

Tide pools constitute an amazingly hardy ecosystem. The life forms must withstand the forces and currents caused by breaking waves as the tide ebbs and flows, cold sea water, occasional rain, and a daily couple of hours of sunshine, or at least clouds. Clearly the denizens must all be happier when the tide comes in and they are covered, but it is an environment they chose to inhabit. Perhaps there are fewer predators there, where the water never gets more than a few feet deep and is always moving. But it is an ecosystem that is susceptible to damage, so we must treat it with respect and care. Please observe and photograph, but take nothing away and leave only footprints behind.

An important and timely study could be made on the effect of purple sea urchins on tide pool life. With their challenging physical conditions, could tidepools provide sanctuary for some species of sea weed, or are the sea urchins stripping them bare as well? Anyone interested?

Brookings

Brookings is the first town we encounter in our south-to-north drive on the Oregon Coast, but one of the last coastal towns established – by more than half a century! Unlike many of the towns farther up the coast, southern Curry County had no road traversing the coastal mountains to the populated areas inland, no large river access to a port, and the beaches have always been impassable for automobile traffic. But the Brookings area has a fascinating history nonetheless, although with a very sad beginning.

Before February, 1853, the Chetco people (a branch of the Tolowa Indian Nation) had long-established villages on both sides of the mouth of the Chetco River and even ran their own ferry service connecting them. Then a settler named A. F. Miller claimed the land around the Chetco village on the south shore with the intention of building a town to serve potential mining interests in the area. After he built his house, he informed the Chetcos they could no longer ferry white people across the Chetco River. This understandably annoyed the Chetco people, even though they had previously been friendly and allowed the settlers to build only a quarter mile away from their village. In February, 1853, fearing trouble from the Chetcos, Miller invited some Indian fighters from Smith River, just south of the California border, to help him out. The group massacred the Chetco men in the village, whose only defensive weapons were the bow and arrow and a few knives that had been made by flattening out bolts and strips of iron taken from old shipwrecks – probably Spanish galleons. The Indian fighters allowed the women and children to escape, but burned their lodges. This was only the first of several shameful massacres of groups of Tolowas in the Curry county-Del Norte County area. I have found no record of what happened to the Chetco women and children. It is likely they escaped to the south to other Tolowa villages on the Smith River.

This understandably annoyed the Chetcos,
even though they had previously been friendly

Even though Miller was apprehended and brought to trial in Port Orford, he was eventually released. At that time of our sad history, Indian testimony was not respected in American courts of law, so testimony by the survivors could not be used against him. By 1857, some 600 Tolowas from the southern Oregon coast and Smith River, California, had been rounded up and marched to the Coast Indian Reservation some 200 miles to the north. Many escaped and returned to Smith River, where many Tolowa people still live. These displacements have been called Oregon's own tragic trail of tears. You can find more of these and other early local events at https://ndnhistoryresearch.com/2017/04/20/massacre-at-the-chetko-villages-1853/

At about the same time, the rich coastal plain between the Chetco and Winchuck rivers was divided up by a group of a dozen early settlers, mainly from the American Midwest. After measuring off the land, they drew lots from a hat to establish claims. No real town was built at that time by the settlers, as they were only a few. Despite a few placer gold claims on the Chetco River drainage, the local mining industry that Miller had anticipated did not pan out. A port was being built at Crescent City which hoped to serve the miners in the Klamath and Trinity River watershed areas.

Unfortunately, the settlers on the coastal plain became involved in the dispute over the Chetco lands they were occupying, leading to one of the early episodes of the Rogue River Indian Wars of the middle 1850s. Battles were fought, leading to the burning of the settlers houses, but there were few casualties. Only after the wars were the land claims resettled. It seemed that a single settler, Thomas Van Pelt, was sympathetic to the cause of the Chetcos. He learned their language and their customs, and even asked the Chetcos at the Winchuck River village if he might build a cabin in the area. For his considerations, Van Pelt was given Amelia, a twelve-year old girl from the Chetco tribe, whom he then married. Although Amelia was forced into the group that was driven up the coast to the Coast Indian Reservation, Thomas was later able to produce a marriage certificate and rescue her. She bore him eleven children. The Van Pelt family continued to be important in the development of the area: I recall that my second grade teacher was a very pretty, part-Chetco woman who bore the Van Pelt surname.

After a few years, a hamlet named Chetco was established in the area, and that was succeeded by a larger hamlet named Harbor in the vicinity of the current boat harbor. These were most likely supplied from the new harbor and town at Crescent City, as the Chetco River estuary was not considered to be a navigable harbor for either sailing vessels or early steamships. Even those supplies needed to be ferried across the Smith River. Later in the nineteenth century a few small lumber mills were constructed, but little commercial development followed, as there was no road and no port. Communication with the towns in the interior was only by a primitive and dangerous stage road from Crescent City to Grants Pass. The coast highway and bridges had yet to be built.

Not until the lumber baron John E. Brookings noticed the local timberland in the area did things really get going. In the 1890s, Brookings was a lumberman operating in the San Bernardino Mountains in Southern California. He had built a lumber mill and 30 miles of narrow-gauge railway to supply it from the nearby mixed conifer stands. Between 1901 and 1911, Brookings Lumber and Box Company was supplying over ten million board feet* annually of cut lumber. However, by 1912 he was running out of trees, and a small forest fire had burned up some of the remaining stand. In addition, his logging operation was becoming unpopular with the local citizens, who wanted to see replanting of the forests in the Santa Ana River watershed. Apparently, some replanting was done, both with pine seedlings and apple trees.

Around 1912 the company started to move their operations to Oregon, establishing a new mill and mill town on the elevated marine terraces just north of the Chetco River. But it wasn't just any old town. John's brother Robert Brookings, a prosperous Midwestern businessman, was financially involved in the venture. This is the same Robert Brookings that supported Washington University in St. Louis and founded the prominent Brookings Institution think tank in Washington D.C. Although it is not thought that Robert ever visited the new town, he engaged the famous San Francisco architect Bernard Maybeck to lay out the town plan and design some of the buildings, of which a few have survived. Bernard Maybeck had previously designed many of the San Francisco Bay Area's most treasured buildings. From 1913 to 1915, shortly after the great earthquake, he created the Palace of Fine Arts Building for the 1915 Panama-Pacific International Exposition in San Francisco, the event's only surviving structure. Designed as an art gallery, in the style of an ancient ruin, the Palace displays Maybeck's flair for drama and his passion for buildings in harmony with their natural surroundings.

A dock had to be built in Chetco Cove

During the next ten years a large quantity of high quality lumber was sawn and shipped via lumber steamer to markets in the California Bay Area and Los Angeles. With neither a road nor a seaport, a dock had to be constructed in Chetco Cove, just north of the river mouth. Short railroads were built up the Chetco and across the river to the south to supply logs. In the summer of 1925, the mill suddenly shut down, leaving the town with virtually no employment. The electric generator that supplied the mill also stopped operating, as there was no longer any scrap wood and sawdust for fuel, leaving

---

"Board feet" is still today the standard measure of lumber volume. One board foot can be thought of as one square foot of rough lumber one inch thick, or one foot of a 1x12 board. A foot of a 2x12 board contains two board feet. Other lumber dimensions are measured similarly by volume of wood. Because boards of different tree species or different dryness can have widely different weights, lumber volumes cannot be accurately measured by the ton like coal or metal ores.

the town without electricity. Brooking's population was down to 250 in a few years, from as many as 1500 during the heyday of O&C (Oregon and California) Lumber Company. Fortunately some of the commercial buildings remained, and these are the ones you see today along Main Street, Highway 101. A small fishing fleet ran out of the Chetco River mouth, but with no highway to markets it never became a viable commercial operation. It was not until the mid-1930s when the Roosevelt Highway connected Brookings with the rest of the world that the town began to recover.

After the demise of the mill in 1925, the Japanese purchased the rolling stock and rails. Why? Probably as scrap iron for the construction of military hardware for their war in the Pacific and East Asia!

Why were the steel rails and rolling stock purchased by Japan?

Early on the morning of September 9, 1942, just nine months after the tragic Pearl Harbor attack, the Japanese submarine I-25 surfaced off Port Orford. Perhaps they had remembered the dense stands of timber in the hills behind the town, from their earlier recovery of the railroad. The crew quickly assembled a specially designed sea-plane, and within a few minutes pilot Nobuo Fujita, observer Shoji Okuda, and two 170 pound incendiary bombs were catapulted air-borne. The plane flew toward Cape Blanco Light and crossed the coastline, then flew southeast for about 50 miles to drop its payload behind Brookings on Wheeler Ridge, becoming the first enemy aircraft to bomb the U.S. mainland. Fortunately, it was a wet fall and the fires didn't catch in the damp forest. The objective seems to have been to occupy the American citizenry in fighting forest fires instead of fighting the Japanese.

But to complete the full cycle of history, Nobuo Fujita, the pilot of the seaplane, was invited to be the grand marshal of the Brookings Azalea Parade in 1962. He surrendered his family's 400 year-old Samurai-type sword to the mayor as "The finest possible way of closing the story, to pledge peace and friendship." You can see the sword on display in the Chetco Community Public Library – on Railroad Street! Nobuo Fujita returned again in 1992 to plant a redwood seedling at the bombed site on the 50th anniversary of the attack.

In the early years the estuary of the Chetco River was not readily navigable except for small fishing craft, and even they had to count on a favorable tide. In 1957 a pair of rock jetties was constructed by the Army Corps of Engineers, enabling the shipment of lumber, plywood, and wood chips by ocean barge. The river itself remains mostly primitive as it winds 57 miles through the rugged Klamath-Siskiyou Mountains and the Kalmiopsis Wilderness. It was awarded federally-designated *Wild and Scenic River* status, one of only a few rivers on the Oregon Coast to be so honored. The tidal estuary itself is less than four miles long.

Even before the jetties were built, the timber industry returned in a big way, harvesting newly opened national forest timber acreage in the Chetco, Pistol, and Winchuck River watersheds. South Coast Lumber Company began operations in 1950, soon followed by Brookings Plywood in 1952. Both mills are still operating and remain major employers in the town.

Each year on Memorial Day weekend, the neighboring towns of Brookings and Harbor sponsor the Brookings-Harbor Azalea Festival. As of this writing (2024) the festival is in its 85th year. Featuring a float parade, the Azalea Queen and her court, and many food and entertainment events spread over three days, it really is a small town version of the Pasadena Rose Festival – except for the football game.

Unlike many rivers farther north, the Chetco River salmon runs were never commercially harvested for local canneries, perhaps because of lack of transportation, leaving the river as a prime sportfishing stream. Five miles to the south, the small Winchuck River, some 27 miles long, also has a small estuary, as does the Pistol River to the north. These rivers also have good salmon and steelhead fishing in the fall and winter.

<u>Library:</u> Chetco Community Public Library, 405 Alder Street.

<u>Playground:</u> Azalea Park, 640 Old County Road.

Azalea Park: Rest stop, playground, stroll. Exit Hwy 101 just north of Chetco River Bridge on N. Bank Chetco River Road; turn left immediately on Old County Road. Continue up the hill 0.1 mile to the park and turn right into one of the two parking lots.

Azalea Park, once a state park but now lovingly maintained by the citizens of the city of Brookings, affords the traveling family a great opportunity to burn off some energy. The park features many beautiful, centuries-old, wild azalea bushes in a grassy park environment, perhaps the largest azalea bushes on the coast. Best blooms are in the spring; they are various shades of white, pink, and coral. You should note the wonderful aroma of the wild azaleas.

You should note the wonderful aroma of the wild azaleas

Landscape azaleas sold in nurseries all over the United States originated in eastern Asia and are odorless. The city has recently built a massive wooden play structure and modern restroom facilities. Hard-surfaced strolling trails run throughout the park. You will find picnic tables and a bandstand which frequently hosts town festivals.

Wildlife habitats: Park, meadow, evergreen forest.

Loeb State Park: Side trip, rest stop, stroll, woodland hike. Exit Hwy 101 on North Bank Chetco River Road just north of Chetco River Bridge. Park entrance 7.5 miles up the Chetco River.

If you didn't have time to stop to see the redwoods in California, this is your last chance on the Oregon Coast to see some large redwoods, as they don't occur any farther north. Will the redwood forest creep up the coast as the climate warms? Good question. They do well in landscape plantings.

Loeb State Park is situated in a grove of ancient Oregon myrtle trees (*Umbellularia californica*). As the Latin name suggests, they also grow along the northern California coast where they are called California bay laurel. The fragrant leaves are often substituted for bay leaves in local cuisine – you can crush a leaf in your fingers and enjoy the aroma. They are not related to the Holy Land myrtle tree (*Myrtus communes*) referred to in the Bible, as the flowers and fruit are quite different, but they are beautiful and fragrant just the same.

You enter the park on the short road to the gravel bar next to the river; people often drive out onto the bar to get their picnic closer to the river and the swimming hole – or earlier in the year to fish for trout, and in the winter for salmon and steelhead. Before entering the gravel bar, there is a parking lot, with primitive restroom on your right. Modern restrooms are found in the picnic and camping areas farther to the right by the meadow, all connected by extensive paved strolling trails.

Chetco River at Loeb Park. *This swimming hole "up the river" at Loeb State Park is where many of the children in Brookings learn to swim. Eight miles inland from the ocean, the park is usually sunny in the summer when Brookings is socked in and cold. The water never gets very warm, but give it a try. During fall and winter, this site is popular for fishing spot for*

salmon and steelhead, and as a launch site for drift boats. It is also one of the few places along the Chetco that the hatchery tankers can drive to the water in order to plant young trout and salmon. Campers, picnickers, fishermen, and swimmers are all welcome, but it never gets very crowded. The varied rocks on the gravel bar (you won't find much sand for your beach blanket) represent the huge variety of rock formations in the extensive Chetco watershed in the Klamath Mountains.

River Trail at Loeb Park. The shady, well-maintained River View Trail runs upstream from the main entrance to the park through a grove of myrtle, maple, and alder trees. All along the trail there are views through the trees to the Chetco River and gravel bars. Sword ferns (shown), maidenhair ferns, and lady ferns line the path, as well as tart-but-tasty wood sorrel at ground level.

Redwood Nature Trail at Loeb Park. *The tumbling creek on Redwood Nature Trail, a beautiful but more challenging trail, extends up the hillside from the end of River View Trail. The trail passes through the northernmost grove of redwood trees in Oregon, well worth seeing if you missed the larger groves in California. A cascading stream waters abundant ferns and mosses at ground level.*

Another interesting trail to stroll is the River View Trail, starting at the sign just into the park entrance. It leads you half a mile through an ancient Oregon myrtle grove with a few tanoaks, alders, bigleaf maples, and a couple of small redwood trees mixed in. You will see many ferns – sword fern, maidenhair fern, lady fern, and a few tiny licorice ferns growing in the moss on low-angle tree trunks.

> ***You will see many ferns – sword fern, deer fern, maidenhair fern, lady fern, and a few tiny licorice ferns growing in the moss on low-angle tree trunks.***

The latter has roots in the moss that taste like licorice. All the way there are views through the trees to the Chetco River. The trail is generally maintained to be stroller-ready, but watch for some exposed roots and rocks.

A beautiful but more challenging rainforest trail is the 1.6 mile Redwood Nature Trail, starting at a trailhead parking lot with a sign, half a mile east of Loeb Park. It takes you up a small tumbling creek and through a grove of old-growth redwoods, but it has 290 feet of elevation gain and is not graded for strollers. There is a primitive restroom at the trailhead parking lot.

Wildlife habitats: River, conifer forest, meadow.

Gardener Ridge: Side trip. From Chetco River Bridge on Hwy 101, drive 5.2 miles east on North Bank Chetco River Road to Gardner Ridge Road, turn left and continue on a steep and windy paved road 4.0 miles to a ridge where the forest opens and gives you a grand view of the Klamath Mountains.

Gardener ridge is a short side trip that is guaranteed to get you above the summer coastal fog, which you may be able to see filling the river valley below. During May and June, pink rhododendrons light the way. There are no restroom facilities here, but there are modern restrooms at Crissey Field Visitors' Center, at Loeb State Park, and at the Chetco harbor. The only strolling opportunity is along the paved road itself, but the road is seldom used. This is your best opportunity to view a broad expanse of the Klamath Mountains from a paved road, and on a clear day they can be visually stunning.

The rugged Klamath Mountains to the east rise to over 4000 feet in elevation and show a few signs of glaciation from the Pleistocene ice age. The rocks are all igneous and metamorphic, having been uplifted from deep in the Earth's crust. There are many abandoned chromium mines in the area, mostly shallow diggings. Much of the terrain in the far distance is included in the Kalmiopsis Wilderness, named for the miniature rhododendron that grows there and nowhere else. It does particularly well on the thin high-magnesium soil that has developed on the serpentine rock substrate. Douglas-fir doesn't thrive there; the mountains to the east have always been more brushy than forested except in the river canyons.

Two enormous forest fires just in the last decade have burned almost the entire area east of the viewpoint; the most recent fire threatened the town of Brookings. The rounded mountain to the south is Mt. Emily, which could be watched from town as it burned. You can still see burn patterns from the forest fires on the slopes. Far to the southeast you can make out the Siskiyou Mountains in California, a taller range of the Klamath Mountains, which was more heavily

*Far to the southeast you can make out the
glaciated Siskiyou Mountains*

glaciated during the Pleistocene. In the near distance you see recently logged patches, burned areas, and areas in various stages of reforestation. Along the road you will see patches of pink and white foxgloves, a widespread invasive flower from southern Europe. Just ahead is a dense, younger, second-growth fir stand with trees in the 6-12 foot range, with some interspersed species: huckleberry, chinquapin, rhododendron, manzanita, salal, madrone, myrtle, and live oak. The Douglas-fir trees will eventually outgrow the broadleaf species, leaving any surviving shrubs as a sparse understory in a dense Douglas-fir monoculture. This progression can be seen in the more mature second growth stand another half mile along the road at the bottom of the slope. There the young forest is quite dense, with Douglas-firs 12 to 18 inches in diameter. Little sunlight reaches the ground. The understory has been reduced to scattered tanoak, sword fern, huckleberry, and a few forbs, but is mostly barren.

Wildlife habitats: Logged land, mountain scrub, second growth conifer forest.

Chetco River Harbor: Rest stop, beach hike, stroll. Located on the south bank of the Chetco River estuary on Lower Harbor Road. Exit Hwy 101 to the east just south of Chetco River Bridge and loop around under the bridge to the south. From the north, exit to the west at the sign. Or from either direction, exit toward the west on Benham Lane a mile farther south.

The harbor complex you see at the mouth of the Chetco River is mostly fairly new, as the jetties were completed only in 1957 and the boat basin after that. But once a harbor was created it became very active as both lumber and fishing port. Salmon, shrimp, and Dungeness crabs have been harvested offshore in large quantities, and there are still two large lumber and plywood mills in town. The boat basin docks and many boats were severely damaged by the tsunami caused by the 2011 Tohoku earthquake in Japan but they have since been repaired.

Chetco Harbor Beach at Low Tide. The sandy, driftwood-covered beach is seen from the south jetty of the Chetco River as the morning fog recedes.

The broad sloping beach and drift log piles indicate both the tidal range and the power of the winter storms, when sea level is also somewhat higher. Note the lack of gravel deposits that dominate the mouth of the Winchuck farther south. The gravel washed down the Chetco River has mostly been deposited on gravel flats upstream in the estuary, where they have been extensively mined.

Parking is available along the beach and sea wall but may be crowded. Additional parking is available on the east side by the boat basin. There is a pleasant half-mile hike along the beach from the south jetty to some rock promontories. You can go a little farther when the tide is low, but watch out as it is a tough scramble up the bank if you get caught by the incoming tide. For strolling, there is a good trail along the low sea wall and around the parking lot with good views of the ocean, the estuary, and the boat harbor. Modern restrooms are located on the north end by the estuary and in the east side parking lot next to the boat basin.

The Chetco estuary is only a few miles long and is dominated by gravel washed down from upstream. Consequently, salt marshes were never formed; the tide flats are gravel bars. Some have long been mined for road gravel and concrete. With its source high in the Klamath Mountains and only a few farms on the small floodplain,

With its source high in the Klamath Mountains and designated as a Wild and Scenic River, the upper Chetco River is inaccessible by road

the Chetco has been designated a *Wild and Scenic River*; the upper watershed is inaccessible by road. It is consequently one of the least polluted rivers in the state. The lower river and estuary are very popular with fishermen, who catch Chinook salmon during the fall and steelhead during the winter. A run of sea-run cutthroat trout enters the river in the summer. Charter-boat fishing offshore for Chinook salmon is popular and can be successful in the summer and fall, before the fish migrate up the river with the first heavy rains. Ocean perch and ling cod are occasionally caught in the lower estuary.

Wildlife habitats: Ocean, jetty, sandy beach, estuary, brushy bluff, harbor. Sea gulls are common, especially on the beach; you often see them following the fishing boats into the harbor.

Easter Lilies (Lilium longiforum)

With its cool equable climate and fertile coastal plain, Brookings has been called the Easter lily capitol of the United States, perhaps even the world. However, more of the crop is currently raised just over the California border on the Smith River delta. Unfortunately for the visitor, the growers discovered many years ago that allowing the plants bloom sapped energy from the bulbs and caused them not to grow as large. Now the blooms are picked at the bud stage and dropped in the row as mulch. Lily fields in full bloom are a thing of the past. Consequently, the Brookings Lily Festival of my memory in the 1950s with its lily-festooned parade floats can no longer be held. Lily fields can still be seen along the ocean side of Hwy 101 between Brookings and the California state line.

The potted Easter lilies you find in the flower shop have had a three-season growing history. It begins with marble-sized bulblets taken from the adult plant when it is dug up – you can see the

The potted Easter lilies you find in the flower shop have had a three-season growing history

bulblets on the underground stem of your potted Easter lily when you pull it out. These are planted in the autumn and harvested the following summer as one- to two-inch diameter "yearlings" with no commercial value. Another year in the ground produces the large bulbs that are sold into the floral industry, where they are finally planted in pots for their third growing season. But Easter lilies don't naturally bloom at Eastertime, nor is Easter celebrated in their native Japan. They prefer to bloom in late spring. The lily plants must be

carefully forced in the greenhouses with artificial light and temperature conditions to be in full bloom at Easter – at whatever date in
the early spring that happens to occur. So you can appreciate why
a fine Easter lily plant with six to ten blooms is fairly expensive.

Strange as it may seem, both the lily bulbs and lily bulblets are
edible and quite tasty – as are bulbs of several other lily varieties,
including the tiger lily you may see on your Oregon travels. Even
the buds and flowers can be consumed; the flowers are said to make
a colorful addition to a salad. Just be sure to stay away from
daylilies, which are unrelated and can be poisonous. Although
Easter lilies are seldom eaten in our country, the Japanese serve
them raw, sautéed, or cooked in a stew. The bulbs had an important
advantage in the days before refrigerated food storage, as they
lasted for long periods underground. Please note that as the intense
pollen of Easter lilies may cause hay fever or even hives in some
people. It is possible that the eating the bulbs may also cause an allergic reaction.

**Harris Beach State Park: Rest stop, beach hike, stroll. Located just
north of Brookings on Hwy 101.**

This state park is comprised of two main parts: the "drive-down"
beach access and the recreation and camping area on the terrace
above, which also has primitive trails to the beach. It is the "drive-
down" I suggest for a rest stop, featuring a large parking lot just
above the beach and the outlet of small Harris Creek. Sea gulls seem
to like such minor creek outlets and can often be seen congregating
there. Perhaps they enjoy the fresh water bath and a drink that they
don't have to desalinate.

Harris Beach State Park in Brookings. *This is the view northward from the beachside parking lot. Like where many small coastal streams cross the beach, a shallow pond forms behind the sand berm that builds up in the summer. As you can see here gulls seem to enjoy a fresh water bath. In the distant offshore there are numerous seastacks; many have been included in the Oregon Islands National Wildlife Refuge. You can see the difficulty in deciding which rocks should be included and which should be left out in the collection of more than 1800 seastacks. The best plan is to stay away from all of them. The largest of them all, Bird Island, is readily visible to the west from this parking lot.*

Just below the picnic tables, a five-minute walk along the beach to the south brings you to a collection of large white rocks. A primitive trail goes beyond but it is hazardous and I don't recommend it. The large white rocks are of igneous origin, apparently related to an ancient volcanic event. Careful examination reveals tiny crystals of quartz and feldspar in a finely crystalline ground mass. On one edge you can find subtle flow structures. It is an unusual rock type for the Oregon Coast. Farther inland, on Mt. Emily behind the town of Brookings, a similar volcanic rock formation has been named the *Mt. Emily rhyolite* – probably another relict of the same ancient volcanic activity. But isn't clear where the volcano was located, as rock outcrops are sparse along the coast. Today the closest known volcanoes are in the Cascades, a hundred miles to the east, and they appear to be much more recent. The hill above the drive-down to the beach is of the same volcanic material – perhaps it is an eroded volcanic neck. When the terrace on which the hill and the campground are located was at or just below sea level, the hill was certainly a seastack looming above the waves. At the seaward edge of the parking lot there is another outcrop of the rhyolite that is very tempting as a climbing rock. People have fallen down the steep seaward face so it has been fenced off. I suggest it should be avoided. With luck, you may find wild strawberries in the meadow area and wild mountain blackberries on the brushy bank, but watch out for poison oak.

Strolling trails here are limited to the large parking lot, but it has a nice view of the beach and the sound of the breakers. You can find more stroller trails and modern restrooms in the campground and rest stop on the terrace above the beach. Bird Island is only 1400 feet offshore. It is called Goat Island on USGS and Google maps, but locals pay no attention to that. It looks like a good place for goats, but I don't know how you would ever get them there. Bird Island is the largest of more than 1800 offshore rocks that make up Oregon Islands National Wildlife Refuge and hosts many varieties of seabirds.

Bird Island is the largest of more than 1800 offshore rocks in Oregon Islands National Wildlife Refuge

On the terrace at the top of the drive to the beach there are several pullovers along the old highway. From each there is a steep trail through the brush to a larger beach below. As there is no road access, this fine beach is never crowded, and it is less exposed to the summer wind. When the tide is out, numerous tidepools can be found at the neck of the flat-topped seastack where it joins the beach.

From the beach parking lot, it is possible to hike 1.5 miles north along the shore, sometimes sandy, sometimes rocky, with some climbing involved, to Rainbow Rock. It takes a bit of a scramble and I don't recommend it except for geologists and mountaineers, but Rainbow Rock is a geological phenomenon well worth the effort for the sure-footed.

Wildlife habitats: Open ocean, seastacks, sandy beach, rocky shore, brushy bluff, brushy creek.

Future Geologist: Rainbow Rock, Boardman State Park. Visible below a highway pullout 4.2 miles north of Chetco River Bridge or 6.0 miles south of Thomas Creek Bridge.

Rainbow Rock is an interesting geological phenomenon, just visible through the brush from a pullout on the west side of Hwy 101. It can only be reached along the shore from Harris Beach State Park, but it is a scramble and I don't recommend it unless you are a geologist, a mountain climber, or otherwise accustomed to such efforts. A primitive trail once reached the beach from the parking area; you may be able to find it. The closest restroom facilities are those at Harris Beach State Park.

Rainbow Rock. *Rainbow Rock, just north of Brookings, a stunning banded chert outcrop. It is poorly visible from the highway, but can be accessed with some rock scrambling from the beachside parking lot at Harris Beach State Park a mile to the south. The banded chert is composed of siliceous marine radiolarian skeletons, deposited in a mud-free environment far from shore. It appears that the deposit slumped down a submarine slope before it became buried and consolidated and became tightly folded in the process.*

Rainbow Rock is a house-sized block of banded chert of various colors and tightly contorted. Wave action has cut tunnels through it. It is clearly out of place in this geological environment, surrounded by marine shale and sandstone – I have not seen any other chert outcrops or chert boulders in the area - or anywhere else along the Oregon Coast. Banded chert is a marine rock made up almost entirely of the opal skeletons of siliceous plankton, in this case radiolarians. A geologist would tell you that the original site of deposition was protected from terrestrial mud, probably far from the modern coastline. It was likely located on a distant seamount that was later pushed against the edge of the continent. Tight folding indicates that the deposit slid down a submarine slope soon after deposition, before it was consolidated into rock. It ended up totally out of place in the deep-water mud rock deposit that now surrounds it. The whole rock formation was then buried thousands of feet, where the original opal was compressed and converted into chert. Finally, the tectonic activity along the west coast pushed it to the surface where it was cleaned up by the waves for us to see. So where did Rainbow Rock come from? There are no clues in the local geology, much of which is covered by brush. Geologists have determined that the rocks along the southern Curry County coast have slid to the north along a large fault, but their exact origin is unclear.

Lone Ranch Beach: Rest Stop, beach hike, stroll. Located 5.2 miles north of Chetco River Bridge and 4.8 miles south of Thomas Creek Bridge. From Hwy 101, turn west at the Lone Ranch Beach sign and follow the short paved road to the parking lot above the beach.

Here we have a scenic half-mile beach walk to the south, down to the rock bluff and back with a mass of driftwood and a brush-covered slope to your left and the open sea to your right. In the rainy season you might need to wade Ram Creek where it crosses the sand, but it doesn't flow all year. Twin rocks, a third of a mile offshore from the bluff, are both seabird habitats, so bring your binoculars. A shorter walk to the north accesses some tide pools along a rocky shoreline, but you may get your feet wet crossing Lone Ranch Creek. Sometimes drift logs provide a bridge there.

A paved loop trail past the picnic tables to the beach

There is a paved loop trail past the picnic tables to the beach, making a nice 10-minute trail for strollers. A primitive restroom is located across the meadow to the north. The vegetation along Lone Ranch Creek affords a good place to look at the riparian species in the brushy creek bottom habitat, here made up of red alder, willow, and a few (non-edible) twinberry bushes. This kind of dense vegetative cover tends to keep the water shaded and cool for the trout. In addition to shade, the trees drop insects into the water that the fish can eat, and perhaps offer protection from ospreys. You can see small cutthroat trout in the pools of the shaded creek if you are stealthy, especially if you have a caterpillar to toss in.

Wildlife habitats: Open ocean, seastacks, sandy beach, rocky shore, coastal meadow, brushy bluff, creek outflow, brushy creek bottom.

Thomas Creek Bridge: Rest stop, scenic viewpoint. Located 10 miles north of Chetco River Bridge and 8.6 miles south of Pistol River Bridge. Parking lots at both ends.

At a height of 345 feet, Thomas Creek Bridge ranks as the highest bridge in Oregon – all to cross a creek that you could easily wade. For comparison, the iconic Golden Gate Bridge is 80 feet lower at the midpoint, although the support towers are far taller. The bridge is only 950 feet across with sidewalks on both sides, providing a short but really scenic stroller trip if it isn't too windy. For more ambitious hikers, a steep trail takes you down to a viewpoint above the beach, then continues south past several more viewpoints as a particularly scenic section of the Oregon Coast Trail. The numerous nearshore seastacks are short and wave washed but may occasionally host some seabirds. There is a primitive restroom at the south parking lot.

Thomas Creek Bridge is eighty feet
higher than the Golden Gate Bridge

Just looking at the Thomas Creek gorge shows you the engineering challenge of building a highway along the southern Oregon Coast in the 1930s. Highway 101 was routed high in the hills to avoid the gorge, reaching an elevation of 1770 feet near Carpenterville, only a couple miles to the east as the sea gull flies. What could have carved such a canyon as the one you see? Thomas Creek certainly doesn't look up to the task. The old Highway 101 through Carpenterville is a slow and curvy but scenic drive through the coastal hills and forest. Motorcyclists may like it. Named Carpenterville Road, it can be accessed either at the north edge of Brookings or at Pistol River. The new highway and Thomas Creek Bridge were built in 1961.

Wildlife habitats: You can see the ocean, a few seastacks, sea cliffs, a stream outlet, and a sandy beach far below, but there is no way to get to them. Both ends of the bridge are in a conifer forest.

Arch Rock Viewpoint: Rest stop, woodland hike, stroll. Located 3.0 miles north of Thomas Creek Bridge, 5.6 miles south of Pistol River Bridge.

As a geologist, Arch Rock Viewpoint is one of my favorite rest stops on the Oregon Coast. A quarter-mile paved loop trail extends from the parking lot to the viewpoint and back, shaded by large Sitka spruce trees with an understory of berry bushes, ferns, and a lovely ground cover of false lily of the valley. But please mind the low wooden fence that has been constructed. A fall down the cliff could be fatal, and a quick rescue nearly impossible by land or by sea. For serious hikers, the Oregon Coast Trail can be accessed from the parking lot.

Arch Rock Viewpoint is a coastal geomorphologist's dream

Arch Rock Viewpoint is a coastal geomorphologist's dream. It is possible to see not only what has happened in the past, but also what is happening right now and what will certainly transpire in the distant future. You can see two, possibly three, close-to-shore seastacks to the south of the viewpoint and two more to the north, and Arch Rock out to sea to the west. The seastacks have flat or gently sloping tops that were once continuations of the mainland and the viewpoint terrace on which you are standing just a few thousand years in the past. Each retains a remnant copse of Sitka spruce and underbrush, carefully nurturing patches of what can only be the original topsoil. Seabirds can be seen resting on them; they afford good nesting sites. It is seastacks like these that Oregon Islands National Wildlife Refuge was created to protect.

Arch Rock. *This view is just off the end of the end of the peninsula at Arch Rock Scenic Viewpoint, reached by the strolling path. Arch Rock is clearly one of the seastack "islands" protected by the Oregon Islands National*

Wildlife Reserve. It no longer retains the original topsoil and mini-forest on the crest and is too wave-washed for secure nest sites, but it provides a temporary perch for pelagic sea birds. You can see a few swimming. In the ocean just in front of the seastack you can see some patches of kelp seaweed that have somehow survived the purple sea urchin onslaught – today an unusual sight along the Northern California and Oregon Coasts. Why the arch? Probably some softer rock got eroded out by the surf, which is seldom calm.

Coastal View South from Arch Rock Peninsula. *In this view to the south of Arch Rock peninsula, you can view a section of primitive cliffed coastline, with a sand beach below and a Sitka spruce forest above the cliff face. The bush in the foreground is a tanoak, with a shore pine to its right and a Sitka spruce to the left. Marine sandstones and mudstones of the cliff are being undercut and eroded by the ocean waves during high tides: the beach sand appears to be composed of residue from the cliff. There is no access to this lovely pocket beach and there are no footprints visible – has it ever been visited?*

Seastacks South of Arch Rock Peninsula. *Three seastacks can be seen in this view to the south from Arch Rock peninsula; the two closer ones still retain their original caps of soil and forest cover. The farther one is a little lower and has had the soil cover washed away by the waves. It is clear in this view that the seastacks were once continuous with the forested bluff on the left; the little copses of Sitka spruce could not have evolved on a bare rock. Pelagic sea birds find opportunities for nests in soil-covered and veg-etated seastacks such as these and on the inaccessible seacliffs.*

In a few more millennia, it is likely that the viewpoint promontory itself will join the family of seastacks, cut off from the mainland by the encroaching sea. Just like the seastacks you observe today, it will initially retain its topsoil, its Sitka spruce grove, and its ground cover of false lily of the valley, eventually becoming another haven for nesting pelagic seabirds. One can observe the process happening today. To the south of the narrow viewpoint peninsula is a small pocket beach, made up of the sand and gravel being actively eroded from the cliffs immediately above them. Note the lack of footprints: it is easy to imagine that there never have been any! This kind of erosion is going on all along the cliffed coastlines of the southern Oregon Coast. That is one reason the water near shore often seems murky, even when the sea is deep blue farther out. One additional advantage of this rest stop: there are wild strawberries growing in the meadow below the parking lot.

Note, however, that despite having only a primitive restroom, Arch Rock is 16 scenic miles south of the next restroom facilities in Gold Beach. There are no restroom facilities provided at the many scenic pullouts along the way.

Wildlife habitats: Open ocean, seastacks, seacliffs, sandy beach, conifer forest, coastal meadow.

Chapter 4

Early People on the Oregon Coast

When settlers began to arrive on the Oregon Coast in the 1850s they encountered many Native American tribes already living there, each with its own customs and unique language. The tribes could be distinguished by the languages they spoke, which belonging to three distinct language families: Tolowa, Penutian, and Salish. These language families are totally unrelated, as different from one another as today's Germanic, Romance, and Slavic language families in modern Europe, with different vocabulary, pronunciation, and even different language structure. Within each language family there were several individual tribal languages.

At least seventeen individual languages were spoken by tribes living along the coast. More than twenty additional languages were spoken just over the coastal mountain ranges in the interior valleys. Perhaps nowhere in the world was there more linguistic variety in such a limited area. Language study can be important to anthropological research: it is more than a medium of communication, but also of cultural identity, an indication of tribal territory, and of tribal history. It is sometimes all we have. An excellent colored map of the western Oregon tribal language areas can be found online at: https://libraryguides.lanecc.edu/americanindianlanguages, published by the Lane County Community College in Eugene.

Several factors have made the investigation of the Native American languages of the Pacific Northwest far more difficult than the study the history of European languages, and therefore less useful in tracking the history of the individual tribes. Foremost is that none were written languages. European and Middle Eastern languages sometimes have thousands of years of written history, some that evolved into languages still spoken today. Many oral histories and legends were recorded, often in religious documents. The oral histories and legends of the Oregon Native Americans have mostly been lost, as most of the tribes were long ago decimated by European diseases, warfare, and brutal colonization practices. Only a few of the oldest speakers are still fluent in some of the languages and dialects; most have none and the tongues are essentially dead. Efforts have been made to resurrect a few Native languages, but this doesn't bring back the legends. A century and a half ago when the legends were still alive, few European Americans were interested in studying them and writing them down. Survivors of the various Native American populations that had been moved to reservations were being encouraged to learn English, adopt Christianity, and forget their Native heritages. Consequently, little has been discovered about the origins of the local languages how they relate to the histories of the small populations that spoke them.

Besides the tribal languages, there is little to go on. Some relevant information can be found in Erna Gunther's book *Indian Life on the Northwest Coast of North America, as Seen by the Early Explorers during the Last Decades of the Eighteenth Century*, but this book, published half a century ago, concentrates mainly on Vancouver Island and Washington, where altogether different languages were spoken. Matson and Coupland's *The Prehistory of the Northwest Coast*, researched and published some twenty years ago, discusses the origins of the three major language families but doesn't get into the individual languages and dialects.

Why such linguistic variety? Probably several reasons. First, the tribes apparently migrated to the Oregon Coast from different areas. Second, the rugged coastal geography makes for difficult travel – the highway you are travelling was completed only in the 1930s. Finally, and perhaps most importantly, the tribes had little reason to move around and interact with one another. The tribal areas all had largely the same resources: salmon, lampreys, and other fish in the many rivers and streams; shellfish in the estuaries and along the rocky coast; seabirds and their nests all along the coast; abundant

wild berries and roots; elk and deer in the forests; and ample building materials derived from the local forests. There was little to trade
with neighboring tribes or to fight over. But the isolation and linguistic variety engendered a grave disadvantage as well: without
effective regional communication and government along the Oregon Coast, the tribes were never able to mount an organized defense
against the settlers as they began to arrive in the 1850s, unlike the
Indian Wars of the American Midwest and Great Plains.

So who lived along the coast before the settlers arrived, and
where did they originate? Starting in the south, in Curry County,
Oregon, and also in the northwestern corner of California, the Native Americans belonged to several tribes of the Tolowa, also called
Taa-laa-wa Dee-ni'. At least in part because of the rugged nature of
the mountainous region and inherent difficulty of travel from one
area to another, regional dialects developed and evolved into more
than a dozen distinct languages, extending inland as far as Mt.
Shasta and as far north far as the Coquille River. Each tended to be
centered on a resource center, often a river estuary such as the
Chetco, Smith, or Eel. There were at least six tribes on the Oregon
coast, three more on the California coast, and several more just inland – each with its own Tolowa-family language. The Chetco and
Winchuck river names come from Chetco, a Tolowa language. My
second-grade teacher in Brookings didn't share any of her Chetco
language with her students – if in fact she knew any.

How did the Tolowa people get there? An oral history recorded
in the *Oregon Encyclopedia* posits that the Tolowa people arrived
from the north by canoe. Based on the limited degree of diversity of
the many local languages and dialects in the language family, some
linguists feel that must have happened around seven hundred years
ago. Other estimates found online put their arrival at between one
thousand and three thousand years ago. Absent from the oral histories is any indication that other tribes were displaced. Perhaps that
remote area was uninhabited. There is little to go on.

Tolowa languages are of the Athabasca language family, tongues still spoken in much of northern Canada and interior Alaska. There is currently a tribe living on the southeastern Alaska archipelago, the Tlingits, who also speak an Athabascan language. They even have a tradition of dugout canoes, made of cedar logs, and some are quite large, said to have been capable of carrying as many as sixty warriors. It is a long trip, but an expedition of Tlingit people must have paddled down the coast to southern Oregon or northwestern California and established a colony there, just as the Vikings colonized England, Iceland and Greenland more than a thousand years ago in longboats of similar size. But possibly not all at once – there are two isolated Athabascan-speaking Native American tribes located along the way, but not, at least presently, on the coast: one at Clatskanie, east of Astoria, and the other in the Willipa Hills of southwestern Washington. There could have been other stops along the way, even colonies, for which we have no information. And the Tolowa were also known to construct large dugout canoes, but of redwood instead of cedar: some up to forty feet in length. Smaller dugout canoes were in use up and down the coast. Because of the many inlets, and the Strait of Juan de Fuca that had to be crossed between southeastern Alaska and Oregon, the migration of new coastal settlers by ocean-going canoes seems essential. The new area they colonized is not so different from the southeastern Alaska archipelago: perhaps even more readily habitable, with a warmer climate, similarly abundant salmon, shellfish, berries, and game resources, and the addition of tanoak acorns as a dietary staple.

Unlike some southeastern Alaskan tribes, the Tolowa didn't construct totems, which would have been useful in cultural identity. But in northwestern California, other ancient Tolowa customs are being followed and their languages are being taught in schools. Recently a feast was held at a tribal gathering in Smith River, a village just over the California border from Brookings. The menu included, in addition to Chinook salmon and elk steaks roasted over an open fire, several traditional foods: sea anemones, lampreys, seaweed, smelt, and acorn bread. This traditional diet was most likely followed by the Tolowa tribes in southwestern Oregon as well and probably by unrelated tribes farther north along the coast.

Continuing north, we encounter a stretch of coast from Coos Bay to Yaquina Bay formerly inhabited by six tribes who spoke Penutian languages, seemingly spilled over from the Willamette Valley. Penutian is a huge language family, with speakers along the Columbia River, the Willamette Valley, and after a gap, the Great Valley of California. Coosan is one of these, spoken by the Coos people who helped out the Dragoons of the schooner *Captain Lincoln* when they were shipwrecked on the Coos Bay's north spit in 1851. Many coastal rivers and lakes have Penutian language names: Coos, Siletz, Siuslaw, Umpqua, Yaquina, Siltcoos, Woahink, and others. Nowadays you can visit one of the two Three Rivers Casinos in Coos Bay or Florence. They are owned and operated by the Confederated Tribes of Coos, Lower Umpqua, and Siuslaw Indians – all Penutian tribes.

North of Yaquina Bay, up to Cannon Beach, we are in the former territories of six tribes who spoke Salish languages. Salish speakers are found in most of Washington, northern Idaho, western Montana, and southern British Columbia. The Blackfeet of Montana spoke a Salish language. Today, the Oregon coastal Salish are separated from the main Salish region by territories of Penutian speaking tribes. How did that come to be – are the Salish invaders, or original inhabitants? It suggests a chapter of local history of which we know nothing. In Oregon, probably the best-known Salish tribe is the Tillamooks, after whom a river, a bay, a town, a county, and a world-famous cheese are all named. It was the Tillamooks that were found cutting up a whale at Ecola Creek and sold some whale oil and blubber to members of the Lewis and Clark expedition.

Finally, just south of the mouth of the Columbia River, we enter the land of the Clatsops, another Penutian-language tribe. Clatsop County is named in their honor. A strip of Penutian-speaking tribes extends along the lower Columbia River to connect to the Willamette Valley tribes that speak these languages.

One final language of the lower Columbia area is *Chinook Jargon*, also called *Chinuk Wawa* or *Chinookian*. This was a trade language used by the Pacific Northwest native tribes and the early fur trappers, who were largely of French Canadian origin. A Chinookian dictionary was composed by local missionaries and published in 1863, but it contains only eight pages. You can access it at https://www.washington.edu/uwired/outreach/cspn/Website/Classroom%20Materials/Curriculum%20Packets/Treaties%20&%20Reservations/Documents/Chinook_Dictionary. Short vocabulary lists were made by early explorers, but the language was never properly documented while it was in widespread use. As Chinuk Wawa is a relatively recently invented language, it has no associated legends of its own, and its precise origin has been difficult to determine. Like other trade languages, it most likely it evolved through time, adopting parts from languages in the large trading area where it was understood, further modified by visitors. *Making Wawa*, a recent book by George Lang, investigates the origins and influences of Wawa, of which there are several:

> The base language is Chinook, a Penutian language spoken by tribes living near the mouth of the Columbia River, a natural trading crossroads for both Native tribes and European visitors.

> As the Chinook owned slaves taken from surrounding tribes, words from those tribal languages may have been adopted.

> In-marrying women from nearby tribes brought vocabulary with them.

> Early European visitors, mainly Spanish and English, came by ship. Nootka Sound on northern Vancouver Island was an important layover. Some learned the local language and brought Nootka words to the growing Chinuk Wawa lingua franca.

> The first land-based visitors were trappers of French-Canadian origin, many of whom took native wives. French words, much modified, came into the language from that source, and their wives from nearby tribes were probably instrumental in creating the lingua franca.

As later arrivals spoke mostly English, that language increasingly permeated Chinuk Wawa. One might suspect that the early Spanish and Russian visitors would have contributed to the language, but if they did, the contributions were very small.

When members of many disparate western Oregon tribes were all pushed into a reservation along the coast in the 1850s, Chinookian turned out to be their only common language. It is currently being revived by the Confederated Tribes of Grande Ronde in a reservation in the Coast Range west of Salem.

There is another factor that may relate to the distribution of the Oregon Coast tribal territories, although somewhat speculative in its possible effect. During what geologists call the Pleistocene epoch, lowered sea level exposed a coastal plain west of the current Oregon coastline some 20 to 30 miles wide. It is reasonable to suppose that the Oregon coastal plain was inhabited during these ancient times, as it lies right on the southward coastal path from Alaska, and ultimately from Siberia. At the time, there may have been no other route south, as the ice-free corridor across Canada is not thought to have been open then. The route southward along the coast of Alaska and Canada can't have been easy, with many glaciers to circumvent, but with canoes the trip should have been possible. From around 15,000 years ago to 7,000 years ago, sea level offshore Oregon – and the entire world – increased by some 350 feet, inundating the Pleistocene coastal plain and creating a submerged continental shelf in its place. Perhaps legends of this same event in Asia Minor led to the Biblical account of Noah's flood (Genesis, Chapter 6).

We know from recent archaeological discoveries that there were humans at Cooper's Ferry, on the Salmon River in western Idaho 15,000 to 16,000 years ago – just up the Columbia and Snake Rivers from the coast. Archaeologists even found bones of horses that have long been extinct in North America: apparently they were never domesticated here. (Imagine how different the history of conquest in North America would have been, had the early Native Americans had learned to ride horses! Did the new Americans eat the horses instead? Fortunately, the early horses, which had evolved on the grasslands of North America, migrated to Asia across the Bering land bridge during the Pleistocene. There they became domesticated and were ultimately returned to North America by the Spanish Conquistadors!

At White Sands National Park in New Mexico, fossil human footprints have been identified in lakebeds between 21,000 and 23,000 years old, based on carbon 14 dating of associated seeds. These findings and others precede the Clovis People and have re-ignited the debate on Native American origins. You can find an excellent review of the subject with a comprehensive map of the early, pre-Clovis archaeological finds at the following link in Live Science: https://www.livescience.com/archaeology/the-1st-americans-were-not-who-we-thought-they-were.

Chapter 5

Gold Beach and the Rogue River

Gold Beach

Gold Beach – what a fine name for a town on the coast, especially a for town that is trying to attract vacationers. There are Gold Coasts all over the world – Australia, Hong Kong, Uruguay, Spain and particularly Africa – but I haven't located another Gold Beach. Maybe you know of one. Around the year 1700, there were six European colonies along the beach of Gold Coast, now the country of Ghana. What a gold rush! Even in the United States, there are several areas referred to as Gold Coast, mostly referring to the conspicuous wealth of the people who live there.

Although Gold Beach is one of the older towns along the Oregon Coast, it didn't acquire its present name until 1890. Originally named Ellensburgh, the town was established at the mouth of the Rogue River in the early 1850's. The name honored Miss Ellen, the daughter of Captain William Tichenor. Tichenor was the captain of the schooner Sea Gull, who established the town of Fort Orford, just to the north. In 1890 Ellensburgh was renamed Gold Beach, in order to avoid confusion with the much larger town of Ellensburg, Washington. But the gold in the name is the real metal, referring to placer gold that was being panned on the beach and on the marine terraces up and down the coast. Tiny bits of gold, and a little platinum as well, were noticed in the black layers of beach sand as early as 1852.

The placer gold didn't originate in that area – much of it appears to have been washed down the Rogue River and its tributaries from the hinterland. Smaller local rivers like the Sixes and Elk may have contributed some as well. Over a span of millions of years, entire mountains with gold- and platinum-bearing veins in the Klamath-

Siskiyou Mountain Range have been eroded down to their roots. The resulting nuggets and flakes eroded from the mother lodes became concentrated in the gravelly placer gold deposits in the rivers that drain those mountains. One of the most productive was Jackson Creek, which runs through Jacksonville, Oregon. Rich placer deposits of gold were found there in 1851, causing a local gold mining boom – there were plenty of prospectors available in the California Gold Country who hadn't yet found their fortunes. Today, Jacksonville is a fine old gold town well worth a visit.

The gold that gets to Gold Beach has been ground pretty fine.

However, it is over 100 rugged river miles from Jacksonville to Gold Beach. By the time the gold gets to the beach it has been ground pretty fine. And the rough Oregon Coast surf diminishes the particle size even further, so that any gold dust remaining is almost microscopic in size. The fine gold particles, because they are very dense, are sorted by the ocean waves into the layers of dense black sand. Along the southern Oregon Coast the black sand layers you find on the beach are composed mainly of magnetite, ilmenite, chromite, and a few other dense minerals. These minerals are historically rich ores of iron, titanium, and chromium in other areas, but on the Oregon beaches there isn't enough to be commercially mined for those elements. Black sands you may have seen on the volcanic islands of Hawaii and in the Caribbean are composed of different heavy minerals and grains of basalt. You won't find any gold on those beaches.

The beach and terrace sands around Gold Beach have been panned and sluiced ever since the 1852 gold rush. Beach placer mines extended for miles north and south of the Rogue River. Like with most gold rushes, the best mines quickly played out, but a 1934 U.S. government report described limited mining activity along the coast even at the time of publication – however, that was nearly a century ago. People still prospect for it, and you may find some even today. New gold-bearing black sand layers are winnowed out by the surf with each tide. Sometimes the waves bring in new sand from beyond the surf zone; the gold certainly hasn't all been recovered. Bring a gold pan and try your luck in the black sand layers.

Before the white settlers arrived, the lower Rogue area had been the home of the Tutuni people, an Athabascan-speaking tribe, who harvested the abundant salmon runs from the Rogue River. The Tutuni population was soon overpowered; by 1856 almost all of the Native Americans along the southwestern Oregon Coast had either been killed in a local battle of the shameful Rogue River Indian Wars or banished to the Coast Indian Reservation far to the north. Many did not survive the journey.

By 1858 Gold Beach (then called Ellensburg) had grown enough to be named the county seat of Curry County – but only after Port Orford, the only other significant town at the time, was unable to finance the building of a courthouse. Gold Beach did build a handsome county courthouse, but unfortunately it became too small when the population of the county grew. The old courthouse was torn down and replaced in 1950. Total population of Curry County at that time could not have exceeded a few thousand, as there were no roads to the interior of the state and none of the rivers rising in the Klamath Mountains were navigable. Even today the lower Rogue River west of Grants Pass is mainly a whitewater rafting and fishing stream and has been designated a national *Wild and Scenic River*.

As mining activity declined, Gold Beach turned to commercial salmon fishing. A salmon cannery was built in 1877, followed in 1880 by the construction of small steamship *Mary D. Hume* to carry the canned salmon to market in San Francisco. However, by the early 1900s the salmon runs had declined due to overfishing. In 1915 drift nets were banned in the river. The *Mary D. Hume* had a long life on the West Coast, initially carrying canned salmon to California and most likely bringing the groceries back on the return trip. Following local cannery closures, the small steamer then worked as a cannery tender in Alaska and eventually as a tugboat in Puget

Sound. In 1978, after almost a century, she steamed back to Gold Beach on the Rogue River, like a salmon returning to the place of her birth. Efforts were ongoing to preserve the ship as a museum ship, but because of a mechanical accident she slipped into the mud where she could not be retrieved, and there she sits today. You may still be able to see her hull near the shore upriver from Gold Beach.

During the middle 1900s, logging and lumbering were economic mainstays for Gold Beach, but the mills are no longer active. The U.S. Forest Service maintains the Gold Beach Ranger District office for the extensive Rogue River-Siskiyou National Forest at 29279 Ellensburg Avenue, which is Highway 101 and the main street of Gold Beach. Information, trail maps, passes, and permits for visiting this varied and fascinating national forest can be obtained there. It encompasses nearly 1.8 million acres in the southern Cascades and Klamath-Siskiyou Mountains. Eight National Wilderness Areas and seven Wild and Scenic Rivers are included within it. Much of the rugged mountainous terrain and the river canyons remain roadless.

Rogue River Estuary and the Isaac Lee Patterson Bridge. This beautiful bridge, designed by Conde B. McCullough and completed in 1931, is the first of several mighty depression-era bridges you will cross as you drive

up the coast. It is also the most architecturally pleasing, with its seven iden-
tical arches rising above the estuary. As the Rogue River is not navigable
upstream, a low bridge could be built here. The bridge abutments are
erected atop dozens of timber pilings, logged from the local forest and driven
into the mud of the estuary floor. The bridge was designated a National
Historic Civil Engineering Landmark in 1982 and later put on the Na-
tional Register of Historic Places.

Today sport fishing for Chinook salmon, coho salmon, steelhead, and sea run cutthroat trout are important activities for visitors, as one run of anadromous fish or another is in the Rogue most of the year. In 1960 jetties and a boat basin were built by the U.S. Army Corps of Engineers, but commercial fishing has never returned to its former glory. Today it is the tourism and retirement industries that are keeping the town afloat. In Wedderburn, just across the bridge, mail boats were formerly launched to carry mail to the tiny town of Agnes, 21 miles up the river at the confluence of the Rogue

Jet boat tours up the Rogue now leave from the Port of Gold Beach

and Illinois rivers. Jet boat tours up the Rogue now leave from the Port of Gold Beach, a trip highly recommended, especially when the beaches are cold and fogged in. You can find some colorful historical accounts of life in Gold Beach on the following link: https://www.curryhistory.com/historic-resources/legends-lore.

Traveling north, you will see the beautiful Isaac Lee Patterson Bridge crossing the Rogue River, the first of many magnificent bridges on the coast highway designed by Conde B. McCullough. Constructed in 1931, it helped to open up the economy of the Gold Beach area. The bridge was completed in a hurry, as it was desperately needed to replace the car ferry *Rogue,* which had been damaged in a flood that year. The bridge is a beautiful early example of steel-reinforced concrete arches with art-deco influences. In 1982 it achieved a listing in the National Register of Historic Places.

Although the north and south ends are based in solid rock, the intermediate piers of the bridge are supported by several hundred locally-produced timber pilings driven into the muddy sediment of the estuary floor - belying the appearance that the bridge is floating on the water. The bridge was constructed for less than $600,000 in 1930-1931, but by 2001 a $20,000,000 rehabilitation project became necessary because of its incipient deterioration in the salt air – a problem that has plagued all the concrete and steel bridges along the Oregon Coast. If you stroll across the Isaac Lee Patterson Bridge on a clear day you can see the estuary entrance to the west across the boat harbor. The vantage point also affords a view into the interior of the Klamath-Siskiyou Mountains, usually hidden behind the coastal foothills. Like other rivers in the hard rocks of the Klamath Mountains of southern Oregon, the Rogue wasn't able to cut a deep canyon during the low sea level of the Pleistocene. Consequently, the estuary is short and there are no significant mud flats or salt marshes.

Engineers may find it interesting that the Isaac Lee Patterson Bridge was the first in the United States to incorporate the Freyssinet method of concrete pre-stressing. This novel construction method had been patented in France in 1928 by Eugene Freyssinet. It allows for the use of smaller amounts of concrete to achieve greater structural strength, and therefore a lighter structure. But as the method turned out to be labor intensive, McCullough didn't use it in his later bridges along the Oregon Coast.

Library: Curry Public Library, 94341 3rd Street.

Playground: Kids Castle, located in Collier H. Buffington Memorial Park off Caughell Street.

Gold Beach Waterfront: Rest stop, stroll. Located in Gold Beach, west of Hwy 101 at the northeast end of town along Harbor Way.

At the Gold Beach waterfront you will find a large parking area shared by Jerry's Rogue River Boat Trips and other commercial ventures. The large building on the river side has restaurants, tourist shops, and modern restrooms available to the public. There are sidewalks for strolling on the parking lot and down to the public small-boat harbor.

Readers will have noticed that I have avoided discussion of commercial ventures; other travel guides have been written for that. But Jerry's Rogue River Boat Trips is one I have done and highly recommended. The jet boats are fast and the weather is generally cool at the Gold Beach end, so you will want a windbreaker.

Wildlife habitats: Harbor, estuary.

Rogue River Mouth and Beach: Side trip, beach hike, stroll. From near the south end of Harbor Way in Gold Beach, drive west 0.4 miles on Oceanside Drive past the end of the small boat harbor to the landward end of the south jetty. Parking is available along the jetty.

The Rogue is one of only three rivers between the Sacramento and the Columbia to make it through the coastal mountains to the Cascades, the other two being the Umpqua and the Klamath. But as it had to cut through the old, hard rocks of the rising Klamath Mountains, it didn't get to create much of an estuary – it is only six miles to the head of tidal influence. The canyon it cut is so narrow and rugged that a road has never been built along it all the way to Grants Pass. The river carries a lot of water from its 5100 square mile drainage area – averaging only 7000 cubic feet per second over the year but reaching more than forty times that during winter and spring runoffs. Consequently, the jetties were built 900 feet apart to accommodate the maximum flow. During the summer, after the snow has melted in the Cascades and the seasonal rains in the coastal mountains have stopped, a sand bar builds, extending northward into the channel from the south jetty, with an ocean-facing beach to the west and the Rogue River estuary to the east. There is usually good viewing for shorebirds on the bar, but I don't recommend walking out on it. In the winter when the Rogue River is running stronger the sand bar can be washed away. It is advisable to stay off the jetty as it is low and there is no pathway. Drift logs lodged on the jetty top is testament to the reach of occasional rogue waves. A beach hike is available toward the south, two miles to the mouth of Hunter Creek. For strollers, you will find a packed-sand roadway just behind the beach and driftwood line, extending 0.6 miles south of the jetty. This is one of the only opportunities on the Oregon Coast to drive a sidewalk stroller along the beach in full view and sound of the sea. You will find modern restroom facilities at the Gold Beach waterfront.

Chinook salmon, coho salmon, cutthroat trout, and steelhead are caught as they make their way upstream to spawn

Both the estuary and the Rogue River farther upstream are popular sport fishing destinations. Presumably because of the spring snowmelt in the Cascades where the Rogue has its source, there are both spring and fall salmon runs. You may see numerous small craft trolling for them. Ocean species such as perch, flounder, and smelt are also caught. Occasionally sea lions follow the salmon, lampreys, and smelt into the estuary, and may even be seen lying on the sand bar. Are the seals and sea lions a danger to the salmon runs? Commercial fishermen believe so, but it has been debated. Sea lions also eat large numbers of lampreys, which are parasitic to salmon. The answer may be different for different rivers.

Just west of the waterfront commercial area, on the way to the beach, there is a public dock and modern restroom. The dock entrance gangway is open to walkers and leads to a pair of shore-parallel floating docks about 100 feet long, but the gangway can be steep during low tide. When I was there in June there were flocks of sea gulls perching on the upstream end of each dock and half a dozen harbor seals lazing on the seaward ends.

Wildlife habitats: Open ocean, sandy beach, jetty, estuary, sand bar, harbor, coastal meadow.

Salmon and the Oregon Coast

Salmon have been caught in the rivers along the Oregon Coast for thousands of years – probably as far back as the initial colonization by Native Americans at least sixteen thousand years ago. The newcomers most likely brought salmon fishing skills with them as they migrated down the coast from Alaska. The salmon runs then were epic – anecdotal stories told of salmon in the rivers that were so numerous you could walk across the river on their backs. Not true, of course, but nothing that could inspire such stories has been seen there for more than a century.

There were five species of salmon native to the Oregon Coast; some have been subdivided into subspecies that come into the rivers at different times. The salmon species names are Chinook (or king), coho (or silver), chum (or dog), pink (or humpback), and sockeye (or red).

Five species of salmon are native to Oregon

The sockeye salmon, however, requires a lake for its spawning run, and there aren't many available in the coastal river watersheds. A small run enters the Columbia, traveling via the Deschutes and Metolius rivers to Suttle Lake in the eastern Cascades near Bend. Efforts are ongoing to reintroduce sockeyes to Wallowa Lake in northeastern Oregon after a century of absence. The run would come up the Columbia and Wallowa rivers. Today, Chinook and coho are the most abundant species in the state. There are also steelhead, a large sea-run rainbow trout, and the smaller sea-run cutthroat trout. Rivers in Japan and Siberia have two additional salmon species, but we don't find them in North America.

Salmon have long been a staff of life for Native Americans who live along the Oregon and Washington coasts, who even today consider them part of their cultural heritage. Both states have passed laws protecting Native American fishing rights and methods. Traditionally, these have included fish traps, dip nets, primitive seine nets, and long spears, some of which had two or three points and barbs. Salmon were smoked or dried for preservation, some even dried and ground up to mix with elk or deer tallow to make pemmican. Sometimes huckleberries were included for added flavor. (Pemmican is a Cree-Choctaw word from the mid-continent, native languages that were not spoken on the west coast. There were likely different words for pemmican in the coastal Oregon tribal languages and dialects. Perhaps you can find one, but the languages are mostly extinct today. The Chinook Jargon dictionary doesn't include a word for pemmican.)

Soon after the coast was colonized by European Americans in the last half of the nineteenth century, salmon canneries were established along the major rivers. The first one was built on the Columbia in 1865. Others followed in the next decade on the Rogue, Umpqua, and other larger rivers. The harvest peaked in the 1880s, after which the runs began to decline. The burgeoning population of San Francisco was a main market for the canned salmon.

Frances Schrader Old Growth Trail: Side trip, woodland hike, stroll. Exit Hwy 101 on Jerry's Flat Road (County Road 595) at the south end of Rogue River Bridge and drive up the lower Rogue River valley 9.7 miles to FD-3300.090, which becomes NF-060, a gravel road. Turn right and drive 2.0 miles to the trail parking lot.

On Jerry's Flat Road you will pass some views of the Rogue River, which has gentle riffles and extensive gravel bars in the lower stretches. The Rogue is considered one of the finest floating experiences in the state, as well as a prime destination for salmon and steelhead fishing. You may spot jet boats on the river, as well as Mackenzie River boats used for float trips. These double-ended craft were designed specifically for the rough rapids encountered on the Mackenzie River in the Cascades. Farther upstream the Rogue flows through a steep canyon and has been designated a *Wild and Scenic River*, both and where it cuts through the Klamath Mountains to the Pacific and again in the headwaters in the Cascade Mountains.

You may see bobwhite quail on the way up the hill. At nearly 1000 feet in elevation and seven miles from the ocean, the Frances Shrader Old Growth Trail assures you of being in bright sun above the coastal fogs of August. This stop treats you to a true remnant of the Pacific Northwest rainforest, with huge Douglas-fir and Port Orford cedar trees. The conifers are intermingled with large

A true remnant of the Pacific Northwest rainforest, with huge Douglas-fir and Port Orford cedar trees

hardwoods, some of the tallest in the state. Some of the Douglas-firs are five to seven feet in diameter and 200 feet tall: several one-log loads on the logging trucks of yore. Along the trail you will see a highly varied understory including sword fern, lady fern, Oregon grape, vine maple, huckleberry, red huckleberry, salmon berry, thimble berry, salal, rhododendron, and wood sorrel. A bridge across a brook in an opening in the forest provides a tempting opportunity for photography. This is the sort of opening characteristic of old-growth conifer forests. The trail is an easy 0.6 mile loop with an earth-and-needle surface suitable for strollers. Keep a sharp eye and watch for the legendary spotted owl. This is the kind of old-growth forest that is being protected for them all across the Pacific Northwest. The location is quite isolated: be sure to lock your car. A primitive restroom is located in the parking lot.

A great adjunct to this side trip is found just 250 feet farther up the river road from the forest turnoff. Turn left on Lobster Creek Road and proceed 400 feet to a small parking lot on your right, with an information sign about salmon, osprey, and wildlife management. From there you can walk out on a bridge crossing the Rogue River that affords views up and down a beautiful stretch of the river. But watch out for logging trucks; they are accustomed to owning the road and are usually in a hurry: the drivers get paid by the load, not by the hour! There are no restroom facilities at this location.

Wildlife habitats: Conifer forest, river, stream.

Future Forester – Douglas-fir

What's in a name? Sometimes quite a lot. Although the Douglas-fir honors the Scottish botanist David Douglas with its common name, it was first documented on Vancouver Island in 1791 by another Scot, Archibald Menzies, hence the Latin name for the tree: Pseudotsuga menzesii. Douglas didn't arrive in Oregon until 1824. Even that name is misleading – the generic name Pseudotsuga suggests some similarity to the hemlock (tsuga), with which it shares the forest but doesn't resemble in the slightest. Perhaps it made sense in Glasgow. Furthermore, it isn't a fir tree at all, so the common name is now hyphenated to clarify matters. There are several true firs in the Cascades and the Coast Range, bearing the characteristic tight cones standing erect on the branch. Douglas-firs have quite different cones. You may be most familiar with the Noble fir (Abies procera), a stately Christmas tree grown mostly in Oregon. But David Douglas achieved fame just the same: his name in the form *douglasii* appears in the Latin names of more than eighty plants and animals he first documented in the Pacific Northwest, all new species.

The Douglas-fir, rightly designated the state tree of Oregon, has long been the basis of the timber industry in western Oregon and Washington, and you will see many of them along your way.

Long the basis of the timber industry in western Oregon

Douglas-fir has the strongest wood of all the American conifers and is used world-wide. Tree farms in western Oregon replant the species almost exclusively. They grow rapidly in the cool damp climate, usually a foot or two each year. Although they can be harvested at thirty years of age, older trees will yield more clear-grade lumber.

But all may not be well with the Douglas-fir forests as the climate warms and dries. They like specific conditions, especially temperature range and soil moisture. Areas where mature trees survive well may no longer suitable for young trees: the mature forest may have got its start a century or two ago, when temperatures were cooler and rainfall more abundant. If the forest is cut down, brush species like manzanita may grow back quickly and out-compete Douglas-fir seedlings. Another modern problem is the bark beetle, a pest that appears to be causing increasing damage to conifers as the climate warms.

These issues are being studied. At Oregon State University in Corvallis, there is a world-famous college of Forestry. Is anyone interested?

Snow Camp Lookout and Vulcan Peak: Side trip, mountain hikes. For directions, map, and current road conditions, consult a Forest Service ranger station in Brookings or Gold Beach.

These two sites, each located some 30 miles by gravel road into the mountains, both afford expansive views of the Klamath Mountains from vantage points above 4000 feet elevation. As such, they are absolutely guaranteed to get you above the coastal fog and into bright sunshine on a summer day. Some walking is required to reach the peaks and the lookouts themselves, but the roads go almost all the way and you don't need to do that. Forest Service maps will show you some well-maintained hiking trails, along with elevation changes.

Graveled Forest Service roads provide access to either from Brookings via North Bank Chetco River Road. Snow Camp Mountain can also be reached from Gold Beach via Hunter Creek Road. These roads are not maintained in the winter due to heavy snow. After they open for the season, you will want to ask the Forest

Service if they are passable for your vehicle and what is currently the best route. You should consider these to be all-day trips, so pack water and a lunch. They are wilderness destinations: you won't find drinking water or restroom facilities.

Vulcan Peak lies within the Kalmiopsis Wilderness, where you may see the miniature rhododendrons for which it is named

Vulcan Peak lies within the Kalmiopsis Wilderness, where you may see the miniature rhododendrons for which it is named. On the north flank, accessed from the road by a rough trail, you can hike to Vulcan Lake, less than a mile away. It appears to be a cirque lake carved out by a Pleistocene glacier, one of only a few in the local mountains. Just below is Little Vulcan Lake, also apparently of glacial origin – possibly a small terminal moraine lake. On the shady south shore you may see a patch of Darlingtonia californica carnivorous plants, also called cobra lilies, if their habitat wasn't damaged by the fires that swept through the area. I haven't been up there since.

Snow Camp Peak affords a magnificent view of the Klamath Mountains to the east, the taller Siskiyou Mountains to the southeast, and all the way to Point St. George lighthouse, off Crescent City, to the southwest, if it isn't fogged in. You are seeing the half-million acre fire scar of two huge fires that went through the range - the Biscuit Fire and the Chetco Bar Fire. Just to the east, in the afternoon shade of Snow Camp Peak, lies Windy Valley. To get there takes a downhill hike of three and a half miles and 1200 feet elevation loss from the road. Unless you are an experienced hiker, perhaps consider it an overnight trip. My interpretation is that Windy Valley was also carved out by a Pleistocene glacier. It was dammed up by glacial terminal moraine, forming a lake, and then slowly silted in by Windy Creek. The end result is a small but beautiful valley with a flat floor, meadows, forests, and a small creek full of cutthroat trout. Sort of a Yosemite Valley in miniature but without the cliffs and waterfalls. Or the crowds. You can save yourself the hike by looking at the great photographic tour on the following link, published by vanmarmot.org: https://vanmarmot.org/2020/10/21/windy-valley-oregon-coast-range-21-oct-2020/

The Pacific Ocean

For much of your journey, your close companion will be the North Pacific Ocean, a sea as rough and wild as any along the United States coastline. So let's get to know it a little bit. The first thing you may notice is that the water along the shore isn't clear and blue like you may have seen on tropical islands or in the Mediterranean Sea. There are a couple of reasons for this. Most importantly, you are seeing water that is unusually rich in plankton, the microscopic organisms that form the base of the marine food chain. They support local commercial and recreational fishing industries that harvest salmon, various species of rock fish, shrimp, and crabs. To say nothing of the salmon, steelhead, cutthroat trout, and sturgeon that eventually migrate up the coastal rivers to spawn and perhaps be caught by anglers. The other reason you may have noticed as you look out to sea from a high bluff: much of the turbidity is concentrated near the shore. As the waves crashing against the sea cliffs, they slowly wear them down, yielding sand on the beach and mud in the water. More importantly, especially during the rainy season, the growing coastal mountain ranges are constantly being eroded away, allowing the many rivers to carry sediment to the ocean. Commercial logging practices in the forests have contributed: gashes and bare soil are often left on steep hillsides, contributing to rapid erosion.

Why is the coastal water so biologically rich? Mainly this is because of upwelling. During the frequent periods of northerly winds, surface water near the coast is pushed offshore. That water is replaced by cold, deeper water that became enriched in nutrients as dead plankton and fish fell through it and decomposed. A related effect of cold upwelling is the cool marine atmospheric layer, where fog often forms in the summer and drifts across the beach. Farther offshore, the surface water may be as warm as 60 degrees during the summer; albacore tuna like that temperature and can be caught there. Nearshore water may only be in the high 40s, very unpleasant for swimmers. Albacore are never seen near the beach.

You will also noticed the constant waves along the shore and the whitecaps farther out. The ocean in the Pacific Northwest has the greatest concentration of wave energy in the United States, possibly excepting the surfing beaches in Hawaii and along the isolated Aleutian Islands. Oregon State University is working on an experimental wave energy project just south of Newport. In addition, the federal Bureau of Ocean Energy Management is investigating the offering of leases for offshore wind farms. However, because the water is quite deep on the Oregon continental shelf, wind generators need to be mounted on floating structures, rather than on sea floor derricks like in Long Island Sound. This makes the installations more expensive to build and maintain. In addition, the mooring cables may present hazards for sea mammals, especially migrating whales. There is a lot of unused wind and wave energy out there – good green energy. We can hope a way can be found to harvest it. There are rewarding future professions here – anyone interested?

Origin of the Oregon Estuaries

Several distinct geographic features define and dominate the Oregon Coast: sandy beaches, rugged cliffed coastlines, seastacks, sand dunes, river estuaries, coastal wave-cut terraces, and the Oregon Coast Range. Of these, the estuaries are of particular interest from a scientific viewpoint. There are many of them and no two are alike. The largest estuaries, like Coos Bay and Yaquina Bay, are important ports and have been modified to enable safe navigation. Others are small, even really tiny, and are largely ignored – except by the salmon and steelhead that migrate through them to spawn in the feeder streams.

In Oregon and in the world at large, estuaries perform a vital function as the "nurseries of the sea." According to NOAA, estuaries worldwide provide critical habitat for most of the fish we eat: some 68 percent of the commercial catch, and even more of the recreational catch. The Oregon estuaries are also home to many varieties of shellfish. Juvenile salmon and steelhead depend on the estuaries with their salt marshes for their transition from the fresh water of the rivers to the salt water of the sea. With their mix of ocean and river nutrients, estuaries are among the most productive biological environments in the world.

Estuaries have been used as harbors for thousands of years. Most important harbors around the world are located on river mouth estuaries. Familiar examples from Europe include London, on the Thames; Liverpool, on the Mersey; Rotterdam, on the Rhine; and Lisbon on the Tagus. On our own Atlantic seaboard, we have Boston, on the Charles; New York, on the Hudson; and Philadelphia, on the Delaware. But the estuaries along the Oregon Coast have one feature that sets them apart from most of the others – sand. Lots of sand. When all this sand get pushed along the shore by a stormy ocean, estuary entrances can become partly filled and hazardous to navigation. It is all tied to the very complex history of the Oregon Coastal estuaries.

The Oregon estuaries we see today haven't been with us for very long in the geologic past

The Oregon estuaries we see today haven't been with us for very long in the geologic past, nor will they be around forever. They have interesting histories that involve plate tectonics, mountain building, ice-age sea level lowering, deep canyon erosion, and Holocene sea level rise. All this has happened in the last thirty million years, a very small fraction of geologic time. In more than four billion years of Earth's history, the world has only occasionally had estuaries like the ones we see today on the Oregon Coast.

Oregon's estuaries have a fascinating story to tell, so we should start at the beginning with some geological history. During the Oligocene Epoch, some 23 to 34 million years ago, the Oregon Coast Range we see today had not yet begun to rise – there was a broad coastal plain in its place, much like the Atlantic seaboard in the southeastern United States.

Plate tectonics got active

So what happened next? Plate tectonics got active. Beneath the sea floor off Oregon and Washington there is what geologists call the Juan de Fuca plate – a large piece of the Earth's crust that is now totally submerged. During the Miocene and Pliocene Epochs, basically the last 23 million years, this oceanic crustal plate has been migrating northeastward toward the North American plate, then diving beneath it. This resulted in compressive tectonic forces (mountain building) that caused the coastal mountains to begin to rise, crumpling and folding as they did. They are still growing today. The process is elegantly explained and illustrated in Sandi Doughton's book *Full-Rip 9.0*. As the ocean ate away at the rising Coast Range and Klamath Mountains, spectacular seacliffs and seastacks formed.

The meandering rivers didn't have time to straighten out; they just eroded straight down as the mountains rose beneath them. These tightly curved river canyons you see on the map are termed "entrenched meanders". Only the much larger Columbia, Umpqua, Rogue, and Klamath rivers were tough enough to maintain their headwaters all the way back to the Cascades. The small rivers couldn't dig fast enough.

The two million-year Pleistocene Epoch ushered in the next phase of estuary development in Oregon, and in much of the rest of the world as well. Continental glaciers and mountain ice caps locked up huge volumes of the world's water as thick ice sheets, causing the lowering of sea level by more than 300 feet. With this lowering of the local base level, the rivers were able to erode their canyons deep into the soft rocks of the coastal mountain ranges. The Oregon coastline advanced twenty to forty miles to the west. The low-relief continental shelf emerged from the sea and became a coastal plain.

Then in the last fifteen thousand years or so, the continental glaciers began to melt; except for a few mountain glaciers and ice caps, they are gone from North America. The thick glaciers on Greenland and Antarctica are mainly what are left of the massive Pleistocene continental ice sheets. Global sea level rose to its pre-Pleistocene level and the new Oregon coastal plain once again became submerged. As this was happening, the ocean advanced into the deep river canyons that had been eroded when the sea level was much lower. Estuaries were formed, larger and deeper than what remain today, as they were only beginning to be filled by sand and mud by the rivers. Today we see flood plains, mud flats, salt marshes, and deltas around the estuaries. All of these are results of the gradual filling of the estuaries since the beginning of the Holocene some twelve thousand years ago. In a few thousand years today's estuary lagoons might largely be gone, filled with river sediments, with the rivers running directly into the sea.

But what of the sand? Sand for the beaches, sand for the sand dunes, and sand covering most of the continental shelf came from two main sources:

1. Erosion of the Coast Range and Klamath mountains by the rivers as the mountains grew. Much of the Coast Range is composed of soft, easily-eroded sandstone.

2. Marine erosion of the seacliffs along the shoreline.

3. The Columbia River, draining parts of seven states and a Canadian province over tens of million years. Additionally, around the end of the Pleistocene ice age, huge ice-dam lakes were formed in Montana. When they burst as the ice melted, massive floods came across eastern Washington, stripped off the sandy topsoil, and carried it down the Columbia to the shore.

The result is copious quantities of loose sand along the Oregon and Washington coasts, deposited as beaches, sand dunes, and sand bars at the river mouths. Problems caused by the river-mouth bars will be discussed in a later section.

What Might Global Warming Do?

What will be the influence of global warming our Oregon estuaries? It is likely that sea level will rise substantially over the next few centuries, or even sooner. How much? The ice caps of Greenland and Antarctica still hold enough water to raise sea level *more than two hundred feet* if they melted right down to the rocks beneath them. That would certainly take many hundreds of years, so we don't need to worry about it right away. But with the current acceleration of global warming, it is already starting to happen. Sea level in some areas has risen almost half a foot just in the last century, and some coastal communities are already feeling the effects. Our coastal estuaries may start to grow again as the sea invades farther up the river valleys. What are now flood plains with farms and towns on them may become new salt marshes or mud flats, finally becoming completely submerged. But we can't be sure of that on the tectonically active Oregon Coast. The coastal mountains are rising too, which would lessen the local effect of relative sea level rise. And who knows – the citizens of the world may figure out how to stop the warming of the global climate before the ice caps melt, and develop the courage to do it. Let us all hope.

Ophir Rest Area: Rest area, beach hike. Located on the west side of the highway 8.4 miles north of Rogue River Bridge, 6.1 miles south of Prehistoric Gardens.

A trail runs through the low sand dunes to the sand beach, where you can hike 2.6 miles to the south, but much of it is adjacent to the highway. To the north, you will be blocked by Euchre Creek in a about a mile, maybe a little more – the outlet changes position each year. Little driftwood has accumulated along the beach. For strollers, there is only a 200 ft. asphalt trail along the seaward edge of the parking lot. It has full view and sound of the ocean, but no protection from the wind. You will find a modern restroom next to the parking lot.

Wildlife habitats: Open ocean, sandy beach, low sand dunes vegetated by European beach grass and coyote brush, brushy bluff.

Chapter 6

Port Orford and Cape Blanco

Humbug Mountain State Park: Rest area, woodland hike, stroll. Located 20.5 miles north of Rogue River Bridge, 6 miles south of Port Orford.

Humbug Mountain State Park is a popular park and campground, somewhat protected from the ocean breeze by its forested canyon setting and Humbug Mountain, at 1765 ft. the tallest peak along the Oregon coast. This state park has several modern restroom facilities. There are fine paved walking and strolling trails in the park along Brush Creek, and a primitive hiking trail to the mountain top. Unfortunately, ocean views from this trail, which should have been spectacular, are said to be mostly blocked by the dense forest. Numerous tidepools can be found along the rocky ocean shore nearby. Although Brush Creek is only five miles long, it is well populated by small trout, and an occasional steelhead has been caught. It provides an excellent example of creekside vegetation keeping the water cool for young fish. Interesting point: The highway goes

After sea level has risen a hundred feet or so, Humbug Mountain will be the largest and tallest island on the Oregon Coast

inland around the mountain but stays at a low elevation. When in the distant future sea level has risen a hundred feet or so, Humbug Mountain will become the largest and tallest island on the Oregon Coast. Will it then become an important seabird rookery like Bird Island near Brookings? Probably not, as populations of predators such as foxes, raccoons, skunks, and even black bears will become isolated on the new island as well, as has happened on the Channel

Islands off Southern California. Seabirds can be seen today on the steep and inaccessible cliffs along the west side of Humbug Mountain.

Habitats: Open ocean, sandy beach, rocky shore, brushy creek bottom, brushy bluff, conifer forest.

Port Orford

When you visit Port Orford (originally Fort Orford) you cannot escape the story of the battle on Battle Rock. That famous but unimposing rock is the tree-covered promontory that juts out from the beach on the edge of town. In June, 1851, nine men were put ashore at Fort Orford from the steamer Seagull out of Portland, which continued on to San Francisco with the promise to return in 14 days with more men and supplies. Unfortunately, the Sea Gull was embargoed for unpaid debt in San Francisco and didn't return when promised.

Sensing that the local Qua-to-mah tribe of the Tututnis didn't want them there, the men barricaded themselves as well as they could on Battle Rock with a few provisions and only a few old rifles and the small ship's cannon for protection. A battle soon ensued in which it is said that some 17 Tututnis were killed by a single cannon blast. After a siege of 14 days the Seagull failed to return as promised. Under assault from some 300 Natives, made up of the local Tutuni tribe and reinforcements from the Rogue River area to the south, the landing party escaped during the night and made their way up the coast on foot to safety, at times relying on friendly tribes for assistance. This must rank as one of the great escapes of wartime history. Only later was a U.S. military encampment established at the present townsite.

The Tututnis refused to carry away one of their dead.

Interestingly, the Tututnis refused to carry away one of their dead, who was wearing a red shirt and had arrived in a canoe with the war party from the Rogue River. "We all remarked that he was very white for an Indian, he had yellow hair and freckles", according to Kirkpatrick, the captain of the band. The narrator states that he turned out to be a Russian survivor from a shipwreck many years earlier and had been living with the Rogue River Tututnis. What a story he could have told! Although this seems quite logical, no evidence was presented in the account. The above paragraphs are summarized from Chapter 3: *The Hero of Battle Rock*, which is Kirkpatrick's fascinating 17 page account of the famous episode, recalled 46 years later in 1897 and recorded in the following online reference: Pioneer History of Coos and Curry Counties, Oregon, compiled by Orvil Dodge. Published in 1898 by the Pioneer and Historical Association of Coos County, Oregon. http://www.orww.org/Coquelle_Trails/References/Dodge_1898.pdf

Apparently William Tichenor, the captain of the Seagull, did eventually return and by late 1851 had established a townsite: one of the first platted townsite on the Oregon Coast south of Astoria. His family arrived from Illinois to join him in 1852. By 1853 gold had been discovered in nearby beach sands, and it is reported that by 1855 there were several dwellings, five hotels, five stores, saloons, two butcher shops, and, strange as it may seem, a bowling alley. By 1856, many of the mines had failed. Like in many boom towns, the subsequent decline was rapid, and in a few years only three families remained. What arrangement was made with the local Tututnis is unknown, but by the late 1850s the Tututnis had all been driven off their lands.

Coastal exploration along the southern Oregon coast had been encouraged by the great wealth in the mining areas around Jacksonville in southern Josephine County. At the time of the Jacksonville gold rush, there were only narrow mountain trails into the area. A road to the sea across the Klamath-Siskiyou Mountains was needed to "enable them to enjoy the profits of the commerce that was destined to become of considerable importance", according to

Orvil Dodge. No road through the coastal mountain ranges was ever built along the Winchuck, Chetco, Sixes, or Elk Rivers due to the ruggedness of the mountains, which range to over 5000 feet tall. Only the Rogue and Klamath rivers completely traverse the Klamath-Siskiyous, but they lie in deep, nearly impassable canyons. The other southwestern Oregon rivers drain only the western slope of this rugged range. A through road from Gold Beach to Grants Pass along the Rogue River was only completed more than a century later. That road must cross a 4600 foot summit at Bear Camp Overlook and is closed in the winter due to the heavy snow. Even today it is not paved all the way, but it is a spectacularly beautiful route. It is advisable to check road conditions before attempting the drive.

Port Orford got its name from George Vancouver's original name for nearby Cape Blanco, which he sighted in 1792 and named for George, Earl of Orford, "a much-respected friend." However, the cape had been mapped previously by the Spanish explorer Bartoleme Ferrelo in 1543, who had previously left his own name on Cape Ferrelo, a promontory just north of Brookings. Vancouver is thought to be the first European to have made contact with the local Tutuni people. Can his visit be why they were so upset with Tichenor's landing party, half a century later? Although Port Orford claims to be the first American town on the Oregon Coast, it has not had an easy history. (This claim apparently considers Astoria to be a river town on the Columbia, not a coastal town.) Named the first count seat of Curry County in 1855, the citizens were unable to get a county courthouse built so lost that honor to Ellensburgh, now named Gold Beach. Having been almost totally destroyed by a forest fire in 1868, further development was slow - in 2024, a century and a half later, Port Orford, with neither a fish-filled river nor a road to the inland towns, remains a very small town. But the town has the honor of giving its name to the Port Orford cedar, a highly prized local tree for lumber prized for its straight grain and its resistance to insects. Port Orford cedar logging and lumbering were important in the town's history for many years. The first lumber mill was built probably in 1853 by William Tichenor, the captain of the Seagull.

Unlike other ports along the Oregon Coast, the harbor at Port Orford is a shallow coastal inlet, somewhat protected from the northwest gales of the summer by the Port Orford Heads promontory and Cape Blanco. However, there is no protection from the southwesterly storms of the winter. With no protected boat basin, the boats of the local fishing fleet are raised from the sea with a crane when they come to port and placed on trailers – the only port on the West Coast, and one of the few in the world, where this needs to be done. You can see them there today just west of town. In the past, lumber schooners used the port to export Port Orford cedar logs and lumber. Even in modern times the Port Orford harbor has been somewhat treacherous. On a stormy winter day in 1937, the 190ft lumber schooner *Cottoneva* was blown away from the dock and ran aground at Battle rock. Today only the ship's propeller remains; it is on display at Battle Rock. Curiously, the harbor is fog-free most summer days when other coastal harbors are fogged in.

How does Port Orford qualify to be included in a book based mainly on estuary towns? The northern part of town includes Garrison Lake, a fresh-water lagoon that is now separated from the Pacific only by a sand bar some 500 feet wide. The surface elevation of Garrison Lake is listed as one foot above mean sea level, which apparently allows for sufficient hydraulic head to allow lake water to seep into the sea through the sand bar, without a stream outlet. There is an ancient channel on the lake floor that is 30 feet deep, or 29 feet below sea level. Clearly the lake was once an estuary of Mill Creek, which runs into the lake at the northeast end. Even today the lake is salty at depth because of an *El Niño* storm event in the winter of 1997 that washed sea water over the sand bar. Nevertheless, fishing in the spring for planted rainbow trout is still said to be excellent. Later in the summer, a second planting includes trout that have been fattened to the 14- to 16-inch size range that have been held in the hatchery for two years. There are, however two small rivers just to the north, the Elk and the Sixes, which enter the Pacific on either side of Cape Blanco. Both have small natural estuaries with no jetty protection and are well worth visiting.

In 1941, Mayor Gilbert Gable, protesting the poor shape of the state roads around his city of Port Orford, suggested that a few counties along the southern Oregon and northwestern California coast should secede and create a new state called Jefferson. Although that movement died with World War II, the concept has occasionally been revisited, with the same name and various southern Oregon and northern California counties included. On both sides of the border, the counties are quite isolated from the respective state capitols Salem and Sacramento and the residents feel ignored by their governments and government spending. Perhaps Port Orford could be made the capitol of Jefferson, to make up for losing the county seat honor to Gold Beach. It needs a boost.

Library: Port Orford Public Library, 1421 Oregon Street.

Playground: Buffington City Park, 14th Street and Arizona.

Battle Rock Park in Port Orford: Rest stop, beach hike, stroll. Battle Rock Park is the city beach park of downtown Port Orford, adjacent to Hwy 101.

The park features Battle Rock, the defensive site of a fierce battle in 1851 between Native Americans of the local Qua-to-mah tribe of the Tututnis and Captain William Tichenor and his men. At 23 sea miles north of the Rogue River and 27 sea miles south of Bandon and the Coquille Estuary, the Port Orford Harbor serves as an emergency refuge for a long stretch of coastline with no other safe harbors. It also provides ready access to fishing and crabbing grounds not readily accessible from the other ports, for both commercial and sport fishers.

Three seastacks only 1000 to 1200 feet
offshore are used by many seabirds

The park includes a long parking lot along the beach with modern restrooms at the south end at the park headquarters. Hikers can take a 20-minute or longer walk along the beach to the south, with seastacks just offshore and a brushy bluff on the landward side, or with some difficulty continue all the way to Brush Creek and Humbug Mountain 1.8 miles to the south. Three seastacks only 1000 to 1200 feet offshore are used by seabirds. However, the highway alongside makes this hike less pleasant than some others. Strollers can use the paved path along the parking lot with a fine view of the ocean or sidewalks in the adjacent town.

Wildlife habitats: Open ocean, seastacks, sandy beach, rocky shore to the south, brushy bluff, evergreen forest, brushy creek bottom. The small creek crossing the beach sometimes attracts numerous seagulls.

Buffington City Park: Rest stop, playground. Located half a mile north of downtown Port Orford. Turn west on 14th street from Hwy 101 and drive two blocks to the park.

Buffington Park is the Port Orford city park with ball fields, picnic tables, and, most importantly, a children's playground with climbing equipment. Modern restrooms are located at the northeast corner of the park.

Future Aquaculturist – Anadromous Fish Hatcheries

Fishing has been an important part of the economy of the Oregon Coast for thousands of years - since long before European American colonization. When the settlers arrived, the rivers still had prolific runs of salmon and steelhead. Other fish and shellfish were harvested as well. As time went on, an unfortunate combination of over-harvesting and watershed damage from logging, farming, and road construction has greatly reduced the natural salmon runs, in some streams nearly to the vanishing point. Although commercial fishing has long been banned from the rivers, sport fishing is still economically important for many towns along the coast.

Can the prolific fish runs be restored?

Can the prolific fish runs be restored? In an attempt to augment the remaining salmon runs, as well as the native trout, a number of fish hatcheries have been established on coastal rivers over the years. They have had some success, especially with trout. But the salmon runs have not come back like before. With intensive commercial fishing continuing offshore and Chinook salmon selling for $24.95 per pound and more in the grocery stores it is doubtful they ever will be allowed to return without severe regulation, and this is unlikely to happen.

But the rivers and estuaries are still there, just with fewer fish. Perhaps aquaculture can restore at least some of their productivity. The Oregon State University Marine Studies Initiative has been looking into this possibility. You can read a recent report on their nascent investigations in the following link entitled *Farming the Waters*: http://terra.oregonstate.edu/2020/02/farming-the-waters/. Presently, the U.S. spends billions of dollars per year on fish imports, much of it from Asian aquaculture. Where I now live in California, most of the farmed Atlantic salmon are imported from Chile, some 4000 miles away. Could we not farm salmon in our own coastal waters and avoid the cost and environmental effects of long-distance transport and refrigeration? Our Pacific Northwest and the southeastern Alaskan archipelago have the necessary mild climate and clean water for aquaculture. Oregon has gotten a start with oyster farming, and seaweed farming is being attempted, but there is room for much more along the coast and in our many estuaries. Fish is presently the largest source of protein in the world's diet, and the standing crop of many species of oceanic fish is rapidly being fished out. There is a lesson in the decline of the Grand Banks cod fishery over many centuries, but it is largely being ignored. There must be some attractive careers here – anyone interested?

Elk River Hatchery: Side trip, short stroll, swimming hole. Three miles north of Port Orford or 0.33 miles south of Elk River Bridge; turn east on Elk River Road. Proceed 7.5 windy miles to the hatchery on your left.

Elk River Hatchery, and ODFW facility, raises Chinook salmon and steelhead for release in coastal rivers. They have several hundred feet of paved paths along the hatchery and around the rearing ponds and a modern restroom. Near the upstream end there is a popular beach and swimming hole in the Elk River, which is normally fog-free all summer. Kayaks can be launched there as well, but the Elk River is a small stream with riffles.

Cape Blanco State Park: Side trip, beach hike, stroll: Location: Cape Blanco State Park entrance from Hwy 101 is 4.3 miles north of downtown Port Orford. From the north, 0.8 miles south of Sixes River Bridge. Drive 4.7 miles west to campground and facilities.

Cape Blanco State Park campground lies along a loop road through a second-growth spruce forest; modern restrooms are somewhat hidden within the loop so watch for signs at trailheads. Along the roadway, some sunshine enters the forest, leading to a profuse understory of huckleberry, salmonberry, salal, and several other shrubs and ferns. You can stroll the half-mile paved loop road through the campground. Even better, you can take the 20-minute paved trail across a coastal meadow to the old lighthouse, with a beacon 256 feet above the Pacific, with grand views of the coast to the north and south. However, there are no restroom facilities at the

The old lighthouse beacon is 256 feet above the Pacific

lighthouse and it is sometimes very windy. Seasoned hikers may like the steep trails to the rocky shore, with beach hikes continuing a mile and a half north to the Sixes River or one to three miles south to the Elk River, depending on where the migrating river outlet is located when you visit. Don't attempt to hike around the cape. Both beaches are littered with driftwood and are backed by low beach dunes. The rocky shore below the cape should have good tidepools when the tide is out, but as Cape Blanco is a coastal promontory and the surf may be rough so you must watch out for large waves. Gull rock, located to the northwest and half a mile off shore, is appropriately named, but the smaller rocks directly off Cape Blanco are wave washed and probably not of much use to seabirds. The beach hike to the north gets you closer to Gull Rock, where numerous seabirds can be seen. South of the campground, a half-mile paved road leads you down to the beach, where there is a parking lot and another restroom. Both the Elk and Sixes river outlets are unimproved, giving you fine views of natural rivers meeting the sea and how they change with the season and the tide.

The crest of Cape Blanco is an erosional remnant of an ancient wave-cut terrace that was uplifted relatively recently, probably within the last million years. Looking to the east, you can see the continuation of the nearly flat terrace. Most of the cranberry bogs between Bandon and Port Orford lie on the same sandy terrace; you will drive by some of them on your way north. At the lighthouse parking lot you can see exposures of poorly consolidated, gravelly beach sand that was deposited on the terrace when it was at sea level. The young beach sand is resting on hard rocks of Cretaceous or Jurassic age, more than 66 million years old. The cape is the westernmost point in the lower forty-eight, but not by very much.

Wildlife habitats: Open ocean, seastacks, sandy beach, beach dunes, rocky shore, coastal meadow, brushy bluff, conifer forest.

Sixes River Estuary and Marsh: Side trip, hike. Located in Cape Blanco State Park; entrance from Hwy 101 is 4.3 miles north of downtown Port Orford and 0.8 miles south of Sixes River Bridge. Drive 1.6 miles west on Cape Blanco Road to the sign and road to *Hughes Historic House*, then 0.5 miles down the hillside to a boat launch and small parking lot next to the estuary, passing the *Hughes Historic House* driveway.

There are two three-quarter mile walks on well-trodden primitive trails along the lower Sixes River estuary. They may be too narrow for some sidewalk strollers. At time of writing, modern restrooms can be found farther west from the Hughes House intersection in the main park campground, as the Hughes House and restroom is closed for Covid restrictions. They may be open now.

The small parking lot by the estuary at the end of the Hughes House road holds only a few cars, but parking on the grassy verge adds to the capacity. The first trail heads northwest through a marsh on the floodplain, with the lower Sixes River estuary alongside most of the way. Cattle grazing is permitted, so there are gates; please close them carefully. The marsh is probably fresh-water dominated except during very high tide, as it is covered with sawgrass, a characteristic fresh-water bog plant. A few willows are becoming established. This is the kind of marsh that may store a lot of carbon in the soil as root mass as sea level slowly rises and flood deposits are added to the surface. After three fourths of a mile, the trail ends where the estuary broadens and a mud flat appears during low tide, very popular with shore birds, particularly gulls. On my first visit there were hundreds of gulls on the mud flat as the tide receded and the water was draining off. The second trail heads directly west from

This is the kind of marsh that may store a lot of carbon in the soil as sea level slowly rises

the parking area to the driftwood-flanked Sixes River Beach, across the marsh and south of the estuary. Half a mile offshore you can see *Gull Rock*, streaked on top with guano and home to many seabirds. *Castle Rock*, a seastack just offshore the river mouth may be subject to surf action, as I saw no sign of birdlife there.

Wildlife habitats: Open ocean, seastacks, sandy beach, shore dunes, fresh-water marsh, coastal meadow, estuary, mudflat.

Flores Lake/Boice Cope Park: Side trip, rest stop, beach hike, stroll. From Hwy 101, turn west on Floras Loop Road, 8.3 miles north of Elk River Bridge. From the north, the turnoff is 1.4 miles south of Flores Creek Bridge. After 0.9 miles turn west again on Floras Lake Road and drive 1.4 miles past an impressive row of old Monterey cypress trees to Woodruff Road Junction, then south 0.1 miles, still on Floras Lake Road, to Boice Cope Road. Turn west 0.25 miles to the parking lot and Floras Lake.

A 0.2 mile path past the end of Floras Lake and through the pines to the ocean beach starts at the bridge crossing the Floras Lake outlet stream, but soon becomes too sandy for sidewalk strollers. Hikers can continue on to the ocean beach, where they can hike two miles south to rocky outcrops north of Cape Blanco. This hike runs along a cliffed beach, where escape from a sneaker wave may be difficult. A longer beach hike takes you seven miles north to the New River outlet. This one is great for bird watching, as it runs along a 600-800 foot wide beach separating the ocean on the west and New River on the east. Pelagic seabirds on one side and shorebirds on the other. However there is no shade after you leave Floras Lake. Strangely, neither beach has much driftwood; perhaps it all gets trapped farther south.

The lake is a good place to observe
abundant ducks and other fresh water birds

Park Road Loop provides a pleasant stroller path of 0.2 mile length along the lakeshore. The lake is also a good place to observe the abundant ducks and other fresh-water birds. They are especially numerous during migrations in the spring and fall, but many are resident. Modern restrooms are located just inside the campground above the day-use parking lot. Wildlife habitats: Ocean, sandy beach, vegetated low sand dunes, lake, stream, evergreen forest, park. I saw two Steller's jays on my visit and many ducks of various species.

Future Botanist – Wild Hazelnuts

If you are from the Willamette Valley, or drove through the Willamette valley on the way from the Portland airport to the Oregon Coast, you may have seen extensive commercial groves of dark-green hazelnut trees, also called filberts. Although these are an important Oregon crop, they are actually a European hazelnut species. Hazelnut paste, or praline paste, is an ingredient in Nutella, but that is hard to find nowadays. The nuts of the wild Oregon hazelnut are smaller and grow on a bush rather than a small tree. The species is called western beaked hazelnut (*Corylus cornuta var californica)*, and grows in western California, Oregon, and Washington. The nuts are little but equally delicious as the commercial filberts. They don't ripen in Oregon until September or October – a bit late for the summer vacationer. They are also a favorite food of squirrels and blue jays—in fact you are lucky to find any before they do! Fortunately, the Western beaked hazelnut grows on bushes low enough to be easily harvested. You just have to find them – they tend to grow hidden on the underside of the branches. To pick them, just twist the pair of nuts so as not to snap the branch. The squirrels will thank you. Tiny filaments protrude from the husk and may stick into and irritate any skin that contacts them, but I haven't found them to cause a rash. The Oregon hazelnut was of course harvested and stored for the winter by Native Americans along the Oregon

Coast, as it is one food that stores well in a damp climate. I recall in my youth on the Oregon Coast finding several hazelnut bushes along the walk home from school.

Future Geomorphologist - Coastal Terraces

Along the southern Oregon Coast, Highway 101 runs between the Klamath Mountains on the east and the impressive sea cliffs on the west. Yet in many places there is still a fairly flat bench on which the road, farms, and the towns have been built. Why is that? These ancient topographic benches are called marine terraces. They have been cut by wave action, just as a new wave-cut terrace is being formed today at sea level. But why are they so high? The terraces record the ongoing uplift of the coastal mountains; the higher terraces are older than the younger terraces. Where they can be dated by carbon-14 isotopic analysis of driftwood fragments, they accurately record the historic rate of coastal mountain uplift. More sophisticated analyses on clam shells, sea urchin spines, and corals can also be used; these fossil materials are much more common than driftwood. The uplift rates have been shown to vary along the coast. Uplift of the high terrace at Cape Blanco seems to be the fastest, currently 4-5 mm per year, but the rate has varied.

Although the terraces are locally quite flat, they tend to change in elevation along the coast. For instance, the main terrace on which the towns of Brookings and Harbor were built slopes gently to the south, eventually diving beneath the sea at Crescent City. In Brookings, there are two higher terraces. The first can be seen at Azalea Park and the nearby high school; it is around 50 feet above the main town. The highest terrace, about 200 feet higher, is still very flat and hosts the local airport. Each terrace provides for us a geomorphic record of a time when the Klamath Mountains were lower than today and the terrace was at sea level. On many of the terraces one can find deposits of ancient beach sand. Often they are well displayed in road cuts. These terrace sands make excellent aquifers –

many people who live on the terraces have dug shallow water wells into the sandy deposits, which are recharged each winter by the abundant rainfall. The terraces also provide much of the arable land in Curry and Coos counties. South of Brookings, Easter lilies are grown on the rich soil of a marine terrace. At Gold Beach, there is barely enough room for the town. Near Bandon, the cranberry bogs are all located on a broad marine terrace, the same one you saw on Cape Blanco.

Fossils in the terraces record the rate of mountain uplift

Geologists have estimated the rate of uplift of the Klamath Mountains along the Coos and Curry County coastline, where the marine terraces are most prominent, at a couple of feet per thousand years, over the last few tens of thousands of years. The rate varies up and down the coast and on different terraces. Unfortunately, older terraces that might have recorded even earlier history of uplift and mountain building have long since been eroded away. But a couple of feet of uplift per thousand years, over a ten million year period, would result in twenty thousand feet of uplift over that period. More than enough uplift to create the tall Klamath Mountains and to cause them to be eroded down to their very cores, which the rocks tell us has clearly happened.

Other areas along the Oregon Coast with marine terraces could be studied with fossils and newer dating techniques to record the amount and timing of tectonic uplift. The results might be useful in earthquake prediction studies. Anyone interested in a geography thesis?

Chapter 7

Bandon and the Coquille River Estuary

Bandon

Bandon is another of the coastal towns that got its start in the 1850s gold rush, but the bonanza there didn't last long. Like at Gold Beach, tiny specks of gold and platinum dust could be panned from the black sand layers along the modern beaches and nearby beach deposits. The black sands are composed mainly of magnetite, ilmenite, and chromite but contain tiny amounts of the precious metals.

The first gold-bearing sands were found at Whiskey Run Beach in 1851 by French-Canadian trappers. That beach is just a few miles north of the mouth of the Coquille River, in what is now Bullards Beach State Park. Things really got going at Whiskey Run Beach by 1853, although the colorful name may have come later. Several hundred men were panning for gold that year. Probably many of them were disappointed Forty-Niners from California. A mining town named Randolf was built, with a lot of tents, a store, a restaurant, the obligatory saloon, and who knows what other entertainment. Gold-bearing black sand was also found in uplifted beach deposits of Pleistocene age. Unfortunately for the miners, a massive winter storm in 1855 stripped Whiskey Run Beach of its black sand deposits, so most of the prospectors moved on to better diggings elsewhere. That was the end of Randolf, but sporadic mining ventures continued in the area for many years. Amateur prospectors with gold pans are finding gold there even today.

For me, the question remains: if a storm could wash away the gold-bearing sand beds, could they be washed back in again by another storm? The gold and platinum grains could not have gone far: they are still out there, somewhere. Maybe just offshore. Even today you can find layers of black sand on the beach up and down the coast, especially after winter storms. Careful panning will reward you with a few "colors" of fine gold dust. Give it a try. You can still pan for gold at Whiskey Run Beach where the first miners had their luck. The entirety of the Oregon Coast is open to the public, and gold panning is allowed on all of the beaches. Just don't plan to pay for your vacation with the gold and platinum you find.

If a storm could wash away the gold-bearing sand beds,
could they be washed back in again by another storm?

But that short-lived town was Randolf, not Bandon. Bandon got started about the same time, on the south bank of the Coquille River with a "donation land claim". The original townsite was called Averill after the initial landowner, although he didn't build a town at that time. Other land claims were taken by Thompson Lowe, who built the first house, and Chris Long. For many previous centuries the Ko-quells, a Tututni tribe lived in that area and along the Coquille River valley, but no record survives of a Ko-quell town where Bandon is now located. Perhaps they found the fishing and the weather better farther upstream. Nevertheless, the river and later the county seat Coquille were both named after them. (The French language spelling Coquille gives credence to the presence of early French-Canadian trappers in the area.) Along with other southwestern Oregon tribes, the Ko-Quells were defeated in the tragic Rogue River Indian Wars in 1856 and banished to the Coast Indian Reservation – an arduous 125 miles hike to the north. Remnants of that reservation are included in today's Siletz Indian Reservation, a scattering of parcels northeast of Newport.

By 1859, the Coquille River Estuary had been shown to be a navigable waterway when the Twin Sisters sailed 40 miles upriver to the forks, just past the head of tidewater. This voyage was considered important, as it promised a port outlet for local agricultural, mining, and forest products. However, the bar continued to be a problem until the captain of the Twin Sisters found he could pull the small craft across the beach, from the Pacific Ocean to the Co-quille Estuary, using oxen and rollers. It couldn't have been much of a boat.

Word of the natural bounty of the area must have spread across the Atlantic. In 1873, Lord George Bennet arrived with his family from Bandon, County Cork, Ireland. Even at that time there existed

> *Word of the natural bounty of the area*
> *must have spread across the Atlantic*

only one small house on the original land donations, all of which he bought for his family. By then the gold rush at Randolf on Whiskey Run Beach was history. Lord Bennet must have liked the area, as in 1874 he changed the townsite name from Averill to Bandon, after his Irish home town on the Bandon River. The climates are some-what similar, with equally cool summers and nearly the same an-nual rainfall. Bennet is infamous for having introduced gorse, the highly flammable, invasive shrub to the area. The following year, more settlers arrived from old Bandon, Ireland. Today, Bandon, Oregon and Bandon, Ireland have a sister city arrangement. Lord Bennet did not bring the whole name of his home town to Oregon, which in the Irish Gaelic language is *Droichead na Bandan*, meaning bridge over the Bandan River. Bandon, Ireland, dates back to 1608 and was once a distilling center for Irish whiskey. Despite the nam-ing of Whiskey Creek, (noting the Irish spelling) there is no record of Lord Bennet bringing the whiskey distilling industry to Oregon.

Bandon has been known for its cheese production for more than a century. Perhaps it got its start as early as 1853 when Chris Long reportedly brought in a herd of 25 cows, a yoke of oxen, and two span of horses all the way from Illinois. (That seems to me a long walk for a milk cow – longer than the cattle drive in *Lonesome Dove!*) These he sold locally to the settlers. More cattle were brought in later from the Willamette Valley. By the 1880s there were already ten cheese makers around the area. But in 2000 the Bandon Cheese factory and brand were bought out and local cheese production was shut down. The factory was eventually demolished, but cheddar and jack cheese with the Bandon Cheese label continued to be made elsewhere. In 2011 the City of Bandon purchased the site of the old Bandon Cheese factory. A new cheese factory was built to reclaim the reputation of Bandon cheese, opening as Face Rock Creamery LLC. It is still operating: occasionally you can find their cheeses in the gourmet section of the grocery story.

In 1884, the federal government appropriated $10,000 to begin the construction of jetties at the mouth of the Coquille River estuary, the waterway having proved navigable up to the new logging and farming towns of Coquille and Myrtle Point. These were completed in 1898. The old lighthouse you can see across the harbor from town was built in 1896 on a rock outcrop, which was in itself a navigational hazard. It operated until 1939, when it was replaced by an automated beacon at the end of the south jetty. Today the lighthouse is part of Bullards Beach State Park and is open to the public; you can reach it from the park entrance north of the Coquille River. You can find an interesting illustrated history of the lighthouse online at https://lighthousefriends.com/light.asp?ID=127.

Bandon may not look like an important shipping center today, but in 1899 Bandon was developing as a principle port between San Francisco and Portland, and a steamship line connected the three cities. Boatyards in Bandon, with a population of 1800, and Prosper, a smaller town just up the river, were turning out propeller-driven steamboats and sternwheelers for both passenger and freight traffic. They journeyed up and down the Coquille River and along the coast as well. Cargoes carried included canned salmon from local canneries, lumber from several riverside sawmills, lignite coal from small mines in the Riverton area, cheese from the local dairies, and output from a local woolen mill. San Francisco was the most important destination for these Coos County products. A published chart shows that 41 ships were active at one time or another on the Coquille

River between 1874 and 1928, most of them built in local boatyards. However, the riverboat heyday eventually succumbed to cars and trucks with the completion of the Roosevelt Highway, now Hwy 101. Bandon lost its importance as a regional and international port to the larger and deeper harbor at Coos Bay. More information on the Coquille River shipping industry can be found online at: https://en.wikipedia.org/wiki/Steamboats_of_the_Coquille_River.

At least partly because of the very thorny and highly flammable gorse shrub introduced by Lord George Bennet, the town has been periodically destroyed by fires. Perhaps gorse thickets were never considered to be dangerous in Ireland, with its frequent summer rainfall, but the dry summers of Oregon's Mediterranean climate have allowed gorse to become a real fire hazard. In 1914, the waterfront business district was destroyed. In 1936, a great forest fire termed locally as the "Bandon Burn" destroyed the town once again and also much of the forest behind it. You can still see the impenetrable and thorny gorse shrubs growing in the area and occasionally along the golf course fairways. If you hit your ball into the gorse, it is gone forever. Or at least until the next wildfire.

Among epicures, Bandon is known for its cranberries. Lots of cranberries. It is said that plantings of cranberries were brought from Massachusetts in 1855 by a discouraged gold prospector.

Bandon is known for its cranberries. Lots of cranberries.

Today, Bandon is the premiere cranberry producer on the West Coast, with more than a hundred growers. You can see extensive cranberry bogs along the highway south of town. Owing to the mild climate and long growing season, the berries get riper and redder than in competing growing areas in Wisconsin and Massachusetts and are valued for their bright red color. Notice the difference in the grocery store around Thanksgiving where Oregon cranberries are marketed alongside cranberries from elsewhere.

It was in Bandon where cranberry bogs were first wet-harvested.

This is done by building low dikes around the bogs then flooding them to float the berries, as they are hollow and float well. If you are there during harvest time in early September, it is a sight not to be missed. Bandon even has a cranberry festival to celebrate the harvest, held on the second weekend in September. Of course the cranberry queen and her court all wear cranberry-colored gowns! In the local restaurants, it is hard to find a meal that doesn't have cranberries in it somewhere.

North of Bandon, across the Coquille River, a couple of square miles of pine-covered sand dunes has recently been converted into the champion-caliber Bandon Dunes Golf Resort, encompassing five courses in all. These are now regarded as among the finest courses in the state and have become a principle economic driver for the area. The courses are public. They are quite expensive to play and caddies are recommended, but if you are a serious golfer you might want to give one of them a shot—especially if you are skilled at blasting out of the sand! At least you won't have to worry about water holes, as sand dunes are highly permeable and don't hold water very well.

Library: Bandon City Library, 1204 11th Street SW.

Playground: Bandon City Park, 11th Street.

Bandon Waterfront: Rest stop, stroll. Located on the Coquille River estuary in the town of Bandon at the foot of Chicago Street, where there is a large shore-side parking lot.

This is a pleasant stop for the whole family, with the estuary, piers, and a small boat basin on one side and the old town on the other. A 600 foot stroll at the foot of Chicago Street follows along the wood-capped jetty enclosing the boat basin. When I visited, there was a great blue heron perched on the rail posing for a photograph. Weber pier, a floating dock extending from the west end

*A great blue heron was perched on
the rail posing for a photograph*

of the parking lot, is popular with recreational crabbers and is also stroller-safe. Modern restrooms are located at the near the center of the parking lot. The Coquille estuary is 2000 feet wide at this point when the tide is in, but at low tide there are mud flats exposed on the far side and you may see people digging clams. On the town side you will find a selection of shops and seafood restaurants.

Bandon and Coquille Estuary. *This image gives you a morning view of a typical mudflat on the Coquille estuary at low tide, with the Bandon Waterfront in the foreground. Tufts of morning fog are typical. The estuary can be seen curling around a large salt marsh in the middle distance, with foothills of the Coast Range in the far distance. It would seem to be a fine clam-digging opportunity on such a sunny day. This and other mudflats are readily accessible from Bullards Beach State Park.*

Wildlife habitats: Harbor, estuary.

Bandon Point and Face Rock: Side trip, rest stop, beach hike, stroll. Located on the Pacific shoreline of Bandon. Turn west on 11th Street and drive one mile to the parks.

At the seaward edge of Bandon you will find a park complex including Oregon Islands National Wildlife Refuge, Kronenberg County Park, Bandon Beach, and Face Rock State Scenic Viewpoint – federal, state, county, and city administered. Parking lots are located at the wildlife refuge at the end of 11th Street and at Face Rock, 0.2 miles farther south on Beach Loop Road. As this is a popular destination during the summer, you may need to park along the street. On 11th Street you will pass through the Bandon City Park, featuring ball fields and modern restrooms. On the north side of the circular road through the park you will find a fine set of playground equipment; on the south side, a dog park. Modern restrooms are also located at the Face Rock parking lot, snuggled in the trees on the northeast side.

The coastal meadow at Oregon Islands National Wildlife Refuge and Kronenberg County Park offers you a flat quarter mile of asphalt trails with interpretive panels and the view and sound of the Pacific below. On a clear day one can see long distances: north, across the mouth of the Coquille River and jetties to Cape Arago,

A flat quarter mile of asphalt trails through a coastal meadow with interpretive panels and the view and sound of the Pacific below

and south to Cape Blanco. Table Rock, only 700 feet offshore, is home to a variety of seabirds. Binoculars will be useful. The terrace appears to be the same as you have been driving along from Cape Blanco through the cranberry bogs, which you will have passed along the highway, but it tilts toward the north and is much lower here. Apparently Cape Blanco is rising at a faster rate than the area around Bandon – perhaps that is why the Coquille River enters the

sea here, much farther north than its headwaters. You can spot ancient beach sand deposits here and there on the terrace, often in the
road cuts. Trails to the north and west of the parking lot lead via
stairs to a driftwood-flanked sandy beach 80 feet below. A beach
hike can lead to the Coquille River mouth and jetties, which you can
see to the north, or past Face Rock, continuing some four miles the
south to the mouth of New River – but you might have to wade
some small streams along the way. Seabirds also frequent the rocks
offshore at Face Rock but in smaller numbers.

*Seastacks at Bandon Point, South of the Coquille River Estuary. At
Bandon Point, there are several close-to-shore seastacks, all easily viewed
with binoculars from the bluff. Populations of nesting seabirds can even be
picked out on satellite images. The two large seastacks in this image can be
reached from the beach at low tide, but are included in the Oregon Islands
National Wildlife Refuge and must not be disturbed. Some have flat or gently
sloping crests still covered with original topsoil, providing excellent habitat
for pelagic seabirds – especially puffins, who like to dig burrows for their
nests. Other seastacks are smaller and jagged, but remain above wave level
and are encrusted with white guano – a sure sign of pelagic sea bird visits.*

How did the river get the French-sounding name Coquille? The simplest explanation might seem to be that the name Coquille derives from "scoquel," a word for the eel-like lamprey that the Native Americans harvested for food, not for the French scallop dish *coquille St. Jacques*. But more likely the origin is another spelling of the Ko-quell Native American tribe who lived along the river. It is unlikely that the local scallops were gathered in any number by the settlers or the coastal Indians tribes, as they are not easily harvested. There are a few species of scallops in Oregon waters, the most common being purple-hinge rock scallops (Crassodoma gigantean), weather vane scallops (Patinopecten caurinus), and spiny pink scallops (Chlamys hastata). You may find their shells on the beach.

Wildlife habitats: Open ocean with seastacks, sandy beach, rocky shore with tidepools, brushy bluff, shore pine forest, coastal meadow.

Salt Marsh on the Coquille River Estuary. *Salt marshes line the lower Coquille estuary in the foreground and on the far shore, with the town of*

Bandon in the distance on the left. These marshes, which become flooded at high tide, are highly productive environments. They provide food and refuge for young salmon and steelhead as they transition to salt water on their migration to the sea from the streams in the mountains. The grass in the foreground is saltgrass, a plant that long ago migrated from a terrestrial environment into the salt marsh. Close examination of the stems reveals a host of microorganisms clinging there that are the base of the salt marsh food chain.

Bullards Beach State Park: Side trip, rest stop, beach hike, stroll. Turn west 0.3 miles north of the Coquille River Bridge on Bullards Beach Road, 3 miles north of Bandon. From the north, 6.6 miles south of the Hwy 101 – West Beaver Hill Road intersection.

Bullards Beach State Park is a popular destination with many hiking and strolling opportunities. At the beach parking lot, several trails lead through the low dunes to the sandy beach. One can hike 1.5 miles south to the Coquille River mouth and lighthouse, or several miles north past the Bandon Dunes Golf Resort and Whiskey Run Beach. Please note the taped off areas, as they are nesting areas for endangered snowy plovers. From the same beach parking lot, there is an asphalted trail of a mile or so through the shore pine groves and meadows back to the campground, mostly protected from the wind. You will find bushes of huckleberries. Yellow lupines are abundant here. Where Bullards Beach Road runs along the estuary, a variety of shorebirds is likely to be seen, sometimes in abundance.

Yellow lupines are abundant here

The entrance to the main campground with modern restrooms and showers is only 0.25 miles from the park entrance, but you need to pay for entry to those facilities. Free modern restrooms are located along the road at 0.8 miles and at the large parking lot behind the low beach dunes 1.4 miles in. You may want to continue to the south another 1.4 miles to the historic lighthouse that you can see from Bandon, but there are no facilities there.

Wildlife habitats: Open ocean, sandy beach, low vegetated dunes, coastal meadow, conifer forest with shrub understory, estuary.

Future Ornithologist - Sea Gulls

You might be surprised to learn that sea gull is not a bird species at all – it is the common name for a whole family of related shore birds that look somewhat alike. Sea gull is a generic term, like duck or sparrow, each group encompassing dozens of individual species. Gull refers to the biological family *Laridae,* containing 57 species in ten genera of gulls and gull-like shorebirds such as terns. Sadly, eight of the species have already become extinct.

As many as nine gull species may be seen on the Oregon Coast in various seasons, some living mainly on the coast and estuaries and others that venture inland to breed. In addition, four terns, three jaegers, a kittiwake and a skua* are occasionally spotted along the coast or in the estuaries. Three additional species frequent the

Four terns, three jaegers, a kittiwake and a skua are occasionally spotted

lakes of central and eastern Oregon but are not seen on the coast. You may remember the legend of sea gulls saving the crops around Great Salt Lake from a cricket (actually a shield-backed katydid) invasion in 1848.

Oregon Coast gulls are all quite similar in appearance, with white breasts, gray backs, a little black on the tail or head, and orange or yellow beaks, often with a red spot. Immature individuals tend to be brown and mottled. Their distinctive white, gray, and black coloration comes in after two or three years. Consequently, it is difficult to tell the juveniles apart. It would seem that eighteen similar shorebird species along a single coastline is somewhat redundant, all competing for the same food resources and nesting areas. To some extent this is true and there can be competition among the species. But considering the variety of coastal environments available – open ocean, sandy beaches with seaweed piles, rocky shores with tide pools, estuaries, tide flats, salt marshes, lagoons, rivers, lakes, agricultural fields, pastures, and domestic garbage dumps – perhaps there is enough to go around. In addition, some gull species are seasonal.

Gulls are famously omnivores, with diets including pretty much whatever they can find in these many environments, both marine and non-marine, and around the city dumps. Gulls can't afford to specialize, as seasons, storms, and tides offer up a changing smorgasbord. You may notice flocks of gulls following the fishing boats as they return to port, squawking, diving, and eating fish remains thrown overboard. They will even steal meals from each other and raid nests. Some are smart enough to drop a live mussel onto rocks in order to smash the shell. Many are scavengers, often to be seen cleaning up parking lots. It will take a good illustrated guide like the Audubon to help you distinguish them. Different gull species frequent the Oregon Coast during different seasons. As gulls seem to have no natural enemies along the shoreline and are very quick to take flight, they tend not to be as fearful of humans as other shore birds.

Options for nesting, for those species that nest on the Oregon Coast, include offshore seastacks, coastal cliffs, sand dunes, salt marshes, estuary shorelines, and, for some species, even trees. For our education and enjoyment, the Oregon Department of Fish and Wildlife has published a fine report on all the gulls and similar shorebirds that are found in the state. It is available online at https://myodfw.com/wildlife-viewing/species/gulls-and-terns. The report includes photographs and descriptions of 23 species of gulls and terns, most of which may be seen along the Oregon Coast.

Perhaps a study could be made on the influence of our garbage-producing civilization on gull behavior: are they eating and redistributing garbage dump plastic into the marine environment and contributing to micro-plastic pollution? Are seagulls suffering from the ingestion of plastics and other components of our garbage?

*Skua is one of the very few words that have come into the English language from Faroese, the isolated Germanic language of the Faroe Islands, a lonesome part of Denmark some 200 miles north of Scotland. A great colony of skuas lives on the Faroes island of Skuvoy. Jaeger derives from the German word *jager*, which means hunter.

Future Oceanographer – Winter Sea Level

One might think that sea level doesn't change over the seasons. This is generally true on an oceanwide basis. But along the Oregon Coast and similar coastlines there are special phenomena that can make sea level quite a bit higher in the winter than in the summer. The result can be to bring the wave swash much farther up the beach. This can potentially cause erosion of the bank, or even flooding of low-elevation towns, especially during storms. That is partly why the driftwood on a summer beach seems so far away from the surf. Four factors contribute:

That is partly why the driftwood on a summer beach seems so far away from the surf.

1. <u>Water Temperature</u>: Oregon coastal water temperature is generally several degrees higher in the winter because upwelling has ceased bringing cold, deep water to the nearshore. As warm water is slightly less dense than cold water, it takes up more space, contributing a small portion of winter sea level increase. The effect is variable both in time and location. For example, a five degree Fahrenheit increase from 40 to 45 degrees over a 300 foot water column would lead to a little less than two inches sea level rise.

2. <u>Coriolis Effect</u>: During the Oregon summer, the coastal

longshore current generally flows from north to south. The Coriolis effect, related to the rotation of the Earth, pushes flowing water to the right in the northern hemisphere. The result is slightly lower water level nearer the coast. During wintertime, the opposite is true. South and southwest winds related to winter storms can cause a north-flowing coastal current. As the Coriolis Effect pushes the flowing water to the right, water level near the shore is slightly elevated.

3. <u>Storm Surge</u>: Because of its Mediterranean climate, severe storms occur almost exclusively in the winter months, or at least in the winter-half of the year. Because of the low-pressure nature of the North Pacific storms, they can bring with them a storm surge of that can exceed four feet.

4. <u>Wave Transport</u>: When surface waves are being created at the ocean surface by the wind, there is a small component of mass transport in the direction of the wind and waves. Therefore, when a winter storm blows in bringing a strong west or southwest wind, sea water can pile up against the shore.

For these reasons, when a winter storm blows in from the west, sea level can be raised quite a bit. When the storm peaks during a high tide, especially a king tide, local coastal flooding can occur and wave damage in low-lying areas becomes likely. Sneaker waves are also more common in the winter. Sea level measurements made over a fifty-year period in Yaquina Bay showed winter sea level to average just under a foot higher than summer sea level. However, during a 1997-98 El Nino event, sea level peaked nearly two feet above summer sea level in January and February. When an El Nino-inspired, higher-than-normal sea level is combined with a winter storm surge and a king tide, coastal flooding can occur. For sure this explains how the piles of driftwood we see can be washed so far up the beach. We are looking at an example of a sea level that might be common some decades into the future – perhaps sooner than we think.

We need to be able to predict variations in sea level along shorelines where people live and where they recreate, and what global warming might bring. It seems like a combination oceanography and climatology problem. At Oregon State University on Corvallis there is a College of Earth, Ocean, and Atmospheric sciences where these things are studied. Anyone interested?

Sneaker Waves on the Oregon Coast

Unless you live on the coast of the Pacific Northwest, you may not have experienced sneaker waves, also called rogue waves when encountered at sea. They are simply very large waves that are taller and contain more energy than the others that are hitting the shore at the time. Consequentially, they can run farther up the beach and be far more treacherous. The danger is real in any season, even when the sea seems calm and orderly. You need to watch for them anytime you are near the shore. Usually the result is only an unexpected bath, but occasionally people are swept out to sea, and some do not survive. Fatalities happen nearly every year on the Oregon and Washington coasts. Sneaker waves are especially treacherous for small children, who are oblivious to the danger and are easily knocked over and washed away by the undertow of a large wave. So it is best to keep them well away from the surf zone unless you have them by the hand. It has not been found possible to predict sneaker waves, but storms at sea make them more likely. Sneaker wave breakers have been known to be as high as thirty feet along the Oregon Coast. They can wash over rocks, tide pools, and jetties and can run up the beach into the driftwood, where they may dislodge logs in a dangerous way.

Why do we have sneaker waves on the Oregon Coast?

Why do we have sneaker waves on the Oregon Coast? Several unrelated factors may contribute to any monster wave, and that is why they are so difficult to predict:

1. Ocean storms. Even during the summer, there are likely to be

storms in the North Pacific between Oregon, Japan, Kamchatka, and Alaska. As I write this section in early May, a satellite weather map shows three storms far out in the North Pacific and a fourth storm approaching the Oregon shore. In the winter, the storms are usually larger and stronger than in the summer. Ocean storms generate waves which radiate outward from the origin in all directions, like rings radiating outward from a pebble splash in a pond. Because the storms can be violent and the winds unpredictable, waves of many sizes and wave lengths are created. The resulting storm waves may travel across the entire ocean, where we see them as swells in the open sea and breakers against the beach, even on calm days with no wind. Since the velocity of a wave in deep water is directly related to wave length, the distance between wave crests, larger waves travel faster and will overtake smaller waves. At the point of overtaking, the combined wave contains the energy of both waves and it will be taller. Physicists call this kind of wave interaction positive interference. Several wave trains could interact in this manner, some originating in different storms and coming from different directions. If that occurs where the waves are approaching the shore, a large sneaker wave might result.

2. Prevailing wind. During the Oregon summer, a strong prevailing north or northwest wind is common, and may blow for days. In wintertime, storm waves often come from the southwest. You can see the result as whitecaps offshore and swells breaking on the beach. The summer winds don't blow at storm intensities, but a fetch of several hundred miles allows large waves to form. Charter fishing boats may not be able to go out for days at a time, although commercial fishermen often brave the elements, departing before dawn when the wind is weakest and whitecaps fewer. Wind energy is being transferred to wave energy and new wave trains are being created. Fortunately, the summer wind and resulting waves run parallel to shore; as the waves diffract toward the beach, their intensity is lessened. But if there are stormy conditions farther offshore, the danger is much greater and the shoreline is best avoided. You can

watch the crashing storm waves from the parking lot or from the bluff above.

3. Sea floor bathymetry. As ocean waves approach the shore, water depth becomes a factor in wave propagation. Where the water shallows, a deep-water wave begins to obey shallow-water wave physics, slows down, and becomes taller. This simple phenomenon causes breakers to form, as the back part of the wave in deeper water overtakes the slower front part of the wave in shallower water. In addition, the bathymetry of the sea floor can cause shallow-water waves to be diffracted as they near the shore. Waves of different sizes will be diffracted differently, as will waves arriving from different directions. A consequence may be that waves may unexpectedly pile up on one another, creating sneaker waves.

All three factors are much more prominent in the Pacific Northwest than on the East or Gulf coasts, where sneaker waves are far less common. The best generality is that if the surf is large, dangerous sneaker waves are more likely, as more wave energy is at play. *So one must always be on guard for sneaker waves when close to the ocean.*

Harbor jetties are particularly hazardous for sneaker waves. The jetties were constructed specifically to allow marine access to the harbors, not for recreational use. The stone jetties have no pathways along the top, so access over the large, rough rocks can be dangerous in itself and a rapid retreat from a large wave nearly impossible. Rescue is difficult if you slip and break a leg. Sneaker waves can wash over a jetty, especially at high tide, washing you or your children into the sea or the river channel. Drift logs you may have noticed stranded atop the jetties indicate the danger. If the tide is receding, a person can be quickly washed out to sea with no one being aware. One must be cognizant that the Oregon and Washington coastline experiences the highest wave energy in the country.

According to a 2023 article in *Nature*, a 58 foot storm wave was recorded by a buoy offshore Vancouver Island in January, 2020. That was in the open sea, miles from land. Imagine what that wave would have looked like as a breaker on the beach! Fortunately, the west coast of Vancouver Island is sparsely populated, and it is unlikely anyone was on the beach that stormy day. But there are storms in the North Pacific even in summer. A wave half that tall would inundate a jetty. Later that year, buoy measurements of sea state off the coast of Norway recorded a wave 68 feet high, more than three times as high as the rest of the storm waves at the time. As tall as a seven-story building. It would have clearly been a sneaker wave if it had occurred at the shore, but that was not observed on the sparsely populated Norwegian shoreline. Although these were among the tallest waves ever accurately measured, there are anecdotal accounts of even taller waves in the past, and there is good reason to believe them.

Efforts are being made to predict rogue waves, as they are still an ocean-wide threat. A recent article in *Science News* (July 18, 2024) points out that during the period 2011 to 2118, "collected eye-witness accounts" attribute 386 drownings and the loss of 24 ships to rogue waves in that eight-year span. Using AI analysis of buoy data, rogue wave predictions can be made up to five minutes in advance, with around 75% accuracy. However, this kind of prediction is of little use to the beach-goer.

I have experienced smaller sneaker waves on the Oregon beach more than once, resulting in nothing more than wet feet and a very wet dog. But my most frightening encounter with a sneaker wave occurred on the southern shore of the Indonesian island of Java. On a sunny day, we had parked the car in a coconut grove well behind the beach. My wife and children were building sand castles while I was attempting to body surf. Suddenly I found myself atop a huge wave. I hollered down at my family, but of course they couldn't hear me. Only because they were watching and the beach was narrow and steep was my family able to dash to safety. When we got back to the car, we found that the wave had come across the coconut grove and up to the floorboards of the car.

On the tropical Indonesian shore of the Indian Ocean, much of the wave energy originates in the stormy Southern Ocean, more than 3000 miles to the south, in an area of consistent, strong westerly winds. Tropical cyclones in the Indian Ocean can be a modifying factor, strengthening the wave trains as they travel northward. They are a well-known danger to swimmers along that coast, and visitors are warned against them. In a similar manner, summer swells along the Oregon Coast may originate more than 3000 miles to the northwest in the Gulf of Alaska, where stormy weather may occur at any time of the year. In December, 1983, sneaker waves caused by a series of winter storms off California even ran into towns in coastal counties. Please beware.

Chapter 8

Coos Bay

South Slough National Estuarine Research Reserve: Rest stop, woodland hike, stroll, visitor center. At 7.0 miles north of the Coquille River Bridge on Hwy 101 you see the sign for Charleston and W. Beaver Hill Road, which becomes Seven Devils Road. Turn west and drive 8.5 miles through a large tree farm in various stages of harvest and regrowth. At 8.5 miles from the junction the entrance to the research reserve appears on the east side, marked by a sign. This route eventually takes you to Charleston and the parks on Cape Arago. From the north, exit Hwy 540 in Charleston onto Seven Devils Road and drive 6.2 miles south to the reserve.

The directions above assume you are traveling along the coast and have decided to follow the coast and skip the town of Coos Bay. You have been passing through a forest carefully managed by the Coos County Forestry Department. The forest is primarily Douglas-fir but includes western redcedar, western hemlock, and various shrubs - including expanses of huckleberry where the trees have been more recently cut. Modern restrooms are available at the research center, which you are encouraged to visit. Entrance is free, and they have several well-designed displays related to South Slough, a pristine arm of the more commercial Coos Bay. The center is open Tuesday through Saturday 10:00am to 4:00pm. It is under joint federal NOAA and state management.

Despite being currently enveloped in a forest, when the visitor center was built it had a fine view of South Slough. But the slough, the forest, and the small feeder streams are all part of a unique ecosystem and they are managed together. What is a "slough"? South Slough is merely an arm of the Coos Bay estuary, a drowned river valley. It includes tidal channels, mudflats, fresh- and salt-water marshes, and vegetated shorelines. Birdlife is abundant. Nearly five miles long, more than four miles of that length is almost totally undeveloped. A pleasant, ten-minute earthen trail starts at the visitor center and loops through the adjacent forest. Berries abound along the trail – huckleberry, red huckleberry, thimbleberry, salmonberry, salal, and wild blackberries. Something should be ripe for you to pick! The trail is not flat but the slopes are gentle and

Berries abound along the trail – huckleberry, red huckleberry, thimbleberry, salmonberry, salal, and wild blackberries

sidewalk strollers should make it OK. In addition, there are more than four miles of more difficult hiking trails from the research center to and along the South Slough. Kayaking excursions (in rented kayaks), guided birdwatching walks, and other activities are occasionally scheduled. There is a lot going on for vacationing families. You can find more information online at southsloughestuary.org, or call Eric Dean, the education specialist, at (541) 888-5558 ext. 126. Reservations are required for the activities.

Also of interest, as the Visitor Center is located within a dense forest, they have carefully modified the surrounding acres to create a defensible space for protection from forest fires, which have been occurring more frequently in the western forests as the climate warms.

Wildlife habitats: Evergreen forest, estuary, salt marsh, mud flat.

Coos Bay, North Bend, and Charleston

The region around Coos Bay, called expansively by some residents "The Oregon Bay Area", has had a long and interesting history. There are presently two good-sized towns located along the bay, but there were others in the past. Like some other towns along the Pacific Coast, the area's first European-American settlement resulted from a shipwreck. The town was called Camp Castaway by the shipwreck survivors, who constructed it and lived there for a few months during the winter and spring of 1852. Here is the fascinating story, summarized largely from Orvil Dodge's 1898 historical account *Pioneer History of Coos and Curry Counties, Oregon*. Dodge may have been able to interview survivors of the shipwreck and Camp Castaway:

The Shipwreck of the Captain Lincoln

In December, 1851, the *Captain Lincoln*, a three-masted schooner of around 300 tons displacement with a cargo capacity of 150 tons, departed San Francisco Bay directly into the teeth of a winter storm. She was serving as a troop transport for the U.S. Army, carrying some 30 troopers belonging to C Troop, 1st U. S. Dragoons, from San Francisco to a military facility at Fort Orford. (Now Port Orford) It appears that a show of force was needed there, as the local Tutunis had proved warlike. The *Captain Lincoln* was an old wooden sailing vessel that had come around Cape Horn from the U.S. East Coast, arriving in San Francisco in poor condition. In addition to the dragoons she was carrying a full cargo of military foodstuffs – barrels of hardtack, salt pork, beans, whisky, and other delicacies. There was no room on board the *Captain Lincoln* for the dragoon's horses, which were transported later on William Tichenor's schooner *Sea Gull*. At the Fort Orford harbor, the horses were dumped into the sea near Battle Rock to swim ashore to the beach, which they apparently accomplished successfully. Not being very seaworthy, the old

The dragoon's horses were dumped into the
sea at Fort Orford to swim ashore.

schooner commenced to leak as soon as she left San Francisco Bay. Crews manned the bilge pumps continuously for the arduous twenty-day voyage to Fort Orford, where the stormy seas made a winter landing too dangerous to attempt. As I pointed out before, the harbor of Fort Orford is well protected from the north and northwest winds and waves that occur mainly in the summertime by the Port Orford Heads promontory and Cape Blanco, but affords little protection from the southwesterly storms in the winter. One could argue that they should have waited for summer weather for the difficult journey, but the voyage was deemed militarily necessary. When the pumping could no longer keep pace with the leaks, Captain Nagle decided to find a beach where the *Captain Lincoln* could land through the surf somewhere north of Cape Blanco and Cape Arago, thus saving the passengers and crew from "a watery grave", as Orvil Dodge avers. The *Captain Lincoln* was finally swept ashore by the heavy seas at night in a dense fog and broken apart just north of the mouth of Coos Bay, at the time variously called Cowes, Kowes, or the Kowan Bay after the Coos people who lived in the area. All aboard were saved. The ship carried only a single whaleboat, far too small for the crew and the dragoons to have used as a lifeboat.

To their good fortune, the ship's crew and the dragoons landed on what is now known as the North Spit of Coos Bay. In the morning the tide was out and the stranded ship could be unloaded of cargo and equipment. A tent camp was established behind the beach, using sails, spars, and rigging from the *Captain Lincoln* for the purpose. The ship's cargo was also stored in tents for protection from the rain, wind and blowing sand. To the delight of the survivors, the cargo, originally intended for the new military fort at Fort Orford and for another facility on Puget Sound, included along with sugar and flour, "…eight or ten barrels of whisky of old times, good and pure, without a heartache in a hogshead, not the 'Tangle foot and kill me quick poison of the present day'." Thus supplies were available for an extended stay. Their foodstuffs were augmented

"...eight or ten barrels of whisky of old times,
good and pure, without a heartache in a hogshead, not the
'Tangle foot and kill me quick poison of the present day'."

by visits from the Cowan people, who lived across the bay near the former town of Empire, now part of Coos Bay. That included, according to Dodge, "...a long pack-train of squaws laden with fish of all kinds, wild geese, ducks, elk and venison..." to barter for various items the dragoons had salvaged and could spare. It seems possible that the dragoons may not have been their first visitors.

Camp Castaway didn't survive as a permanent settlement. After all, it was basically a military encampment for dragoons without their horses, there were no women or children present, and the sandy spit where it was located provided no opportunities for agriculture – not that the dragoons were prepared to initiate farming with no equipment and no seeds. Even their horses were waiting for them some fifty miles away in Fort Orford, but of course they didn't know that right away, and the dragoon's mounts probably wouldn't have taken kindly to becoming draft horses anyway. Although much of their food was bartered from the Cowan Indians, their bartering stores couldn't last forever. So after waiting for four months for orders which never came, they figured they had been assumed lost at sea. Or perhaps they ran out of whisky. (Note Dodge's spelling of *whisky* – does this imply real Scotch whisky? His description implies that it was a step up from American corn whiskey.)

There are two accounts of what happened next. According to Dodge's history, the entire brigade then trekked to Port Orford, their original destination, some fifty miles to the south. That wasn't a simple hike – they had to cross Coos Bay, the Coquille River estuary, and the Elk and Sixes rivers, without any boats or horses. Dodge doesn't say how they crossed these water bodies, but rafts could have been readily made using driftwood and lines salvaged from the *Captain Lincoln*. It took them ten days to cover the distance, which appears to have allowed time for raft-building. Another account holds that Captain Nagel, the skipper of the *Captain Lincoln*, was able to successfully sail the schooner *Nassau* across the Coos Bay bar to the bay side of the Camp Castaway – the first recorded crossing of the Coos Bay bar. But how did he manage to get to the Nassau? There may be some truth in both histories, but I like Dodge's account better. In either case, Camp Castaway was left deserted. In 2010, after more than a century and a half, archeologists using ground-penetrating radar discovered and excavated evidence of the camp. A monument was erected, Oregon archaeological site 35CS277. You may be able to find it on Coos Bay's North Spit, but there isn't much to see.

Current Oregon residents will recall the shipwreck of the *New Carissa*, a 640 foot Panama-flagged freighter, in nearly the same spot in 1999. Not unlike the *Captain Lincoln* more than a century before, the New Carissa was waiting out a winter storm that prevented her from entering safe harbor, this time Coos Bay. The New Carissa dragged anchor, ran aground, and broke apart in the storm, causing oil pollution on the beach of the North Spit. The majority of the wreck was not removed until 2008 after many attempts and a lot of legal wrangling. A fine article describing the event can be found online at https://en.wikipedia.org/wiki/New_Carissa.

Coos Bay's subsequent history started not long after the wreck of the *Captain Lincoln*. According Orvil Dodge's history, an exploring party left the gold-mining town of Jacksonville in May of 1853, a year after Camp Castaway was deserted. They were looking for a harbor on the Pacific coast that would serve the growing population of Jacksonville and the Rogue River Valley. Apparently the Klamath-Siskiyou Mountains and the lower Rogue River canyon itself proved too difficult as routes to the shore. An outdoorsman named P.B. Marple claimed to be familiar with the Coos Bay area, but he may have gotten some of his information indirectly from the survivors of military Camp Castaway or other early explorers, such as the French-Canadian trappers. Marple started out with a pack train of forty men and eighty horses. Going was easy north to the Umpqua Valley, but the seventy-mile trek across the Coast Range to the coast proved more difficult and many turned back. Once reaching Coos Bay, they endeavored to plan a townsite near Empire – across the bay from Camp Castaway. The Dodge report is silent about any actual attempts to establish Coos Bay as a seaport for the Rogue Valley: perhaps he needed to talk to pioneers in Jacksonville, and that was outside of the area of his historical research. Today, only two towns remain, Coos Bay and North Bend. Unincorporated Charleston, near the mouth of the bay, serves as the fishing and recreational boating center for the area.

Timber, Fish, Agriculture, Shipbuilding, and Coal

The Coos Bay region turned out to be richly endowed and soon attracted settlers. As extensive stands of cedar and Douglas-fir covered the area, sawmills were soon built. Forest products have been important to the Coos Bay area for more than a century. Several small rivers run into the bay, and these carried runs of salmon for new fish canneries. Their floodplains were turned into rich farm and pasture land. The first cattle were brought to the area from the Willamette Valley as early as 1953. Coal mines were developed, making the Coos Bay basin an important contributor of lignite coal to the San Francisco market, competing with mines around Puget Sound. San Francisco's own local supply at Black Diamond Mine near Antioch, the largest coal mine in California, couldn't supply the growing demand. And all of this right around the finest natural harbor between San Francisco and the Columbia River. Logging and milling continue to this day, but at a far lesser scale than earlier; one can still see barges and ships being loaded with forest products and chips along the Coos Bay waterfront. Lignite coal is no longer mined, but commercial salmon fishing and crabbing continue to support the economy. As an adjunct to the early maritime trade out of Coos Bay, many sailing ships were built there – tall ship festivals are still held today.

The Coos Bay Estuary

Coos Bay is the largest estuary on the Oregon Coast. It has over thirteen thousand acres of surface area, but much of it is shallow and exposed as mud flats during low tide. Some of the flats are covered with eelgrass. Heavily vegetated salt marshes are found along the estuary, especially in the numerous sloughs. Over the years, many of the salt marshes and mud flats have been filled and converted to agricultural, industrial, or residential use, which is unfortunate as these constitute important biomes. Many local marine fishes breed in the bay, and the salt marshes are important to them. Dredging of ship channels, dumping of dredged material on the mud flats, and industrial pollution are additional problems, but these have been recognized and are being addressed.

Trapping Dungeness crabs is popular

The watershed area draining to Coos Bay is listed at 605 square miles. Sport fishing in the system is popular year-round for a variety of fish – particularly Chinook salmon, coho salmon, striped bass, shad, and sturgeon. Trapping Dungeness crabs is popular. Steelhead and sea run cutthroat trout pass through the bay but are mainly fished in the rivers and sloughs. In addition, some typically oceanic fish species such as halibut, ling cod, rock fish, and varieties of perch are caught as they occasionally enter the bay. Many of them feed on the mud flats and in the salt marshes during high tide and congregate in the deeper channels during low tide. Altogether, more than sixty fish species have been found in the estuary, many of them coming in from the ocean to spawn in the bay, the salt marshes, the sloughs, and the fresh-water tributaries. The extensive mudflats yield a variety of oysters and clams. Gapers, littlenecks, butter clams, cockles, and several other species are harvested by recreational clam diggers.

Today, oysters are grown commercially in the bay for the

wholesale market and for local consumption. The oysters start out
as tiny larvae and kept in huge salt-water tanks for a few days until
they can attach to old oyster shells that have been fastened to stakes.
Next the stakes are placed in shallow areas of the bay that have been
leased, where the young oysters grow for a three-year period before
being harvested. You can find the tasty fresh Pacific oysters in the
local fish restaurants. But the odds of finding a valuable pearl are
low – perhaps one in a million.

Sloughs

Several tidal sloughs extend inland from Coos Bay, features not
seen in most of the estuaries along the Oregon Coast. These are basically small estuaries that flood the lower valleys of small streams
that enter the bay. Each has an array of biological habitats, making
them ideal for bird watching. They also provide safe areas for canoe-
ing and kayaking, secluded and protected from ship traffic on the
open bay. South Slough, near Charleston, is a prominent example.

Bird Life

As one of the largest enclosed bays along the Pacific Coast, Coos
Bay with its many sloughs serves as an important rest stop for varieties
of waterfowl on their biannual migrations from the Canadian and
Alaskan tundra to the tropics and back. Some make it all the way to
Patagonia or farther; others only fly far enough south to find warmer
weather, and may even winter in Coos Bay. Annual surveys by the
National Audubon Society have identified nearly a hundred bird
species on and around the bay – some resident and others migratory.

Research Institutions

Such a rich array of habitats and marine life has understandably
attracted marine research institutions. The Charleston Marine Life

Center, located right on the waterfront in Charleston, offers a small

Charleston offers a small family-friendly
aquarium with touch tanks for the youngsters

family-friendly aquarium with touch tanks for the youngsters. Oregon Institute of Marine Biology, a branch of the University of Oregon, is located here. Farther south on South Slough you will find the South Slough Reserve, formally the South Slough National Estuarine Research Reserve, with a great array of exhibits and activities and both strolling and hiking trails. The South Slough Reserve was established in 1974 and is managed by NOAA and the state of Oregon.

Wildlife habitats: Open ocean, sandy beach, rocky shoreline, jetty, estuary, mud flat, salt marsh, conifer forest, and pasture, and park.

Library: 525 Anderson Avenue, Coos Bay; 1800 Sherman Ave, North Bend.

Playground: Pirate Park, 1010 N 10th CT, Coos Bay.

Estuaries and Sea Level Rise

Many of the Oregon estuaries still have salt marshes within them – totaling several thousand acres in all. As sea level rises, the seas will invade farther up the current river valleys and a new era of estuary development will be ushered in. Lands that are now floodplains will become submerged and converted to new mudflats and salt marshes – at least where the rate of sea level rise is greater than the rate of uplift of the coastal mountain ranges. Both of these rates are uncertain, highly variable, and poorly documented.

Both present-day and future estuarine salt marshes may have an interesting beneficial response to the ever-increasing atmospheric carbon dioxide and sea level rise. As salt marshes trap organic and inorganic sediment, a richly organic soil is created. When the water level increases, the top surface of that soil becomes higher. As I point out in a letter to the editors and published in American Scientist, carbon dioxide will be removed from the atmosphere and stored forever by this process – although probably not enough to significantly alter the warming climate. It does, however, emphasize the importance of preserving the estuarine salt

This carbon-trapping process should be active in estuaries

marshes. This carbon-trapping process should be similarly active in estuaries, deltas, and coastal salt marshes across the world – with areas far larger than that of the small estuaries of Oregon.

Related studies have been published in New Zealand and Chesapeake Bay, but few other coastal areas. We need to look into it on our tectonically active Oregon Coast. At Oregon State University on Corvallis there is a College of Earth, Ocean, and Atmospheric Sciences. Anyone interested?

Future Fisheries Biologist - Oysters in Peril

Oysters and clams are highly sensitive to water conditions – they are more delicate creatures than their hard shells suggest, and their thick shells may be part of their problem. Both start life as floating eggs that hatch into tiny free-swimming larvae that build tiny calcareous shells from dissolved carbonate in the water. Unfortunately, some 30 percent of the carbon dioxide being expelled into the atmosphere is being dissolved in the world ocean, making the ocean more acidic. Acid can dissolve thin shells and may make it more difficult for them to form shells, both as larvae and as adults. At what point will it no longer be possible?

The ocean acidification problem also affects other shellfish and their larvae. Detailed studies need to be made on the effects of ocean acidification on the entire oceanic ecosystem. The College of Earth, Ocean, and Atmospheric Sciences at Oregon State University in

Corvallis would be a good place to start. Anyone interested?

Cape Arago Parks: Side trip, rest stop, stroll. Driving south along the coast from Charleston on Cape Arago Highway (Hwy 140) you encounter several scenic parks and overlooks in a six-mile stretch.

Several state parks and scenic overlooks lie along the four-mile coastline of Cape Arago south of Charleston. There are modern restrooms and paved trails for strolling at Sunset Beach, Sunset Beach State Park, and Shore Acres State Park. Shore Acres includes a historic rhododendron garden surrounded by tall Sitka spruce and Douglas-fir trees. Flanking the entrance are the largest Monterey cypress trees you will ever see outside of Monterey. You will find a modern restroom in the trees next to the parking lot.

Of marine biological interest is Simpson Reef overlook near the south end of Cape Arago Highway. It features a view of rock outcrops immediately offshore with abundant sea birds and sea mammals – the sea lions and harbor seals can even be seen in online satellite photos. There are no beach access or restroom facilities at the overlook, but there are primitive trails along the bluff to the north.

Some interesting clues about the geologic history of Coos County

You can't drive out to the parks on Cape Arago without being impressed by the spectacular rock formations. On the rocky shores and seacliffs along Cape Arago you can see some interesting clues about the geologic history of Coos County. The east-tilting sandstone beds you see on the seacliffs were deposited as beach and river sands some forty million years ago in the Eocene epoch. They are part of the Coaledo Formation, which also includes the coal beds that were extensively mined over a century ago south of Coos Bay. The coal layers may have started out as salt marshes or fresh water swamps like we see today around Coos Bay. Covered by layers of sand and mud, the whole deposit was buried and turned into the rocks you see.

Clam shells in the sands contributed calcite for the cement. Subsequent tectonic compression and the building of the Coast Range during the Miocene epoch, starting around twenty million years ago, pushed the Coaledo Formation back to the surface, showing the faults and folds that are typical of a growing mountain range.

Sunset Beach Unconformity. *At Sunset Beach, south of Charleston, a beach cliff has exposed beds of soft sandstone and mudstone dipping to the east and cut by small faults. The outcrop displays several fascinating episodes of local geologic history. They include deposition of mud and sand in horizontal layers, burial and lithification into rock, mountain building and tilting to the steep angle seen here, eventually followed by uplift and erosion to create the flat unconformity visible near the top of the cliff, with thousands of feet of rock having been eroded away. When the unconformity was at sea level, the ocean advanced across it and deposited a layer of beach sand on the terrace where the Sitka spruce trees are growing. Gentle uplift of the terrace allowed the sea to advance once more and erode the cliff face you can see. Now a new unconformity is being eroded at the base of the*

cliff with beach sand and gravel being deposited on it. A whole course in geology visible in one outcrop!

Sunset Beach Sandstone. *This picture provides another view of the same unconformity as in the previous image, with mostly sandstone in the dipping beds. The thick sandstone beds may represent an ancient river sand deposit. At the upper right, below the unconformity surface, a channel can be seen cutting into the sandstone beds. Above the unconformity surface a thin beach sand deposit supports the Sitka spruce forest. Weathering below the soil layer is visible in the orange-colored zone.*

The next phase was a period of relative quiescence, encompassing the last few million years. This allowed the sea to erode the flat marine terrace you see above the sea cliffs, when that surface was at sea level. It is the same terrace that extends all the way to Cape Blanco, where it is much higher. You can still see layers of ancient beach sand lying on the terrace – a nascent unconformity. Finally, the whole coastline got uplifted, so the terrace is now above sea level. Today the waves are cutting into the soft rock formation, eroding it away, and creating a new wave-cut bench at today's sea level. Future mountain building may elevate this bench as yet another terrace, with recent beach sand lying on it.

Wildlife habitats: Open ocean, seastacks, seacliffs, rocky shore, sandy beach, conifer forest, park.

Morgan Creek Fish Hatchery: Side trip, stroll. Located in the Coast Range east of Coos Bay. At the southern ege of the city of Coos Bay on Hwy 101, turn east on State Route 241/Newport Lane. Proceed to a drawbridge across an arm of Coos Bay; cross the bridge and follow Route 241 north to Route 241/D Street. Turn right, following Route 241 past Catching Slough toward a taller bridge crossing the Coos River. Just before the bridge, turn left on South Coos River Highway/Lane and continue to the east under the bridge along a flood-control and land reclamation dike. Continue 4.4 miles to Daniel Creek Road, turn right, and continue 1.8 miles to Morgan Creek Road. Turn left at the hatchery sign and proceed another mile to the hatchery.

A visit to the Rumreich-Morgan Creek hatchery gives you a scenic drive through the valley farms and foothill forests of the Oregon Coast Range, where you may find pleasant sunny weather on days when the coastal attractions are cold, windy, or foggy. Despite the complicated route, it is only about eleven miles from Hwy 101. The drive is most beautiful in the fall when all the bigleaf maples have turned bright yellow. You will see several "sloughs", or tidal streams, along the way, some with abundant waterfowl. Most of the salt marshes and mud flats have been diked off and turned into rich pastureland. All but the last mile is on good paved roads. Just

*The drive is most beautiful in the fall when
all the bigleaf maples have turned bright yellow*

before the last turn, by the hatchery sign, you can see a steep hillside
to the right that has been logged a few years ago and is now re-
growing with western hemlock, an unusual choice, as Douglas-fir
is a more valuable crop in this area. No hikes in the area, but stroller
paths around the hatchery are available. The hatchery has an interesting history, which you can explore on the website:
https://www.morgancreekfishhatchery.org/morgan-creek-
history.html. Like at other ODFG (Oregon Department of Fish and
Game) hatcheries, families are welcome and modern restrooms are
provided.

If you want to continue your local explorations, upon returning
to the bridge across the Coos River you can proceed across the
bridge and turn left at the first opportunity on East Bay Road, following signs to Cooston. This route winds along the east side of
Coos Bay, through the village of Cooston, eventually rejoining Hwy
101 at the little town of Glasgow at the north end of the main span
of the Coos Bay Bridge. Parts of this route run along Coos Bay and
provide several great opportunities to observe the abundant waterfowl that frequent the estuary. It is a slow drive, but only ten miles
long and quite scenic.

Wildlife habitats: Meadows, conifer forest, river, estuary.

**William M. Tugman State Park and Eel Lake: Rest stop, woodland
hike, stroll. The turnoff at the sign is 11.0 miles north of Haynes
Inlet Viaduct, 5.5 miles south of Winchester Bay, on the east side
of the highway. Proceed 0.4 miles to the parking lot at the
lakeshore and boat launch.**

This is a superb park, situated on the western shore of 365-acre
Eel Lake, offering a dock, boat launch, and picnic tables both open

and under a shelter roof. Asphalt trails run through the park, camp-ground, and down to the dock. Modern restrooms are located some 400 feet south in the field, beyond the playground equipment. A stroller-accessible earthen trail extends 1.5 miles along the lake south of the park, staying in the forest but with lake views; there are a few exposed roots to watch for and it is a little muddy after rains. It starts at the wooden bridge downstream from the restroom build-ing and fish-management structure; you have to look for it. The for-est is secondary. According to the park ranger it was logged around sixty years ago and not touched since. It still gives you a true rain-forest experience with tall Sitka spruce, western redcedar, western hemlock, Douglas-fir, alder, and bigleaf maple. A few of the ever-greens are several feet in diameter. Perhaps they were too small to harvest in the original logging and have had extra time to grow. Un-dergrowth includes a wealth of berry bushes: huckleberry, red huckleberry, thimbleberry, salmonberry, and salal. Nothing was ripe in June when I visited, but there should be something to pick all summer. Sword ferns and lady ferns line the trail. Eel Lake is one

A few of the evergreens are several feet in diameter; perhaps they were too small to harvest in the original logging

of the many dune-trapped lakes on the central Oregon Coast, drain-ing to the sea through the small Eel Creek. The surface elevation is 66 feet; the maximum depth is 65 feet in the submerged channel, which is close to today's sea level. Waterfowl are abundant in the lake, es-pecially during the spring and fall migrations. You will find good bass and crappie fishing in the warm season both from the shore and from boats; ODFW stocks rainbow trout in the spring. Native cutthroat trout may also be taken. Although Eel Creek, the outlet stream to the ocean, is quite small, coho salmon migrate up the stream and through the lake to the tributary streams. Unfortunately, if you catch one it must be released in order to help build up the stock. But catching a silver salmon is an experience in itself. Careful observers may be able to see migrating salmon in the creek in the fall. You can find a comprehensive fishing report online at https://www.bestfishinginamerica.com/or-eel-lake-fishing-oregon.html; other fishing reports are posted online as well. South of the main day-use parking lot, beyond the restrooms, there is a salmon-steelhead-lamprey management structure with excellent educational displays.

Eel Lake at Tugman State Park. Eel Lake is representative of many dune-trapped lakes nestled in the sand dunes of the Oregon Dunes National Recreation Area, the fifty-mile stretch of sand dunes between Coos Bay and Florence. Although most of the area was logged more than half a century ago; thick second-growth forests of mixed conifers and hardwoods have grown up: Sitka spruce, Douglas-fir, western hemlock, western redcedar, red alder, bigleaf maple, and a luxuriant understory. Some of the lakes, like Eel Lake, are connected to the ocean by small streams and host runs of salmon, mainly coho. Eel Lake was named for the lampreys that also migrate through the lake to the feeder streams, although they are not true eels.

Did you know that even though the lake is called Eel Lake, there are no eels there but lampreys instead? Lampreys are primitive, cartilaginous, eel-like fish. They have sucker mouths with which they attach to salmon and other fish in order to suck their blood. They actually spend their early life as larvae in the mud and migrate to the ocean as adults. Lampreys then come back to the rivers to prey on the returning anadromous salmon, and finally to spawn.

Wildlife habitats: Park, lake, conifer forest, brushy creek; a flock of resident Canadian geese was grazing the lawn on my visit in June.

Chapter 9

Winchester Bay

Reedsport, Winchester Bay, and Gardiner

In 1791, the American captain James Baker sailed into the Umpqua estuary and traded with the local Native Americans for a few days. Little history was recorded for the next sixty years. There are reports that smallpox and measles were introduced to the coastal Native American populations in the 1800s – possibly from Baker's crew? The Umpqua population may have been much smaller when American settlements began. Today there are three small towns along the lower estuary of the Umpqua River, now called Winchester Bay. They all date back to the early 1850s and each has a history of its own – yet today they seem to function as parts of the same town.

Gardiner was established in 1850 – because of a shipwreck!

Gardiner was the first. The town was established in 1850 on the north bank of the estuary a few miles inland from the ocean – because of a shipwreck! Gardiner was named for the owner of a merchant ship, the Bostonian, which became shipwrecked at the mouth of the estuary on October 1, 1850. Gardiner wanted to trade along the Umpqua River, which is navigable for some distance, but apparently was unable to get his sailing ship across the bar at the river mouth. Despite being shipwrecked – I am guessing she may have simply run aground near shore – Gardiner was able to save most of his cargo and moved it to the location where the town now stands. Using materials salvaged from his ill-fated schooner, he built a house, called it a town, and named it after himself. A year later, in 1851, the Umpqua customs district and a post office had been established in what was by then called Gardiner's City, later Gardiner City, and finally Gardiner. Many early buildings have been preserved, now enshrined as the *Gardiner Historic District*. Since 1994 almost all of Gardiner has been listed in the *National Register of Historic Places*, and it is well-worth seeing.

One can speculate why a customs district office was thought necessary along the remote central coast. It is likely that the Umpqua River was seen as logical shipping access to Roseburg, a growing town some 100 river miles inland. Roseburg was also a new town and had neither rail nor river connection to the growing population centers in the Willamette Valley. However, the Umpqua never reached its promise as a navigable waterway – only one steamship, the *Swan*, ever made it all the way from the Pacific Ocean to Roseburg, and that was not until 1870. Consequently, the town of Scottsburg, located at the head of tidewater on the Umpqua, became the seaport for Roseburg. At Scottsburg cargo was transferred from schooners and steamships to mule trains for the remainder of the trip upriver.

Only a short time after the Bostonians ill-fated voyage, Herman Winchester left San Francisco on an expedition to the Oregon Coast on the schooner *Kate Heath*. It was not a well-planned voyage. Looking for the Klamath River, considered a possible route to the gold fields in the interior, they first entered the Rogue River, where they found no gold and had considerable difficulty with the Tutuni people who lived in the vicinity. Even today, neither the Klamath nor the Rogue rivers have proved to be navigable upriver to the inland valleys.

Captain Winchester and the *Kate Heath* finally crossed the bar into the Umpqua estuary, apparently missing Coos Bay along the way. He immediately founded a town on the south bank and called it Winchester Bay. That location had been a "trading point" previously called West Umpqua, where trading between the local Kuitsh Tribe, who had a village there, and the Spanish had occasionally been taking place at least as far back as 1791. Spanish galleons had been sailing annually from Manila to Acapulco since the northern route was discovered, taking advantage of the east-flowing North Pacific Current and favorable westerly trade winds to aid the crossing. Stopping at first land in Oregon to replenish their water supply was not illogical, though it was north of the normal route, so why not trade with the locals for some pelts at the same time? It doesn't appear that the Kuitsh people were totally enamored by the White men they dealt with. In 1828, they attacked and nearly wiped out the Jedediah Smith party that had been exploring the Oregon Coast all the way up from Brookings. Sadly, the Kuitsh were deported from the area to a desolate reservation near Yachats in the 1850s, thereby allowing the Umpqua Valley to be opened for settlers. Winchester Bay has since been developed as a major small-craft port, hosting a large commercial fishing fleet, many pleasure craft, and a Coast Guard station.

Winchester Bay Fishing Fleet. *This is only a small part of the huge commercial fishing fleet working out of Winchester Bay. A variety of fish are landed here by commercial and recreational anglers: Chinook and coho salmon, rock fish, ling cod, both white and green sturgeon. Currently, sturgeon must be released. Crabbing and clam digging are also popular in the estuary.*

Reedsport, now the main town of the area and headquarters of Oregon Dunes National Recreation Area, was established in 1852 by Alfred W. Reed, but didn't really get going until around 1900. Along with Gardiner, it thrived for more than a century as a lumbering center. You will see an extensive area along the river just east of Gardiner where large lumber mills were dismantled. A salmon cannery built in Reedsport in 1910 lasted for a few years.

The Umpqua has not been kind to ship traffic. Over the years from 1850, when the Bostonian ran aground, and 1924 when the jetties were built, the Umpqua claimed ten schooners, three steamships,

The Umpqua claimed ten schooners, three steamships, two barques, two brigs, a tugboat, a barge, and a sternwheeler

two barques, two brigs, a tugboat, a barge, and a sternwheeler, mostly wrecked trying to cross the treacherous bar. What was the attraction for all this ship traffic? Besides the unnavigable Rogue and Klamath rivers, the Umpqua is the largest river between San Francisco and the Columbia. It is 226 miles long, crossing the Coast Range to reach its headwaters in the Cascades near Crater Lake.

A 92-foot lighthouse was completed in 1857 next to the river mouth, using materials brought up from San Francisco, as part of a string of lighthouses all within physical view along the Oregon Coast. Unfortunately, the foundation in the sand was poorly planned. By 1861 it had begun to tilt during a January storm and flood, and was officially abandoned in 1864. Shortly after, the lighthouse crashed to the ground just as the lantern room was being dismantled. For thirty years there was no lighthouse along the sandy central coast. The present 65-foot lighthouse was completed farther inland on high ground in 1894 on a stable foundation. It was fitted with a modern Fresnel lens, once again completing the string of navigational aids stretching from the Columbia River to the St. George Reef lighthouse off Crescent City, just south of the California border.

Library: Lower Umpqua Library, 395 Winchester Avenue, Reedsport.

Playground: Henderson Park, 9th Street and Greenwood Avenue, Reedsport.

Umpqua Lighthouse State Park: Side trip, rest stop, woodland hike, stroll. Entrance 15.3 miles north of Coos Bay/Haynes Inlet Bridge and Viaduct. Turn west on Lighthouse Road, and in 0.4 miles turn west again also on Lighthouse Road. Continue 0.3 miles to the campground entrance, then 0.2 miles to the campground. From the north, turn west on Lighthouse Road, 0.9 miles south of Winchester Bay, drive 0.6 miles to the campground entrance, then south 0.2 miles to the campground.

Umpqua Lighthouse State Park and Campground lies above the lovely 10-acre Lake Marie, one of many dune-trapped lakes along the central Oregon Coast. The lake is completely surrounded by a dense secondary forest of Sitka spruce, western hemlock, Douglas-fir, western redcedar, and shore pine. Undergrowth includes sword fern, deer fern, bracken, false lily-of-the-valley, and in marshy areas, expanses of skunk cabbage and horsetail. Near the southwest end you will see a great example of a western hemlock growing out of an ancient stump and enveloping it with its roots. As the lake is entirely within the park there has never been any commercial or residential

A great example of a hemlock growing out of
an ancient stump, enveloping it with its roots

development. Even the campground is out of sight, up the hill from the lake, which is accessible by road only at the north end where there is a small bathing beach and boat launch – no power boats please: that would break the tranquility. Modern restrooms with showers are located in the campground loop. Visitors have posted online photographs of strings of rainbow trout they have caught in

Lake Marie, some of them quite large. A one-mile earthen trail goes around the lake, suitable for strollers and well protected from the wind but with a few roots and, in rainy times, a little mud. Longer hikes continue through the dunes to the beach and the south jetty of the Umpqua River, less than a mile to the west, and from there five miles south along the beach to Tenmile Creek. The historic lighthouse is a short distance farther west along Lighthouse Road and is definitely worth visiting. The lighthouse gift shop also has a public restroom.

Umpqua River Jetties. *This view of the stone jetties protecting the mouth of the Umpqua River and Winchester Bay shows efforts by the U.S. Army Core of Engineers to protect commercial and recreational navigation into and out of the harbor. Construction began in 1933, nearly a century ago, using a railroad to transport the rocks to the ends of the growing jetties. However, subsea hazards still exist in the form of sand bars built up by the waves, tides, and river flow. These must be periodically dredged.*

Wildlife habitats: Conifer forest, lake. I saw squirrels and Steller's blue jays along the trail.

Future Oceanographer – Harbor "Bar"

In the histories of the Oregon Coast, frequent references are made of a "bar" protecting the mouths of the estuaries from easy passage in and out of the harbor. This is a shallow area within the mouth of an estuary characterized by shifting currents and often by breaking waves. Many ships, particularly sailing ships but modern vessels as well, have been wrecked while attempting to cross one of these bars. Perhaps the first was the heavily armed Navy schooner *USS Shark*, wrecked while trying to cross the Columbia River bar in 1846. Another early casualty was the propeller steamer *Sea Gull* which foundered after crossing the bar at Humboldt Bay in northern California in 1852. This is the same *Sea Gull*, captained by William Tichenor, which figured prominently in the early history of Port Orford.

What is the big deal about river-mouth bars, and what causes them?

So what is the big deal about river-mouth bars, and what causes them? Up and down the Oregon Coast the bars still constitute major navigational hazards in modern times, and these are the reasons: First, there are vast quantities of sand along the Oregon Coast. Much of the sand came down the mighty Columbia River, particularly during the Pleistocene era. Rivers draining the Coast Range and the Klamath-Siskiyou Mountains also contributed sand to the shore. Extensive sand dunes in the Oregon Dunes National Recreation Area south of Florence were generated from these copious supplies of coastal sand. Second, nearshore oceanic currents are caused by both summer and winter wave action. These longshore currents move the sand north or south along the beach, depending on the season and the wind and wave direction. Finally, sand is carried in and out of the estuaries by river flow and tidal currents. At the mouths of the rivers and estuaries, where the tidal flow meets the marine wave energy, the migrating sand tends to pile up and block the entrance in the form of a submerged sand bar, or several sand bars. Changing oceanic conditions cause them to move about unpredictably, so they must be repeatedly dredged out to allow ships to enter the harbors. Small rivers like the Winchuck are blocked completely during periods of low river flow and the river water has to seep into the sea through a subaerial sand bar. But in the larger rivers that are used for ports, the sand bars are submerged and become perennial navigation hazards. Waves tend to break on the submerged sand bars, making a ship's passage even more difficult - or even inadvisable during stormy weather.

Still today, even with stone jetties, "crossing the bar" on entering or leaving a coastal estuary can be an ordeal if the sea is stormy. My own experience on the MV Acona, a small oceanographic vessel once operated by the School of Oceanography at Oregon State University, included a scary 45 degree roll while crossing the bar at Newport, Oregon, coming into the harbor at Yaquina Bay during a storm. An even scarier 60 degree roll was reported as the Acona crossed the Alsea River bar at Waldport; fortunately I wasn't aboard.

So what to do about it? The standard practice is to erect a pair of long rock jetties well into the sea, beyond the reach of the longshore currents, and then periodically dredge out any sand that accumulates between the jetties. Usually that is effective for the estuary entrance itself, but this process is an imperfect solution to coastal management. On the "upstream" side of the jetty, often on the north, the sand tends to accumulate, building a wider sandy beach out toward the end of the jetty. As a result, the downstream side becomes starved of its traditional sand supply, sometimes resulting in severe beach erosion. Houses have been lost. You can see the geographic results on recent satellite maps of the coastline, or merely by standing on one of the jetties and looking across the channel to the beach on the other side.

More detailed coastal geomorphological studies could be made of sand flow along the beach near river mouths, along with the contribution of sand from the river itself. And what, if anything, can be done to mitigate the annual accumulations of sand that make navigational hazards and must be dredged. Anyone interested in doing such a study?

Umpqua Discovery Center. Located at 401 Riverfront Way in Reedsport. From Hwy 101, drive east a quarter mile on Hwy 38 (Umpqua Avenue) to E. Railroad Avenue. Turn north and continue a third of a mile to Riverfront Way, then right a tenth of a mile to the Discovery Center parking lot on your left.

Although there is an entrance fee, ($8 for adults, $4 for children aged 6-16, free for preschoolers), the Umpqua Discovery Center is a small museum well worth the price. Modern restrooms are located inside. The museum was established by the City of Reedsport and is run by volunteers from the town. You will find fine displays of both people history and the natural history of the lower Umpqua area. And, of course, a nice gift shop that is worth perusing. The museum features extensive natural history murals which are themselves worth the price of admission. Outside, there are stroller boardwalks along the estuary and out onto the boat docks. A couple of restaurants have located along the boardwalk. The Discovery Center is open Tuesday through Saturday. For a public restroom, the Oregon Dunes National Recreation Area Visitor Center is nearby at 881 Hwy 101 and is open weekends.

Wildlife habitats along the boardwalk: Estuary, harbor.

Future Ornithologist - Cormorants

Cormorant. The very name sounds like a military title, not a bird. The word has origins in the medieval Latin term *corvus marinus*, which meant "sea raven". From there it went to Old French "cormoran" and finally into Middle English, where the *t* was attached to the end, possibly to get away from the French nasal pronunciation.

One can readily see why they were called sea ravens. Most of the forty or so species living worldwide have glossy, all black plumage like ravens and are of similar size. A few species are lighter, and some, like the pied cormorant of Kangaroo Island, Australia, and other far southern cormorants, even have striking white breasts.

Along the Oregon Coast, you may see three species of cormorant: Brant's cormorant (*Phalacrocorax penicillatus*), double-crested cormorant (*Phalacrocorax auritus*), and pelagic cormorant (*Phalacrocorax pelagicus*). Brandt's cormorant is the one most common seen along the Oregon Coast in the summer, especially in the estuaries. They are also called shags, a common name for cormorants in the English-speaking countries. Cormorants are excellent divers and harvest their fishy meals that way. Consequently, they are said to taste like fish and are not considered good to eat. This is probably to their advantage.

Following a dive, cormorants may be seen on a rock or a piling with their wings spread to dry, as they have less waterproofing preen oil than other sea birds. (You may have seen turkey vultures

Cormorants have less waterproofing preen oil than other sea birds

behaving this way in cool mornings, but they are only trying to capture sunlight to warm up.) Brandt's cormorants are seen nesting in colonies on Oregon's many offshore rocks, also on protected cliffs on the shore. You aren't likely to get very close, but with good binoculars you may be able to see their small, bright-blue pouch at their throat and their bright blue eyes. If the pouch is orange, you have spotted a double-crested cormorant. These are common all over Oregon near rivers, estuaries, and lakes. They may nest in trees or on the ground. Pelagic cormorants have white plumage on their lower back; they also have a blue pouch but their eyes are green rather than bright blue.

Brandt's cormorants, found all along the Oregon Coast, have a distinctive, recognizable flight pattern. They often leave their nesting colony in small groups and fly rapidly in a straight line at a short distance above the water like a squadron of fighter planes. But when fishing, they dive from the water surface – not from the air like pelicans.

Cormorants are commonly seen in the estuaries, often perching on abandoned timber pilings. Crab Pier on Winchester Bay is a good place to observe them close-up. Is there a way to work out how important their role is in the estuarine environment? Are they negatively affecting the populations of young salmon and steelhead on their return to the sea? Anyone interested in such a study?

Cormorants at Winchester Bay. *At the end of Crab Pier on lower Winchester Bay, several timber pilings from a previous dock make ideal roosts for cormorants as they dry their feathers between dives. Pigeon guillemots and gulls may also be seen there and on the adjacent stone jetty, while coots swim about. Barnacles encrust the lower parts of the pilings where daily submergence is guaranteed but they are still above the normal range of predating marine snails.*

Oregon Coast Range

The Oregon Coast Range has been the focus of many geological studies, as it is a classic example of a linear, folded mountain range forming above a subduction zone. But first, just what is a subduction zone? The crust of the earth is made up of discrete tectonic plates that slowly drift around, hence the common term *continental drift*. Some plates are very large, like the North American continental plate, which is very thick and mostly composed of familiar rock types like granite, sandstone, and limestone. Others are much smaller, like the Juan de Fuca oceanic plate offshore Oregon and Washington. Oceanic plates are thin, located below the deep sea floor, and are composed of layers of basalt overlain by mud. When an oceanic plate drifts into a plate of thick continental crust, it will typically be thrust, or subducted, beneath it, continuing downward at an angle until it is eventually destroyed by the temperature and pressure. The collision zone and the sloping fault zone that separates the two plates are the main components of a subduction zone.

Off the coast of Oregon and Washington, the Juan de Fuca oceanic plate is diving beneath the western edge of the North American continental plate. The action is localized in the Cascade subduction zone, which reaches the earth's surface and forms a bathymetric trench at the foot of the continental slope, a few tens

The Juan de Fuca oceanic plate is diving
beneath the North American continental plate

of miles offshore. But as the Juan de Fuca plate gets subducted, some of the sediments get scraped off and pushed up into a coastal mountain range, replete with folds and faults. That is the origin of the Coast Range of Oregon and Washington. You may have driven across the range and seen folded and faulted layers of sandstone and mudstone in the road cuts and river banks. Some of these sedimentary rocks were originally deposited on the deep sea floor of the Juan de Fuca plate before being plastered against the North American plate. Much of that material was originally eroded from the rising mountains and carried to the ocean by the rivers you have crossed; it is a continuing cycle of erosion, deposition, continental accretion, mountain uplift, and more erosion.

The subducted Juan de Fuca plate doesn't stop at the Coast Range, but continues downward at an angle until it becomes physically and chemically unstable. In the Pacific Northwest, that is happening around a hundred miles inland beneath the volcanic Cascade Mountains. There, sea water carried in with the sediments on the descending plate starts percolating upwards toward the surface, dissolving and recrystallizing minerals along the way. Semi-liquid magma bodies form in the shallower subsurface, which occasionally erupt gas and lava to form volcanoes. A line of more than twenty of these volcanoes in the high Cascades now extends from California's Mt. Lassen in the south to Washington's Mt. Rainier and beyond. Most appear to be dormant, but Mt. Lassen erupted as recently as 1917. Mt. Saint Helens explosive eruption in 1980 is the most recent. It is still smoking, and volcanologists tell us it may erupt again. You can find more information on the Cascade subduction zone in Sandi Doughton's excellent book *Full rip 9.0: the next Big Earthquake in the Pacific Northwest*. Doughton points out that this whole process is not gentle, but accompanied by major earthquakes occurring every few hundred years, and that the next big one might be due soon.

Dean Creek Elk Viewing Area: Side trip, rest stop. From Reedsport, drive 3.5 miles east on Hwy 38 to the viewing area on the right of the highway.

This is a fine stop for the family, as a herd of Roosevelt Elk is usually in view in the extensive meadow. Two viewing areas, managed by the Bureau of Land Management, are connected by a half-mile asphalt driveway. At the main viewing area near the entrance, the BLM has supplied excellent interpretive panels. Modern restrooms are maintained at the main viewing area; the second viewing area has primitive facilities. However, there are no strolling trails. Tidal channels flow through culverts under the highway, which runs along a low dike separating the Umpqua River from the elk meadow, part of which appears to be salt marsh and, at the southern margin, fresh-water marsh. It is likely completely flooded when the river is running high. The herds of elk may be at some distance away, so grab your binoculars. You are also likely to see ducks of various species in the tidal channels.

The Roosevelt elk (Cervus canadensis roosevelti) you are watching are the largest of the six original North American elk subspecies: Roosevelt, Manitoban, Rocky Mountain, Tule, eastern, and Merriam's. The eastern elk of North America have long been extinct: the last one was bagged in 1880. Merriam's elk once roamed Arizona, New Mexico, and northern Mexico, and were hunted out a short time later. Two more elk species still live in Asia.

Roosevelt elk seem to like the Pacific rainforest, living in northwestern California, western Oregon and Washington, and coastal British Columbia. They have been transplanted from Olympic National Park to Afognak Island, Alaska, next to Kodiak Island, where they have multiplied. With antlers that can span four feet and weigh twenty pounds each, male Roosevelt elk can reach 1100 pounds. Seems like quite a weight to be carrying around on your head and steering through the dense forest! If you are travelling farther north to Olympic National Park, the Hoh rain forest is also a good elk viewing area.

Roosevelt elk can reach 1100 pounds

What about wapiti? This is a traditional name for elk that comes from the Shawnee and Cree word "waapiti" meaning "white rump". It was probably first applied to the eastern and Manitoban elk subspecies.

Wildlife habitats: Salt marsh, fresh-water marsh.

O.H. Hinsdale Rhododendron Garden: Side trip, stroll. From Reedsport, drive 4.7 miles east on Hwy 38 to the entrance to the garden on the left, a mile past the elk viewing area. There is no parking in the garden – parking is available mainly on the opposite side of Hwy 38, which has a 55 mph speed limit that is often exceeded, <u>so caution must be exercised</u>.

Hinsdale Rhododendron Garden is a privately operated garden next to the Umpqua estuary with 55 acres of rhododendrons of many varieties. The bushes were collected from around the world; some are huge, 15 to 20 feet tall. They have a modern restroom and earthen strolling trails with packed wood chips, but no other hiking opportunities. Entrance is free. The garden is most beautiful in the

The rhododendron bushes were collected from around the world

spring, but some varieties bloom in the summer as well. You will find useful websites at https://traveloregon.com/things-to-do/outdoor-recreation/birding/o-h-hinsdale-rhododendron-garden/ and an extensive photo tour online at Hinsdale Rhododendron Garden/ images for hinsdale rhododendron garden. Before visiting, call to find open hours, at (541) 756-0100. On select days there may be a shuttle service from the main parking lot at Dean Creek Elk Viewing Area just to the west, but you should check.

Wildlife habitats: Park, estuary, fresh water marsh, salt marsh.

Future Aquaculturist – Anadromous Fish Hatcheries

Fishing has been an important part of the economy of the Oregon Coast for thousands of years - since long before European American colonization. When the settlers arrived, the rivers still had prolific runs of salmon and steelhead. Other fish and shellfish were harvested as well. As time went on, an unfortunate combination of over-harvesting and watershed damage from logging, farming, and road construction has greatly reduced the natural salmon runs, in some streams nearly to the vanishing point. Although commercial fishing has long been banned from the rivers, sport fishing is still economically important for many towns along the coast.

Can the prolific fish runs be restored?

Can the prolific fish runs be restored? In an attempt to augment the remaining salmon runs, as well as the native trout, a number of fish hatcheries have been established on coastal rivers over the years. They have had some success, especially with trout. But the salmon runs have not come back like before. With intensive commercial fishing continuing offshore and Chinook salmon selling for $24.95 per pound and more in the grocery stores it is doubtful they ever will be allowed to return without severe regulation, and this is unlikely to happen.

But the rivers and estuaries are still there, just with fewer fish. Perhaps aquaculture can restore at least some of their productivity. The Oregon State University Marine Studies Initiative has been looking into this possibility. You can read a recent report on their nascent investigations in the following link entitled *Farming the Waters*: http://terra.oregonstate.edu/2020/02/farming-the-waters/. Presently, the U.S. spends billions of dollars per year on fish imports, much of it from Asian aquaculture. Where I now live in California, most of the farmed Atlantic salmon are imported from Chile, some 4000 miles away. Could we not farm salmon in our own coastal waters and avoid the cost and environmental effects of long-distance transport and refrigeration? Our Pacific Northwest and the southeastern Alaskan archipelago have the necessary mild climate and clean water for aquaculture. Oregon has gotten a start with oyster farming, and seaweed farming is being attempted, but there is room for much more along the coast and in our many estuaries. Fish is presently the largest source of protein in the world's diet, and the standing crop of many species of oceanic fish is rapidly being fished out. There is a lesson in the decline of the Grand Banks cod fishery over many centuries, but it is largely being ignored. There must be some attractive careers here – anyone interested?

Chapter 10

Florence and the Oregon Lake District

Tahkenitch Lake Campground: Rest stop, woodland hike, stroll. Located 6.1 miles north of Umpqua River Bridge and Gardner, 13.4 miles south of Siuslaw River Bridge. Turn west at the sign, which comes up suddenly.

Tahkenitch Lake Campground is located in a second-growth portion of the Pacific Northwest rainforest. Logged a century ago in the 1920s, the trees have had the opportunity to grown quite large since then – often they get logged again after only thirty or forty years. Douglas-fir, western hemlock, western redcedar, Sitka spruce, and red alder are all present. To the left is the day-use area, trailhead for a three-mile hiking trail to the beach through the forest, and a primitive restroom. The loop to the right takes you through a managed campground with modern restrooms. Hard-surface roads through the area provide a shaded stroller walk protected from the wind. The hike to the beach is listed as difficult, but the first few hundred feet is good earthen trail albeit with a few roots. A primitive trail leads to Lake Tahkenitch, only a quarter mile away, but you must first cross the highway. A sign reminds you that a recreation pass is required for the day-use area, available online. A Golden Age Passport is accepted.

Wildlife habitats: Evergreen forest. Note the 15 foot rhododendron bush to the right of the entrance.

Jesse M. State Park: Side trip, rest stop, stroll. Located 17.6 miles north of Haynes Inlet Viaduct and 2.3 miles south of Siuslaw river Bridge; turn west at the sign.

Jesse M. Honeyman State Park is one of the jewels of the Oregon state park system. The day use area has modern restrooms, picnic tables, canoe and paddle boat rentals, sand dune access, and a beach for swimming on tiny Cleawox Lake – but don't expect the water to be very warm. Like many of the small lakes in the Oregon sand dunes, the lake is fed mainly by rainfall seepage through the dunes. The park is also a favorite campground.

Jesse M. Honeyman State Park is one of the jewels of the Oregon state park system.

The park is nestled in a forest of Douglas-fir, western redcedar, western hemlock, and shore pine with an understory wax myrtle, cascara, rhododendron and a profusion of berries - huckleberry, salmonberry, wild blackberry, thimbleberry, and salal. Something should be ripe all summer, and the huckleberries last into the fall. You can use the extensive asphalt road system for strolling. Hiking trails lead to a sand dune field half a mile to the west; you can continue to the beach a little more than a mile farther. You may encounter speeding dune buggies when you leave the park, so watch out! There is a $5.00 entrance fee per car, but this one is well worth it.

Half a mile east of the highway on Canary Road there is another day use area on much larger Woahink Lake, complete with a dock, boat launch, and modern restrooms. Camping is allowed there as well. Fishing for trout and a variety of warm-water species can be excellent, partly because it is quite deep for the dune-trapped lakes at 72 feet. As the surface elevation is only around 43 feet, the deep point appears to be an ancient stream channel, 29 feet below sea level, which preceded the damming of the lake by the sand dunes.

Wildlife habitats: Lake, park, sand dune, beach, open ocean, conifer forest. Woahink Lake is a fine place to observe ducks and other waterfowl from the shore.

Future Limnologist – Dune-trapped Lakes

The science of limnology is the study of lakes – their origin and decline, their sediments, their chemistry, their biology, and especially how these attributes change with time and human influence. A unique set of lakes is found on the central Oregon Coast, between Coos Bay and Florence. Some forty lakes, termed sand dune lakes, are located just landward of the Coos Bay dune sheet. They lie in the ancient coastal valleys of small rivers and streams where they have been separated from the ocean by migrating sand dunes. Even today the surfaces of most of these lakes are only a few feet above sea level, approximately at the local water table. The original stream courses can be detected on the lake floors of most of them, extending several feet below sea level. These include several beautiful lakes that are visible from Highway 101, such as Tahkenitch Lake and Woahink Lake. Others are off the highway within the Oregon Dunes National Recreation Area.

Some forty lakes are located just landward of the sand dunes

Unfortunately, these lakes and their forested watersheds have not escaped the notice of the recreation, real estate development, and timber industries. These have led to changes in the water quality of some of the lakes, especially the larger ones that are outside the national recreation area. Originally all were oligotrophic lakes – well oxygenated with low concentrations of the nutrients nitrogen and phosphorus. The low supply of essential nutrients limited the growth of lake biota, so although the lakes were clear and pristine, neither zooplankton nor the fish that ate it were abundant. Only a few of the larger lakes have drainage to the sea, via small creeks through the sand dunes. The rest of the lakes, despite the high annual rainfall along the central coast, are able to drain through the permeable sand dunes to the ocean.

Siltcoos River Estuary. *Not all of the estuaries on the Oregon Coast are large like Winchester Bay and protected by jetties. Many, like the Siltcoos River estuary shown here, are really tiny and are only really open to the ocean during high tide. Nevertheless, some harbor small runs of salmon and steelhead. Anadromous fish must wait for high tide to enter the estuary, when it is being refilled with sea water. These little rivers present a challenge to the homing skills of the salmon and steelhead that spawn in them. Siltcoos Lake, drained by the Siltcoos River through the estuary, remains slightly above sea level and contains only fresh water. Once the fish migrate upstream to Siltcoos Lake, they still have to find the feeder streams in which they were hatched.*

Real estate development has changed water quality for the worse. Housing developments now dot the shores of the larger lakes. As there is no regional sewer system to serve some of them, many houses rely on a septic tanks and drain fields. While these systems are effective in the primary treatment of household sewage, dissolved chemicals such as detergents are not removed in the process. The cleaned-up water still includes nitrogen and phosphorus, along with many other chemicals. If you look at the content lists on the bottles under your sinks at home, you will discover literally dozens of chemical constituents that are routinely flushed down the drain. The problem here is that the highly permeable sandy soil in the developments around the lake allows this chemical-laden water to eventually drain from septic systems into the nearby lakes. Visible results have been diminished water clarity, invasion of nuisance water weeds, and even occasional eutrophic conditions that have resulted in algae blooms. None of the Oregon dune lakes has yet reached the severely eutrophic condition found in Lake Erie, but the potential is clearly there.

Septic tank pollution of Oregon's dune-trapped lakes is a serious and continuing problem, and a solution needs to be found. One could hardly ask for a more beautiful place to conduct field studies. And there are untold thousands of lakes elsewhere in the United States, many of which need help. Anyone interested in a limnology career?

Florence Old Town: Side trip, rest stop, stroll, restaurants. Located along the Siuslaw River Estuary just east of the north end of the Hwy 101 Bridge. To access from the south, turn right on Maple Street and drive down to Bay Street, which runs along the waterfront. There is a large parking lot at the bottom of Maple Street, but on busy summer weekends you may need to find street parking a block or two away.

Florence is one of only a few towns along the Oregon Coast that have retained colorful old-town historic districts along their estuaries, and it is one of the best. In just a few square blocks of the old "Port of Siuslaw" you will find shops, restaurants, galleries, and pubs quite separate from the modern commercial district built nearby along the new highway. The "Dockside Restroom" is located across Bay Street at the foot of Maple Street, a modern facility maintained by the town. Stroller walks are limited to the sidewalks, which may be crowded in the summer. Any hikes would be of an urban sidewalk variety.

Before the European American settlers arrived, the Siuslaw people had lived there for thousands of years, gleaning rich harvests of fish, shellfish, game from the forest, and various berries and roots. They now remain in the area as part owners of Three Rivers Casino, just out of town on the highway to Eugene. You can see the town history at the fine Siuslaw Pioneer Museum at 278 Maple Street in the old town area. The museum displays one of the best collections on the coast of the apparel and tools of the White settlers, as well as that of the first people before them. There is even an authentic dugout canoe. How old must that be?

The museum displays an authentic dugout canoe.

The Siuslaw River extends 110 miles into the Coast Range to a source just southwest of Eugene, but that distance is as the salmon swims. It is a very crooked river, with several entrenched meanders in its upper part. In the beautifully illustrated book *Rivers of Oregon* by Tim Palmer, you can find a detailed description of a four-day, 77 mile canoe trip on the upper Siuslaw starting at Siuslaw Falls and ending at Mapleton. He noted clearcutting on privately-held land and buffer violations, allowing muddy runoff from steep logged land to flow into the Siuslaw River. Previously the Forest Service had allowed "overcutting of old growth forest that could never be sustained". Eighteen log jams to navigate on the first day likely resulted partly from careless logging practices, on both public and private land. In addition, the Siuslaw River and estuary are likely to run brown during and after rainstorms.

The Siuslaw estuary is long and narrow; as defined by tidal influence it extends inland 32 miles to just past the town of Mapleton. Surface area is only 3040 acres, relatively small for the size of the river, so mud flats for clamming are limited. However, there is a five-mile stretch of nicely developed salt marshes just upstream from Florence. In the late 1800s, salmon canneries and sawmills were built near the towns; large quantities of canned coho salmon were shipped out before the salmon runs declined due to overfishing. An informative pamphlet entitled *History of Fishing on the Siuslaw* by Trygve O. Nordahl, a long-time local fisherman, was published by the Siuslaw Pioneer Museum in 2000. Nordahl describes the sequentially declining populations of Chinook salmon, coho salmon, steelhead, striped bass, shad, smelts, herring, and ocean perch in the Siuslaw estuary over his 70-year fishing career. He attributes the declines to seal and cormorant predation. Perhaps there is some truth to that, but overfishing is never mentioned. Today, fishing for Chinook salmon is popular both in the estuary and offshore; steelhead and cutthroat trout are caught in the Siuslaw River and its tributaries.

Florence hit the national news in 1970 when a dead 45-foot sperm whale washed up on the ocean beach. As the beaches in Oregon had been declared a state highway, it was up to the highway department to deal with it. Dynamite was their tool of choice, presumably to break it up so some of it could wash back out to sea and the seagulls would take care of the rest. Their reasoning has not been published. Apparently the half-ton charge used was too large, as the explosion

The explosion caused whale flesh to fall from the sky

caused whale flesh to fall from the sky as far as 800 feet away, some landing on spectator's automobiles. One wonders what kind of highway signs they erected afterward! But despite the smell, Florence took it in stride and built a park to commemorate the event.

Wildlife habitats: Estuary, urban.

Library: Siuslaw Public Library, 1460 9th Street.

Playground: Miller Park, 1681 18th Street.

Darlingtonia Wayside: Scenic stop, rest stop, stroll. Located close to Hwy 101 at Mercer Lake Road, 5.7 miles north of Siuslaw River Bridge, about 2.5 miles north of Florence, and 5.9 miles south of Sea Lion Caves.

Darlingtonia State Natural Site is the only state park property dedicated to the protection of a single plant species – *Darlingtonia californica*, commonly called "cobra lily" because of its strange hooded appearance. This small botanical park provides parking, a boardwalk circling a small fen crowded with these strange plants, and a primitive restroom. A stop here is highly recommended. Cobra lilies are the only carnivorous pitcher plant known to grow in Oregon. Darlingtonia is a variety of pitcher plant that lives in swampy areas of northern California and coastal Oregon, but it is not common. I have seen them before only at Little Vulcan Lake, high in the Klamath-Siskiyou Mountains east of Brookings, where it enjoys the serpentine rock soil. As you will see on the informative sign, the colorful cobra lilies trap insects and dissolve them for their nutrients. You can learn more on the website at https:// appliedeco.org/darlingtonia-wayside-meet-the-pitcher-plant/.

Cobra lilies trap insects and dissolve them for their nutrients.

The five-minute boardwalk path from the parking area traverses a dense secondary forest of cedar, hemlock, shore pine, and alder with an understory of salal, huckleberry, and rhododendron. Along the path you will also see skunk cabbage, another local marsh-loving plant that looks like something out of a tropical jungle. It has yellow flowers resembling calla lilies, huge flexible leaves, and a distinct aroma of skunk. It is reported that the Native Americans had many medicinal uses for skunk cabbage, some of which persist in modern herbal medicines, and also ate the roots.

What visitors will see in this little garden of multi-colored horrors (for insects) is a plant with yellowish-green hooded leaves that form erect, 10- to 20-inch hollow tubes. Insects are attracted to a potential nectar feast through a hidden opening near the top of the stalk, just beneath the curved hood of the leaf. It appears that they cleverly designed their hoods to keep out rainfall. Once inside, the unfortunate insect becomes confused by the transparent "windows" that appear to be exits. It's all downhill from there, as the insect eventually tires and drops into the lower part of the tube where a pool of water awaits it. An enzyme dissolved in the water decomposes the prey, yielding nitrogen and other nutrients to be absorbed by the pitcher plant.

Wildlife Habitats: Conifer forest, wetland.

Brown Pelicans

A wonderful bird is the pelican,
His bill will hold more than his belican,
He can take in his beak
Food enough for a week,
But I'm damned if I see how the helican.

This limerick, composed more than a hundred years ago by the American humorist Dixon Lanier Merritt, describes perfectly our image of the pelican. The description is accurate – a pelican can actually hold far more in his beak pouch, also called a gular pouch, than his stomach will hold. (Note the word similarity to gullet – both words come from the Latin word *gula*, or throat.) No other bird can come close. Quite handy for a take-out dinner for the family. You have heard that a camel is a horse that was designed by a committee. The pelican may be a seabird designed by that same committee. Brown pelicans frequent coastal waters, where they feed on fish, catching them at or near the water surface. They are gregarious birds, travelling in flocks, hunting cooperatively, and breeding in colonies.

The brown pelican was saved from extinction by Rachel Carson with her 1962 book The Silent Spring

In the late twentieth century the American brown pelicans were endangered. They were almost certainly saved from extinction by Rachel Carson's 1962 book *The Silent Spring*, and the environmental movement that followed. It was found that eating fish that had been contaminated by the insecticide DDT affected their calcium metabolism and caused their eggs to have thin shells, which were broken in the nest before hatching. It did not help that brown pelicans incubate their eggs by essentially standing on them, warming them with the skin of their feet! The current abundance of this pelican species in the United States represents a stunning success story for conservationists, who succeeded in vastly limiting the use of DDT and other persistent pesticides both here and around the world – to the advantage of us all.

Cape Creek Bridge. This beautiful Romanesque bridge appears to run straight into a forest, but beneath the forest there is a basalt ridge called Devil's Elbow that required a 700 foot tunnel, necessitating a very tall bridge for a very small creek. The old road that crossed Cape Creek and climbed over the ridge was very difficult to drive, especially in rainy weather. If you have been here before 1991, you might be struck by the new metallic gray color of the bridge; it has received a sacrificial zinc coating to protect the cement rebar from corrosion. Cape Creek Bridge was added to the National Register of Historic Places in 2005, along with other coastal bridges designed by Conde B. McCullough.

There are only eight species of pelicans in the world, really a small family compared to ducks and sparrows. The two that live in North America seem to have signed non-competition agreement. The brown pelican (*Pelecanus occidentalis*) we see along the Oregon Coast in the summertime is a true shore bird, feeding on fish in the open ocean and in brackish estuaries, and is therefore limited to the immediate coastline. In contrast, the American white pelican (*Pelecanus erythrorhynchos*) prefers to fish in a fresh water environment, both near the coast and in the many rivers and lakes of the United States and Canada. American white pelicans do not currently live on the Oregon Coast, but you may see these beautiful birds on the high-desert lakes in central and eastern Oregon.

So it is only the brown pelicans that you will see on the Oregon Coast, and then mainly in the summer. You may see them flying in formation just above the waves as they watch for fish that have strayed too near the surface. Sometimes they exhibit an awkward but spectacular dive when prey is seen. It appears that this plunge from 30 to 60 feet above the water is capable of stunning fish as deep as six feet below the water surface.

A mature brown pelican may weigh over ten pounds and have a wingspan of seven feet. It is by far the largest sea bird you will encounter on your trip. Often you will see them perching atop pilings or an offshore rock, quite striking because of their size. Unlike cormorants, which are more wary, pelicans may be found resting on beaches, sand bars, or in shallow water. They have occasionally been reported to be scavengers, even accepting handouts from fishermen. Perhaps because they are the largest birds in the area they have less fear.

So how did pelicans get here in the first place? They are thought to have evolved in the Old World and spread into the Americas. Pelicans on both sides of the Atlantic prefer warm environments. On the U.S. west coast, brown pelicans are only known to nest on the Channel Islands, offshore southern California. Most of them nest farther south in Mexico.

So how did pelicans get here in the first place?
Floating on a log? Maybe so.

American brown pelicans are commonly found in the summertime as far north as Vancouver Island on the Pacific coast and Long Island on the Atlantic coast. American white pelicans like even warmer coastal waters, from Southern California and Mexico to Florida, although they may breed in southern Canadian lakes during the summer. As American pelican species neither live nor breed in boreal climates, spreading from Siberia across the Bering Sea to Alaska and then down the coast, seems unlikely. Europe and Africa separated from the Americas long before pelicans evolved, so they couldn't have walked across from Europe. And it is a long way to fly across the Atlantic Ocean. Unlike albatrosses, pelicans are not seen on the open sea. Though for a bird that can sleep on the water, perhaps it would not be impossible – except for the fact that the Gulf Stream flows the wrong way.

Modern DNA evidence shows that the new world and old world pelican species split apart very early in pelican evolution. American brown pelicans and American white pelicans diverged genetically next, apparently after they arrived in North America. Consequently, it appears that a single emigration or period of emigration from the old world to America was sufficient. No DNA evidence has been found to support later emigrations and cross-breeding.

People who lived on the Oregon Coast in the years after the 2011 Japanese Tohoku earthquake and tsunami probably have a good idea how the pelicans got here, and I think they are correct. During the following year, tons and tons of Japanese flotsam washed up on the Oregon beaches, pieces as large as trees and entire wooden docks. Whole populations of western Pacific marine life came along for the ride. It does not seem unlikely that one or more breeding pairs of early pelicans followed the same route after an ancient Japanese earthquake and tsunami, riding on patches of floating debris. There are fish to be caught along the way, and brown pelicans with their built-in desalination filters don't need fresh water to drink. The journey in the east-flowing North Pacific Current could have taken all summer, but pelicans are long-lived. And it only needed to happen one time. It is thought that the swimming iguanas of the Galapagos Islands must have similarly arrived on floating logs millions of years ago: it can be done.

Of course there is always another possible explanation in scientific arguments. The earliest pelican-like fossil, found in France, is from the early Oligocene epoch, 30 million years ago. Northern hemisphere climate was much warmer then, before cooling to a climate more like that of today. Perhaps it was possible for Oligocene pelicans to work their way around the northern margin of the Pacific. However, new world and old world pelicans are much too similar to have separated so long ago in their evolutionary history. I prefer the Japanese flotsam story.

There must be a way to determine the origin of the brown pelican in North America and how it became separate from Eurasian pelicans. Detailed genetic studies might help. Anyone interested? Another useful study might investigate the brown pelican's ability to deal with climate change, especially the warming of the surface water of the Pacific and related biological changes. How does that affect their food supply and, consequently, their distribution along the Oregon Coast?

Chapter 11

Yachats and the Cliffed Coast

Heceta Head Lighthouse: Rest stop, stroll. Heceta Head Lighthouse State Scenic Viewpoint is located 12.5 miles north of the Siuslaw River Bridge at Florence; turn east 200 feet north of Cape Creek Bridge at the sign. You will curve around past the overflow parking lot and under the bridge to the beachside parking lot. Southbound travelers turn west at the sign 13.3 miles south of Yachats River Bridge and proceed down the hill to the main parking lot.

Heceta Head Lighthouse State Scenic Viewpoint is one of the scenic stars along the Oregon Coast. Not only are there a lighthouse and lighthouse keeper's houses, but a pocket beach, cliffs, and seastacks where seabirds are nesting – common murres are seen there. Bring your binoculars for a close up view. Gulls seem to like the terminus of the Cape Creek estuary where it flows across the beach at low tide. As small as it is, Cape Creek still hosts a run of winter steelhead, possibly salmon as well.

A well maintained, quarter-mile, hard-surface trail climbs 150 feet to the base of the lighthouse; the trek is highly recommended for the fine view. The promontory is said to be a prime place to watch for migrating whales in the spring and fall, perched as it is directly above relatively deep water. A short trail climbs the bluff above the lighthouse, where you can view the Fresnel lens closer to eye level. For those that don't wish to climb to the lighthouse, there is a 500ft paved trail along the beach side of the main parking lot with a close view of the beach, ocean, and seastacks. Modern restroom facilities are located at the north end of the parking lot.

From the parking lot you can see the Romanesque Cape Creek Bridge

From the parking lot you can see the rather unusual Cape Creek Bridge, one of the many bridges designed by Conde B. McCullough and built during the Great Depression. You can't see the bridge as you cross it. Construction was especially difficult because the bridge needed to be quite high and runs smack into a basalt bluff that required a 700 foot tunnel. Because of its age and its Roman aqueduct-like appearance, the bridge was added to the National Register of Historic Places in 2005. The unusual name of the promontory honors the Basque explorer Bruno de Heceta y Dudagoitia, who explored the Pacific Northwest coast for the queen of Spain in 1775, some 115 years before the lighthouse was constructed. He is not thought to have come ashore here.

Brown Pelicans Sharing the Beach with Sea Gulls at Heceta Head. *This is the beach view from the parking lot just south of Heceta Head lighthouse. More seabirds can be seen on the seastack just offshore, an important nesting site. Pelagic seabirds also frequent the seacliffs around Heceta Head*

and can be easily viewed from the shore, but binoculars will be useful. Cape Creek, with a short estuary, reaches the ocean here; gulls like the brackish water flowing across the beach. These brown pelicans are fair-weather friends, spending only the warmer months along the coasts of Oregon, Washington, and southern Vancouver Island. The only nesting area on the U.S. West Coast is on the Channel Islands south of Santa Barbara.

You may notice that the bridge is shiny and appears metallic. As Cape Creek Bridge is quite close to the ocean, it is particularly exposed to salt spray when the winter storm gusts sweep up Cape Creek canyon. It has been found that the reinforced concrete in the Oregon coastal bridges is permeable to salt water: the chloride ions soak into the concrete and corrode the steel rebar. When this happens, the rebar expands and can cause the concrete beams to spall and weaken. In order to prevent further corrosion, Cape Creek Bridge and other coastal bridges have been coated with a paint that contains zinc. The process is termed sacrificial cathodic coating and provides electrochemical protection to prevent further corrosion of the rebar. Other Oregon Coast bridges have been given this treatment to prolong the life of the superstructures: they are approaching a century of age but still appear to be in good shape.

Habitats: Open ocean, seastacks, beach, small estuary, brushy wetland, evergreen forest with salal understory.

Carl G. Washburn Memorial State Park: Rest stop, beach hike, stroll. Turn west at the sign 2.2 miles north of Cape Creek Bridge, 11.3 miles south of Yachts River Bridge.

This is the day-use area of the park; the camping area is east of the highway. A 0.2 mile drive loop has parking and a modern restroom on the west side. Strolling is limited to the loop, somewhat out of the wind but with no view of the beach. For hikers, primitive trails through the low sand dunes opens up beach hikes 1.4 miles south to Heceta Head or 1.0 miles north to Big Creek, where you

would need to wade to go farther. Located just offshore is Cape
Perpetua Southeast Marine Protected Area, where fishing is limited
in order to help maintain fish stocks up and down the coast.

Wildlife habitats: Open ocean, sandy beach, vegetated low sand
dunes, coastal conifer forest.

**Cape Perpetua Visitor Center – Siuslaw National Forest: Rest stop,
woodland hike, stroll. Located 11 miles north of Cape Creek
Bridge, 2.6 miles south of Yachats River Bridge. Turn east at the
sign on the driveway and proceed 0.2 miles up the hill to the parking lot and visitor center.**

The visitor center is a great stop for traveling family along the
Oregon Coast, especially in inclement weather. It offers a large in-
door facility with well-designed and informative displays, a collection of books and pamphlets, and friendly foresters on site to answer
questions. Modern restrooms are located indoors. It is operated by
the U.S. Forest Service, a division of the Department of Agriculture
– a fine example of your federal tax dollars at work. The visitor center is virtually surrounded by coastal scenic attractions: Cape Perpetua, Cape Perpetua Lookout, Cape Perpetua Scenic Area, Cape
Perpetua Marine Garden, Thor's Well, Devils Churn, Cape Cove
Beach, Spouting Horn, and the rainforest itself. Some are accessible
by trail from the visitor center. Immediately offshore, a large area
has been designated Cape Perpetua Marine Reserve.

On the north side of the visitor center building you will find the
start of Giant Spruce Trail, which runs for more than a mile through
the densely forested canyon of another Cape Creek – a true rainforest experience. The upper story of the forest consists of unusually
tall red alders and Sitka spruce, sheltering a varied mid-story that
includes salmonberry, thimbleberry, huckleberry, salal, and red elderberry. There should be something to pick all summer, but I caution against the elderberries, as they are somewhat toxic to people
and don't taste good anyway. Those are the ones that look like

bunches of tiny red grapes. If you are both sneaky and lucky you may encounter a flock of wild bandtail pigeons enjoying them. At ground level you will see skunk cabbage, wood sorrel, sword fern, lady fern, deer fern, maidenhair fern, and numerous smaller forbs. Although the trail is earthen and descends to creek level, it is not steep and is kept in good shape. Sidewalk strollers should be fine, but watch for roots. For the less adventurous walkers, the large three-level

At ground level you will see skunk cabbage, wood sorrel, sword fern, lady fern, deer fern, and maidenhair fern.

parking lot is located in the shade of the same forest and provides a pleasant setting for a shorter stroll on a paved surface. The Pacific Coast Trail can be accessed there, but the trail is steep and less well maintained, especially to the north. I don't recommend it for casual walkers.

Only half a mile farther north, the Devils Churn parking lot on the west side of the highway offers a fine view, trail access to the beach and the rocky shore, and another modern restroom. However, the trails to the beach are steep and have stairs.

The Cape Perpetua name has an interesting history. Captain Cook first saw the cape from the sea on March 7, 1778, as he was searching for the fabled Northwest Passage. Although he did not come ashore, he bestowed the prominent feature with the unusual name Cape Perpetua in order to honor the early third century Christian martyr Vibia Perpetua on her name day. Vibia Perpetua, an educated noblewoman only 22 years old who was nursing her infant son, along with Felicitas, a pregnant enslaved woman, were imprisoned in Carthage and put to death for their beliefs. Vibia left behind a diary of her travails, thought to have been at least partly written by her in prison around the year 202. An English translation is available online at: https://www.amyrachelpeterson.com/Groups/1000004968/Read_Perpetuas_Prison.aspx. It makes fascinating reading, revealing that Vibia's son was rescued her by relatives. It is thought to be the first diary written by a woman that has been preserved. Today there isn't much left of the Roman city Carthage besides some ruins along the northern coast of the city of Tunis, the modern capital of Tunisia.

Native Americans have lived around Cape Perpetua since long before Vibia Perpetua's imprisonment, likely for thousands of years. Shell mounds in the area indicate that they harvested mussels, crabs, clams, and sea urchins from the rocky coast. The Alsea name of the cape was Halqaik, thought to have meant "exposed place". Old photographs show Cape Perpetua to have been quite bald; it has since been overgrown by the young Sitka spruce forest you see there.

Wildlife habitats: Evergreen rainforest, open ocean, sandy beach, rocky shore, brushy creek, brushy bluff.

Pacific Temperate Rainforest

As you travel along the Oregon Coast, you are passing through the western edge of the world's largest temperate rain forest, the Pacific Temperate Rainforest. But you need to look fast, as it is disappearing, and what remains in Oregon is endangered. Still, there are bits of the original rain forest that have been preserved. One of the finest is in the Siuslaw National forest at Cape Perpetua, where the foresters are managing a must-see educational facility just up from the highway. It is in an area next to the ocean that is so steep and rugged that it never got logged off. A full suite of Douglas-fir, Sitka spruce, western redcedar, western hemlock, bigleaf maple and red alder can be seen there, along with several shrubs in the understory.

A full suite: Douglas-fir, Sitka spruce, western redcedar, western hemlock, bigleaf maple and red alder

The Pacific Temperate Rainforest extends along the coastal mountains, from the redwood forests south of Eureka to the northern part of the archipelago of southeastern Alaska. Most rainforest maps include the western slope of the Cascade Mountains as well, patches of redwood forest as far south as Santa Cruz, and the immediate coastline as far north as Kodiak Island, Alaska. The definition of a temperate rain forest is imprecise. How much rain do you need? Over the whole 1600 mile length the rain forest enjoys a mild, wet climate. Along the Oregon Coast, annual rainfall averages around 100 inches, but it is somewhat higher in the coastal mountains. Parts of Olympic National Park receive more than 180 inches a year; on Vancouver Island some areas get as much as 260 inches per year. In Ketchikan, Alaska, it rains 234 days in the average year, although not all day and much of it falls as snow.

Why is it so rainy? A main climatic influence is in the relatively warm North Pacific Current. This current is a continuation of the Kuroshio Current off Japan, which transports warm water from the subtropical Pacific Ocean northward to sub-polar latitudes – much like the Gulf Stream in the Atlantic. It is a broad current that crosses the North Pacific at about the latitude of the Columbia River. It then splits to become the warm Alaska Current flowing northward along the Washington and Canadian coasts, and the California Current that flows southward along the coasts of Oregon and California. West winds pick up huge quantities of moisture from the warm ocean water and dump it as rain and snow as the storm systems cross the coastal mountain ranges. Most winters also include atmospheric rivers bringing additional moisture from the tropics.

A large variety of conifers dominates the Pacific Temperate Rainforest, certainly the largest variety in the world. You might identify eleven conifer species in the coastal forests along the Oregon Coast, from the small Pacific yew in the understory to the majestic Douglas-fir that dominates the forest in Oregon and the redwoods in northern California. Another twelve conifer species are found in the forests of the western Cascades and the Klamath Siskiyou Mountain Range. However, many of these live mainly in high-altitude areas or on the dryer edge of the rainforest and are only occasionally seen in the rainforest itself.

Other temperate rainforests exist around the globe, but most are managed as grand timber farms. Perhaps the most similar is the rainforest along the mainland and islands of southern Chile. It lies nearly as far south as our Pacific Temperate Rainforest is north and has a similarly rainy climate. The trees, however, are totally different, having evolved independently south of the tropics. The few conifers include the Araucaria, commonly called the monkey puzzle tree, and the alerce, a lone species of cyprus that rivals the sequoia in size and age. It is thought that the biome of southern Chile and Argentina has survived since the splitting of the Gondwanaland supercontinent during the Cretaceous Period, some 140 million years ago. Most of the trees there are of broadleaf varieties not found anywhere else.

Future Forest Ecologist – Tree Planting to Save the Earth

You will be seeing few stands of large trees as you travel along the Oregon Coast but instead areas where the original forest has been logged off and young Douglas-firs have been planted. According to Thomas Crowther, an ecologist at the Swiss Federal Institute of Technology, planting a trillion or more trees may be the most effective and by far the least expensive method for combatting global warming (July fifth, 2019, online issue of *Live Science*). He calculates that there are at least 3.5 million square miles of unused space in various countries where this could be done – without reducing the acreage of farmland. Fast-growing trees capture and put into long-term storage massive amounts of carbon, all taken from the carbon dioxide in the atmosphere. Not only do the tree trunks and branches store carbon, but the root systems store additional carbon in the ground. The United States, Russia, Canada, Australia, Brazil, and China are the countries with the most acreage where Crowther avers this kind of massive planting could be done. However, I might add that planting trees is one thing; keeping them watered and protected until they become established is quite another.

Of the trees that grow along the Oregon Coast, Douglas-fir, Sitka spruce, red alder, and bigleaf maple might fit into Crowther's scheme for "carbon planting". Each grows rapidly in the rainy climate, has a long lifespan, and can store a lot of wood in the trunks and roots. Clearly, areas of the Pacific Northwest rainforest where the trees have been logged and the land left fallow would benefit from Crowther's "carbon planting" with these native species. Current research shows that planting a variety of trees is more effective at above-ground carbon capture and storage, possibly because the different trees utilize soil resources differently. Other climates will favor other fast-growing trees. Planting programs have already been started in Pakistan and in the Sahel of Africa. The *Live Science* article doesn't mention the beneficial oxygen that would be liberated into the atmosphere as the trees grow. That would be, molecule per molecule, the same as the carbon dioxide removed – another advantage of Crowther's scheme. The general formula for cellulose, the main ingredient of wood, is $(C_6H_{10}O_5)_n$. The general process that trees use to make cellulose is simply:

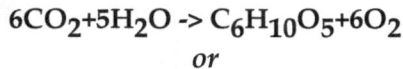

$$6CO_2 + 5H_2O \rightarrow C_6H_{10}O_5 + 6O_2$$

or

Carbon dioxide plus water yields wood plus oxygen

You can see from this reaction that a wet environment will be advantageous. Many forest ecologists would be needed to guide such worldwide planting programs for best advantage; that might be a growing field of employment. Trees must be planted where they will grow quickly and well with little or no care and where they will fit into the natural and social environments. At present, deforestation and the accompanying slash burning are major contributors of carbon dioxide into the atmosphere. As a society we are going the wrong direction.

As all of Switzerland experiences adequate rainfall for forests, it is possible that Professor Crowther has not considered carefully all the requirements for his trillion trees in other areas. Much of the un-used land in the United States lies fallow because of lack of sufficient water for crops or even for grazing, let alone trees. Grassy rangeland often is too dry for trees to grow well. Grasses are not so demanding. That is not a problem for western Oregon, and particularly along the Oregon Coast, but much of the high-desert area east of the Cascades in Oregon and Washington is not favorable for forests. Some of Crowther's mapped areas of forest potential in Canada, Alaska, and Russia are tundra, often underlain by permafrost, where trees grow very slowly, but this could change for the better as the climate warms and permafrost melts. Unfortunately, melting permafrost yields methane to the atmosphere, so the forestation effect there may get canceled out. Nevertheless, any tree planted will create a carbon sink and the proposal deserves consideration. You can follow the link below to find Thomas Crowther's article in *Live Science:* https://www.livescience.com/65880-planting-trees-fights-climate-change.html

At Oregon State University in Corvallis, there is a world-renowned College of Forestry. Is anyone interested?

Yachats

When you visit a town, you want to know want it is called. This one is simply pronounced Yah-hots. No accent. The name is thought to have come from Ya'hatc in the Alsi language, once spoken along the coast and the Yachats River. Unfortunately, there are no longer any Alsi speakers so this will have to do, as the Ya'hatc band of the Alsi Indian Tribe was largely wiped out by 1860, more than a century and a half ago. They were apparently victims of European diseases, maltreatment, starvation, and exposure, while being overseen by U.S. government agencies. Why the odd *ch* in the middle of the name? My own theory is that the German-speaking settlers in the Alsea River Valley may have had something to do with it, rhyming Ya'h with Bach. Yet the town of Yachats was called Oceanside as late as the early 1900s. Only in 1917 did the inhabitants realize that name was too common for a coastal town, so the current name Yachats was adopted, honoring the original inhabitants. The original Ya'hatc

The original Ya'hatc appears to have been a very old village.

appears to have been a very old village. Native American burial grounds uncovered during road construction in and around modern Yachats have been dated to as early as the year 570 CE. It turns out that the town is largely built on kitchen middens and ancient cemeteries. Certainly the Alsi tribe habitation in the area began even earlier. Wooden artifacts that are often used for radio-carbon dating don't survive well in the coastal climate; there were no caves to keep them dry or anoxic bogs to protect them from decay.

Because of its isolation, modern Yachats didn't really get going until the early 1900s. There were earlier homesteads along the Yachats River, but there was no road farther inland from there. Much of the Oregon Coast could be accessed along the beach, but Cape Perpetua blocked beach travel to the south between Yachats and Florence, the first road around Cape Perpetua being completed by the Forest Service around 1914. Even Waldport was difficult to reach until the highway to Corvallis was completed in 1919. Only with the Great Depression and the construction of the Roosevelt Highway (now U.S. Highway 101) and bridges over the estuaries could Yachats begin to grow as a town and become the delightful tourist destination you see today. You can see online a great illustrated history of Yachats by Claire Hall at the following site: https://www.yachatsoregon.org/DocumentCenter/View/124/Yachats-History-Presentation—-Claire-Hall-PDF_

Here is a bit of early Yachats history you won't find in the guidebooks. According to the well-researched book *Holy Rollers: Murder and Madness in Oregon's Love Cult* by T. McCracken and Robert B. Blodgett, Edmund Creffield once came here. Creffield, who also called himself Joshua, and eventually God's Elect, was the founder and head of the tiny Holy Rollers protestant sect. After starting the strange cult in Corvallis in 1902, being tarred and feathered, run out of town, and finally spending 17 months in the state penitentiary for adultery, Creffield gathered together what remained of the faithful, mostly young women, and headed to Yachats where a couple of the women had lived as children. They set up camp on the beach on the south side of the Yachats River and proceeded to burn all their clothes and don sack-cloth gowns.

The Holy Rollers camped here in 1904

Unfortunately for them, a running account of the Holy Rollers' escapades and Creffield's treatment of wives and daughters had been carried in the Oregon newspapers. The farmer who lived on the north side of the river recognized the group and ran Creffield out of town once more, leaving his followers to fend for themselves. Creffield was later shot and killed in Seattle by the brother of two of his converts, who was then tried for murder in King County. A "small fortune" having been raised by the citizens of Corvallis and elsewhere in Oregon for his defense, the brother was acquitted of the murder charge – but one of his sisters shot him dead at the train station as he was returning home.

Although little is made of it, Yachats is actually located on an estuary, the tiny Yachats River. When the tide is out, you can see the river flowing across the beach just south of town; seagulls like to congregate there. At high tide, the short estuary is refilled with the reverse flow. The river is only 15 miles long, draining a watershed of 44 square miles, and the estuary extends only a couple of miles inland.

Library: Yachats Public Library, 560 W 7th St; phone (541) 547-3741.

Playground: Yachats Commons Park, La De La Lane off 5th Street

Yachats River Road and Covered Bridge: Side trip. Exit Hwy 101 east 0.3 miles north of Yachats River Bridge.

   A drive up Yachats River might be a good side trip if you want to get away from the coastal weather for a little while, with an old covered bridge as a reward. Yachats River Road is paved. Drive seven miles to a T intersection, turn left on a one-lane gravel road, and continue a mile and a half to the covered bridge. (Cars will do fine, but the road will not accommodate RVs well.) You can park there for photographs or to walk onto the bridge, but please don't drive across to park, as the property across the bridge is privately owned. A walk back down the access road along North Fork Yachats River is a good choice, well-shaded by Douglas-firs, bigleaf maples, and red alders. If you are lucky you might see an American dipper fishing for nymphs on the bottom of the stream. There are no rest-room facilities along Yachats River Road or at the bridge, but you will find them at Yachats State Recreation Area in town.

   The North Fork Yachats Covered Bridge was built in 1938 with a queenpost truss, one of the few of this type remaining in Oregon. It was faithfully restored in 1989, and again in 2014. Look up the hillside above the bridge for a view of a giant old-growth Spruce tree that is 350 years old. If you make this trip in the early morning or in the evening, watch for elk grazing in pastureland along the river, shared by goats, sheep, horses, and belted black cattle.

   Wildlife habitats: Estuary, brushy wetland, stream, river valley farm, second-growth forest, logged forest.

Yachats State Recreation Area: Rest stop, stroll. At the southern edge of town, 0.3 miles north of the Yachats River Bridge, turn west on Ocean View Drive, which takes you 0.25 miles along the estuary outlet and a rocky shore to the parking lot.

   Yachats offers two nice rest stops as well as the side trip up the

Yachats River. The state recreation area has modern restrooms in the meadow to the east of the parking lot. On the western edge there is a 600-foot paved trail just above the beach, driftwood, basaltic rocks, and breakers.

An even better stop for a stroll is located a little farther north, still within the town of Yachats. At 1.1 miles north of the bridge, turn west on a street called Sunset Road to State Park and proceed 0.2 miles to the parking lot at Smelt Sands State Recreation Site. There the "804" paved trail runs to the north some 3500ft in a coastal meadow, along the edge of the terrace and separated by the town from the highway traffic. It looks down on a long rocky shore with small

Low tide will expose sea life clinging
to the rocks and some nice tide pools

pocket beaches visible at low tide. Low tide will also expose sea life clinging to the rocks and some nice tide pools, so be sure to carry a tide table. But be careful, as waves can suddenly wash up onto the tiny beaches and leave you with a quick scramble up the rocks. Modern restrooms are found just east of the parking lot.

Wildlife habitats: Open ocean, rocky shore, sandy beach, estuary mouth, coastal meadow.

Beachside State Recreation Area: Rest stop, beach hike, stroll. Located 5.4 miles north of Yachats River Bridge and 3.4 miles south of Alsea River Bridge. Turn west at the sign to a loop road through the campground; day-use parking is to the right.

This park and campground is a popular stop for access to a beach that, due to its fine sand, can be more than 900ft wide when the tide is out. It offers a two-mile beach hike north to the Alsea River estuary or 3.5 miles south to Yachats along a mostly developed shoreline. The park road is paved, offering a half-mile stroll down and back through the campground, mostly protected from the wind.

A modern restroom is located in the trees just south of the day-use parking lot, and another is located in the campground.

Wildlife habitats: Open ocean, sandy beach, scrub conifer forest.

Seacliffs on the Oregon Coast

You may wonder, especially if you are visiting from the American Mid-continent or East Coast, why the Oregon Coast has such an impressive display of seacliffs and seastacks. Like with so much of Oregon's history, there is a really interesting tale to tell – and an even longer story. For at least 30 million years, the sea has been chewing away at the western edge of the Coast Range as soon as it began emerging out of the Eocene coastal plain. Then a couple million years ago the Pleistocene ice age caused the sea level to drop, by more than 300 feet! That moved the beach and the breakers twenty to forty miles to the west, exposing a narrow, low-relief coastal plain. Of anthropological interest, it is along this coastal plain that the various Native American adventurers and colonizers must have migrated south from Alaska and Canada. Unfortunately, any Native American villages and other signs of this great migration have since been covered by the advancing sea and washed away. Apparently they didn't build stone buildings like the Pueblo and Hopi civilizations of the American Southwest. There is no Atlantis to look for offshore Oregon.

There is no Atlantis to look for offshore Oregon

Eventually, sea level began to rise during the Holocene, mainly between 10,000 and 6000 years ago, as the North American and European continental ice sheets melted. This event was very rapid from a geological viewpoint. Was this the flood that led to the legend of Noah and his ark? This sea level rise allowed the beach to advance back to its present position, allowing the surf to crash against the seacliffs just as before.

Local geology has a profound effect on what kind of seacliffs we see. Along the southern Oregon coast, south of Bandon and the Coquille River, the rising Klamath Mountains run right up to the beach. These mountains are composed of older, harder, rocks, so tall rugged seacliffs and rocky coasts are the rule there. Along the central coast, between Bandon and Florence, younger and softer sedimentary rocks of the Coast Range prevail, so seacliffs are not common – marine terraces and sand dunes are dominant. North of Florence, tall seacliffs of Miocene-age basaltic volcanic rocks punctuate the coast. Some of these old lavas have snuck in all the way from the Miocene-age basalt flows that dominate the Columbia River Plateau of eastern Oregon, Washington, and Idaho - one of the greatest outpourings of basaltic lava the world has seen. Others, like Haystack Rock near Cannon Beach, may be volcanic necks of local origin. Even farther north, in the Clatsop Plains just south of the Columbia River and the Willipa Bay area to the north, the massive influx of sand from the river becomes dominant and the coast becomes sandy again. Whenever the coastal mountains are rising rapidly and are composed of hard rocks, seacliffs and seastacks will dominate the shoreline.

Chapter 12

Waldport and Alsea Bay

Waldport

Waldport didn't get started quite as early as most of the other towns along the Oregon Coast. Agreements had first to be worked out with the people who already lived there – the Alsi Tribe (now generally spelled Alsea). The Alsis lived in several villages along the Alsea River and estuary, which provided a rich harvest of salmon and shellfish. Using cedar dugout canoes, they also harvested marine mammals in the estuary and in the open ocean. Although agreements with the Alsis were made on a local level and the Alsis were apparently forced into compliance, no treaty was ever ratified in the U.S. Congress, so no appropriations were sent. The tribe was essentially abandoned in a prison-like reservation, where many died of exposure and starvation. By 1875, even that was terminated to make room for White settlers, and the Alsis were once again forced out. This bureaucratic "oversight" was corrected in federal court with a lawsuit in 1959, and some compensation was received by the descendants of the Alsi survivors – *nearly a century later!*

A curious custom among the Alsi people was forehead flattening, which was done by applying slight pressure to the forehead of an infant in the cradleboard over the first year of life. This custom was also practiced among the Flatheads of Montana, presumably leading to their name. Meriwether Lewis noted this trait among many of the native groups that the expedition encountered west of the Rockies some 50 years earlier. You can read more in this link to a fascinating article by Meriwether Lewis written in 1806. http://www.lewis-clark.org/article/1016.

Where did the unusual name *Waldport* come from? It appears that many of the first settlers in the 1870s were of German heritage. They had settled in the broad Alsea valley farther upstream as early as 1855. Waldport was first laid out by David and Orlena Ruble and chartered in 1880. Ruble is an old German name originating in the western German province of Westphalia, situated on the Rhine River. The Rubles apparently took the term "wald", meaning forest, from their German language and attached it to the English term "port" to form a descriptive name for their new town.

Where did the unusual name Waldport come from?

But the town grew slowly, having a population of only a couple of thousand more than 150 years later. We can perhaps attribute the slow growth to Waldport's isolated location between Newport to the north and Florence to the south. Each of those larger towns has an improved harbor with stone jetties and a long-established highway across the Coast Range to the Willamette Valley. The Alsea River still has no jetties; the bar is dangerous and is difficult to navigate safely. State Route 34, connecting Waldport to Corvallis, was completed only in 1919. It is a slow and curvy road climbing over the south flank of Mary's Peak. But in Route 34's defense, an article in a motorcycle magazine states that "This [60-mile] road is an absolute delight." Oregon's transportation and tourism commission has recently designated the route as the "Mary's Peak Scenic Byway", and I fully agree. From the 1230ft pass you can take a side trip to a large, flower-studded alpine meadow near the top of 4097ft Mary's Peak, the tallest peak in the Oregon Coast Range – a highly recommended trip through the forest. There is a primitive restroom at the south end of the parking lot. An easy trail takes you to the crest of the peak. The view from the either the parking lot or the mountain top is spectacular, encompassing the whole of the Willamette Valley and the volcanoes of the Cascades beyond. Interestingly, the conifers near the crest include alpine species characteristic of the Cascades at the same elevation. But be sure to start with a full gas tank and pack a lunch, as there are no services for many miles.

It was only with the Great Depression that Waldport was really opened up to the world. CCC funds during the depression sponsored the finishing of Highway 101 along the coast and the construction of bridges across the many estuaries and rivers. In 1936 the first automobile bridge across the Alsea estuary was designed and built by Conde B. McCullough, who also designed other remarkable bridges you have seen along the Oregon Coast. (A railroad trestle preceded the automobile bridge during the WWI Sitka spruce logging episode.) Although completed the same year as the San Francisco Bay Bridge, the Alsea Bay Bridge was apparently not maintained so lovingly and deteriorated in the harsh Oregon Coast weather. It had to be replaced in 1991 by the handsome concrete span you see today. Before 1936, historical records show a series of ferries operating on Alsea Bay as early as 1915. You can see a picture of the *Roosevelt*, taken in 1930, at the following link: https://oregondigital.org/sets/lchsa/oregondigital:df65vq874

Like most Oregon coastal towns, Waldport's history is steeped in salmon canning, logging, and lumbering. Salmon canning was big during the 1930s; more than 137,000 pounds of salmon were netted in 1937. By 1957, commercial salmon fishing had been closed. Nowadays, there is still some logging, but the mills and canneries are gone. It had always been a disadvantage to local lumber milling that only small vessels could navigate Alsea Bay's shallow bar on entering the bay, and particularly on leaving the bay when fully loaded. A few small sailing schooners were built on the Alsea. The largest of the local fleet was the W.H. Harrison, launched around 1875 but measuring only 90 feet in length. After a short time in service, she was wrecked on the Alsea Bay bar, not the only boat to suffer that fate.

Waldport may be small, but its history had some interesting episodes, beginning with the First World War. The coastal forests in the area had great stands of very large Sitka spruce trees, which were in great demand for aircraft construction for the war effort because of the woods strength and light weight when cured. A war-effort lumber mill was built by the U.S. government in Toledo, on Yaquina Bay, and a railroad was constructed to Waldport and the timber stands to the south of Waldport. But by the time in mid-1918 when everything was ready, the armistice was about to be signed and the spruce lumber was no longer needed for aircraft. The logging train kept operating under private ownership for a while, but today the mills and the railroad are all gone. By the Second World War, spruce lumber was no longer being used in warplanes, having been replaced by aluminum, a practice that prevails today.

During the Great Depression, CCC camps were established along the coast south of town at Angell and Cape Creek. A large amount of conservation work was done by the men. Trails were built in Siuslaw National Forest; most of the elaborate stone buildings and fireplaces you may have seen on your rest stops were also CCC products. As WWII got going in the early 1940s, the depression was over, the camps were closed, and many of the men joined the military. During the war there was a conscientious objector camp at Waldport. It is said that there were basically two kinds of objectors: those with religious objections, who were willing to work hard, and draft dodgers who were more interested in writing anti-war tracts.

Alsea Bay and river host runs of Chinook salmon, coho salmon, steelhead, and cutthroat trout. The Alsea River extends some 49 miles into the Coast Range. The estuary is 9 miles long to the head of tidewater, but it is the wide, lower 4 miles that has salt marshes and mud flats. Crabbing is good in the lower estuary; flounders may also be caught there. Public docks for crabbing, fishing, and moorage, a launch ramp, Robinson Park and picnic area, are among the facilities available in the port area. Many private marinas along the river provide similar services.

Library: Waldport Public library, 460 N Hemlock Street.

Historic Alsea Bay Bridge Interpretive Center: Rest stop, stroll, museum. In Waldport, turn west at the traffic light on Hemlock Street. After one block turn right at the bank of the Alsea River estuary and proceed one block to the parking lot.

This is a small museum with interesting displays related to Oregon Coast history – especially some fine examples of the legendary logging tools and engines used over a century ago to harvest Sitka Spruce in the local rainforest. The main attraction is a model of the new Alsea Bay Bridge and explanatory panels related to its construction from 1988 to 1991. Of the many spectacular bridges built in the 1930s crossing the estuaries along the Oregon Coast, this is the only one that has needed to be replaced. You may have noticed that with their beautiful designs, these great bridges appear to be standing on the water surface, but of course this is not true. The Oregon estuaries have thick deposits of mud, deposited during the Holocene sea level rise since the end of the Pleistocene ice age some 10,000 years ago. As there is no rock to support the piers that hold up the road deck, each is built on a bunch of timber pilings, treated with preservatives and driven 40 or 50 feet into the mud.

An infestation of marine boring organisms so weakened some of the pilings that the bridge was in danger of collapsing

In the case of Alsea River Bridge, an infestation of marine boring organisms in 1967 so weakened some of the pilings that the bridge was in danger of collapsing, so it had to be replaced. So far, the other coastal bridges have avoided this problem. You can find an excellent review of the construction of these bridges in the book *Crossings – McCullough's Coastal Bridges* by Judy Fleagle and Richard Knox Smith.

No hiking trails start here except for the sidewalks on the bridge itself, although access to the high arch is easier from the wayside at the north end of the bridge. Strollers have access either to the bridge or to the sidewalks in Waldport.

Eckman Lake - W.B. Nelson State Recreation Site: Rest stop, stroll. Located on Oregon State Highway 34, 2.3 miles east of Hwy 101 in Waldport. Proceed to SE Nelson Wayside Drive, turn south then immediately east into the parking lot.

This 45 acre lake was once a slough off the Alsea River estuary, but was diked off by construction of Highway 34. It is now a small fresh-water lake, often with abundant waterfowl. You will find a primitive restroom by the parking lot. If you are heading to Corvallis, this is your last public rest stop for many miles of slow driving. There are no hiking trails here, but strollers can go out on the 180 ft. boat dock.

Wildlife habitats: Lake and fresh-water marsh.

Salt Marsh on Alsea Bay. *This is an excellent example of an estuarine salt*

marsh during high tide on the Alsea River estuary, with the wooded Coast Range in the distance. The waxing tide has flooded the marsh, a rich habitat for a wide variety of aquatic plant and animal life. Salt-tolerant grasses and sedges dominate the marsh. Farther seaward, mudflats are more common, with their own biota. In the middle distance, Sitka Spruce trees demonstrate their tolerance of salt water-saturated soil; other conifers could not live here.

Future Forester – Sitka Spruce

You will find Sitka spruce (*Picea sitchensis*) all along the Oregon Coast, mainly close to the ocean. Sitka spruce range from northern California all the way to Kodiak Island in Alaska, enjoying the wet and cool marine climate. They seem to like the salt air. How many trees have been named after a city? The Sitka spruce is one of the few. It is usually the other way around. But it is much more complicated than that. Sitka is a town is southeastern Alaska on Baranof Island – an island heavily forested with Sitka spruce and hemlock. Although the population is small, it has an interesting history worth exploring. The town was established by the Russians in 1799, only 68 years before Alaska was purchased by the United States in 1867, and was made the capital of the Russian territories in North America and far eastern Siberia. The Russians were not interested in the wealth of timber in the area so far from Moscow, but valued more highly the pelts of the sea otters. The current town's name is not Russian – they originally named their outpost Fort St. Michael, then Novo-Arkhangelsk, probably after the Russian city Arkhangelsk on the White Sea north of Moscow. Sitka was derived from the Tlingit word Sheet'ka, which also as other spellings in English and a history of its own in Tlingit.

Some Sitka spruce trees in the nearby Tongass National Forest exceed 700 years in age. As you might suspect from the size of the spruce trees you have encountered along the coast, the Sitka spruce ranks as one of the largest trees in the world. Heights of over 300 feet have been recorded, with trunk diameters of 18 feet. Because they grow rapidly in challenging soil conditions, they have been naturalized in many countries as a timber crop, especially in the British Isles, the Scandinavian countries, and New Zealand. Sitka spruce even do well in Iceland, where they are one of the tree species being grown to replace the forests of birch and willow trees that were cut down by the Vikings more than a thousand years ago.

You can see along the Oregon Coast how the Sitka spruce is able to grow on offshore rocks where the soil is splashed by salty spray during storms, and where the winds are the strongest. Other Oregon conifers don't thrive in those conditions. As one can guess from its geographic range along the coast, the Sitka spruce needs a cool, moist environment and tolerates salty soils.

The Wright brothers used Sitka spruce in the Wright Flyer

As Sitka spruce wood has a very high strength-to-weight weight ratio, it was once used extensively in aircraft manufacture. The Wright brothers used Sitka spruce in the frame of the *Wright Flyer*, along with bamboo. Straight-grained spruce was a favorite construction material for aircraft for many years through World War I. At the *Evergreen Aviation and Space Museum* in McMinnville, Oregon, you can see the Spruce Goose, the largest wooden airplane ever constructed – but it actually is built mainly of birch. It is a giant seaplane with eight engines, built to ferry troops to Europe during World War II and avoid the German U-Boats that were prowling the North Atlantic. Unfortunately for the innovative concept and engineering of the Spruce Goose, the war was over before the giant aircraft was finished. It flew only once, after the war was over, with aircraft designer Howard Hughes at the controls. With a wingspan of 320 feet and a length of 218 feet, the Spruce Goose still ranks as one of the largest aircraft ever built. Yet because of the all-wood construction of the airframe, it weighs only 250,000 ponds – little more than half the weight of a Boeing 747. Think of the number of soldiers the extra capacity might have accommodated!

The distribution of Sitka Spruce along the coastline and its rela-
tion to soil salinity or moisture content would make an interesting
study. Or are other nutrients that are blown inland in the foam also
important? What are the key characteristics of the topsoil remaining
on the bluffs and seastacks that permit Sitka spruce to thrive there
when other conifers do not? Anyone interested in such a study?

Future Pharmacologist – Medicine from Trees

Medicine from trees? How primitive! But you have probably
used them more than once. Aspirin is the most familiar example. At
least 4000 years ago, the Assyrians in Asia Minor found that chewing on willow bark relieved fever and pain – apparently because of
the salicylic acid in the sap. The Assyrian Kingdom was centered in
the Tigris-Euphrates valley, now controlled by Iraq, Turkey, and
Syria – the ancient Fertile Crescent. Willow trees grew abundantly
along these rivers.

Eventually, acetylsalicylic acid was isolated by German chemists
and put into pill form, whereupon Bayer sold it as aspirin. We can
see the relationship in the Latin name for the willow tree family, Sal-
icaceae, and the genus name Salix. Like most organic remedies, the
drug is now made in exclusively the laboratory. Although willows
are abundant along the stream banks in western Oregon, I have not
found evidence that the local Native Americans took advantages of
its medicinal properties as was done in some other Native American
societies. Perhaps the local willow trees were of the wrong variety.
Maybe they had other remedies. Young willow shoots were, however, used in basketry. And you may see them sold at flower shops
as pussy willows.

Another useful medicine was made from the bark of cascara
buckthorn tree (*Rhamnus purshiana*), commonly found all along the
coast of Oregon and Washington. It was used both by Native Americans and early European settlers to prepare a very effective laxative.
It is reported that Spanish explorers in the 1600s found Native

American groups in the Pacific Northwest using cascara bark. Peeling cascara (also called chittem) bark has been a common way to make a little extra money in the spring for a long time. My young friends and I made our spending money that way. We would cut the small trees, peel off the bark, and dry it in the sun. At the time, in the 1950s, we could get as much as 35 cents a pound for a gunny sack of dried bark from the local hardware store. Sometimes they shook and carefully felt the bag to see if a heavy rock was hidden in it, but we were mostly honest. We always suspected that the more common name "chittem" was related to its laxative properties, but I haven't been able to prove it. Cascara bark was an important laxative ingredient until the late 1900s, and is still available online as a ground bark product.

A much more recent tree-derived medicine is paclitaxel (sold as Taxol), an important chemotherapeutic remedy for a number of cancers. Taxol was first isolated from the bark of the Pacific yew tree (Taxus brevifolia), a spindly understory conifer found in humid forests all over the Pacific Northwest, including the Oregon Coast.

Taxol was first isolated from the bark of the Pacific yew tree

This medicine was considered truly groundbreaking when it was developed in the late 1900s at the behest of the National Cancer Institute. But it requires a huge amount of bark for a tiny vial of paclitaxel, and it was once feared that the entire yew population could be decimated. Fortunately for the yew trees, paclitaxel has been synthesized in the laboratory. As the thin, red bark is considered poisonous, it seems surprising that its medicinal properties were investigated at all. Chewing the bark of the Pacific yew tree won't be curative like chewing willow or cascara bark.

There are thousands of distinct plant species in the forests and brushlands of the Pacific Northwest; dozens of them are trees. Each has a distinct chemical makeup; some have been used by the Native Americans as cures. Perhaps future pharmacologists will isolate additional medicines from some of them. Anyone interested in looking for them?

Oregon Hatchery Research Center: Side trip, rest stop, stroll. From Waldport, drive east 26.6 miles on State Highway 54 to County road 714. Turn north and proceed 2.4 miles to the hatchery.

Oregon Hatchery Research Center is a joint research project between the Oregon Department of Fish and Wildlife and Oregon State University. The research center supports basic and applied research comparing wild fish and hatchery fish. You will find numerous fish tanks, artificial stream channels, and a laboratory. Lots of fish to see and feed – big ones. On my visit, the main tank next to the research building had trout and steelhead up to two feet long and a few white sturgeon. You are welcome to feed them – but bring quarters for the fish food dispenser. Modern restrooms are inside.

Lots of fish to see and feed – some really big ones

A graveled road extends 0.2 miles past the residence to water control equipment and a fish ladder, making a short stroller walk. The site has a resident bald eagle; the occasional visits by an osprey have made it necessary to cover the artificial streams with netting. A large pasture on the way up Fall Creek often has a herd of elk. So far inland, this site is a guaranteed escape from coastal fog and wind of the summer, and it is a beautiful drive as well. Fill your gas tank and pack a lunch before you leave Waldport.

The mission of the research center is to investigate the differences between wild salmon and steelhead, and those reared in a hatchery, with as close to natural conditions as possible. Available pamphlets explain it well. There are many other questions being addressed in a scientific manner in the universities of the Pacific Northwest: Can hatchery fish, raised only on food pellets, learn to harvest wild food, or should they be fed caddis flies as well? Do they understand how to avoid predation by ospreys and eagles?

Will they spawn successfully with the wild fish? Must there be a release of hatchery salmon in each potential spawning stream, or is releasing them into the main river sufficient? A quick investigation of the literature finds hundreds of articles on these subjects. After all, raising salmon in a the artificial conditions of a hatchery, to successfully start the complex life cycle of the many wild salmon populations is not the same as dumping hatchery trout in a river or lake to be caught by anglers the next weekend. Evidence has shown that hatchery-reared salmon have traits that can be disadvantageous in the wild, and that these traits show up in the DNA after only a few generations. Cross-breeding with native salmon stocks can then affect the population in the river. The research center is to be commended for their innovative approach toward solving some of these issues. It is clear, however, that hatcheries are successful in increasing the numbers of trout, salmon, and steelhead in the coastal rivers.

The research facility provides a great opportunity for a future fisheries biologist to see research in action – to see what biologists really do. Anyone interested?

Driftwood Beach State Recreation Site: Rest stop, beach hike. Located 1.9 miles north of Alsea Bay Bridge, 11 miles south of Yaquina Bay Bridge. At the sign turn west into the parking lot.

Driftwood Beach State Recreation Site is mainly a beach access site for the northern neighborhoods of Waldport, and has a modern restroom. Stroller walking is limited to a 700ft sidewalk around the large parking lot. A primitive trail leading to the beach opens up a 3.0 mile beach hike south to the north spit of the outlet of Alsea Bay. Unlike most large estuaries along the Oregon Coast, there are no jetties protecting the outlet to the sea. Consequently, it is a dangerous crossing and little used by commercial and recreational watercraft. To the north, a 1.5 mile hike takes you to a rocky point, beyond which you may find both a sandy beach and a rocky shore with tide pools when the tide is out.

Wildlife habitats: Open ocean, sandy beach, low vegetated sand dunes, scrub conifer forest.

Seal Rock State Recreation Site: Rest stop, beach hike. Located 4.5 miles north of Alsea River Bridge at Waldport, 8.8 miles south of Yaquina Bay Bridge at Newport. At the sign turn west into the parking lot.

Seal Rock State Recreation Site is a lesser-known jewel of a park for the naturalist, with a sandy beach, beautiful tidepools protected by a nearshore rock reef, and close-by seastacks for seabirds to land on. You are likely to see sea lions and seals on the reef only a few hundred feet offshore. A couple of short asphalted trails lead to the beach.

You are likely to see sea lions and seals on the reef only a few hundred feet offshore.

Seal Rock itself extends onto the beach, but it falls within the Oregon Islands National Wildlife Refuge, so please don't climb on it and disturb the seabirds. Hikers can wander five miles south to the north spit of Alsea Bay, but there is a little rock scrambling needed. To the north, once you climb down the rocks to the beach, you can hike two miles along the beach to Beaver Creek. A modern restroom sits in the meadow next to the parking lot.

Elephant Rock at Seal Rock State Park. *On the edge of the beach you can reach Elephant Rock, a seastack included in the Oregon Islands National Wildlife Sanctuary, but you should leave it alone; nesting seabirds frightened from their nest and eggs or fledglings may never return. In this image, and even on satellite imagery, you can see many seabirds nesting on the sparsely vegetated crest. Smaller seastacks in the area provide temporary perches for seabirds. Elephant Rock is an erosional remnant of a basalt sill: hardened basaltic lava that was injected between layers of the sedimentary rocks. As the lava sill cooled, it contracted, leading to the prominent vertical columnar jointing. At the base, next to the beachcomber on the left, you can see a "quick-frozen" layer which is the bottom of the sill.*

Wildlife habitats: Open ocean, seastacks, sandy beach, tide pools.

Ona Beach State Park: Rest stop, beach hike, stroll. Located 6.3 miles north of Alsea River Bridge; from the north, 7.0 miles south of Yaquina Bay Bridge. Turn west into the parking lot at the sign, just opposite N. Beaver Creek Road.

The main park occupies a small peninsula surrounded by Beaver Creek estuary; the estuary outlet and sandy beach are nearby. Hard-surface paths lead from the parking lot past the modern restroom and picnic areas in the meadow next to the narrow Beaver Creek estuary, finally converging at a 180 foot arched plank bridge that crosses the estuary to the sandy beach. The bridge seems to provide a fine vantage point to watch for salmon and steelhead migrating

A 180 foot arched plank bridge crosses the estuary to the sandy beach.

upstream in the fall and winter, as the marsh is likely to filter any mud from Beaver Creek and leave it clear. Hikers can trek seven miles south on the open beach to the mouth of the Alsea River or six miles north to Yaquina Bay – but be sure which side of Beaver Creek you start on or you will have to wade. The trail to the beach may be too sandy for sidewalk strollers. Shorebirds can be seen in the estuary and the estuary outlet where it crosses the beach.

Wildlife habitats: Open ocean, sandy beach, vegetated low sand dunes, estuary, estuary outlet, scrub conifer forest.

Beaver Creek Natural Area: Side trip, rest stop, woodland hike, stroll. From the south, 6.3 miles north of Alsea River Bridge; from the north, 7.0 miles south of Yaquina Bay Bridge. Turn east on N. Beaver Creek Road and drive 1.25 miles to the park entrance and parking lot.

The fresh-water marshes along Beaver Creek are unusual for the Oregon Coast: most marshy areas are tidal. A parking lot, park head-quarters, and a primitive restroom lie atop a small hill, from which there is a broad view of an extensive fresh-water marsh watered by Beaver Creek and its tributaries. A quarter mile farther along the road there is a small parking lot, another primitive restroom, and a boardwalk that extends a few hundred feet into the marsh. Kayaks can be launched there, but a much better launch site is located at the parking lot off N. Beaver Creek Road just east of the highway, where there is more open water. Across the access road from the park headquarters there are some hiking trails in the forest. The marsh here and along the N. Beaver Creek Road is habitat to beavers, river otters, muskrats, nutria, and, in season, abundant waterfowl. Nutria are large invasive rodents originating in South America, brought

The marsh here and along the N. Beaver Creek Road provides habitat for beavers, river otters, muskrats, and nutria.

to the United States to raise for fur more than a century ago. You may also see deer or elk along the margins of the wetland. As the natural area is only a couple of miles from the ocean, you might not escape the summer fog, but it is somewhat forested and the wind should be less intense. Although the parking lots have only primitive restrooms, there is a modern restroom at Ona Beach, just across Hwy 101 from N. Beaver Creek Road.

Wildlife habitats: Fresh water marsh, second growth evergreen forest.

Beavers – The Official Oregon State Animal

Beavers were a source of wealth in Oregon long before farming in the Willamette Valley and gold mining in Jacksonville. As early as the 1700s, beaver pelts were a trading commodity when the occasional Spanish galleon visited coastal Native American communities. In the early 1800s, French Canadian trappers are known to have trapped beavers in the Coast Range. The beaver was elected to be a state symbol, and is the mascot of Oregon State University – although I never saw one there. Even at football games. Because of their fresh tree-bark diet, they must be difficult to keep as pets.

As the state became more settled in the late 1800s, beavers were heavily trapped, and in some places exterminated as a nuisance. However, they are still present across the state and a few are still found in the Oregon Coast Range. It is becoming understood that beavers with their dams and channels are excellent environmental engineers. Beaver dams store water for the dry season and especially for droughts. Flooded stream valleys serve as effective fire breaks. At the same time, ground water recharge is occurring using water that would otherwise have run into the sea. The ponds also provide habitat for trout and young salmon. When beaver ponds eventually become filled with silt, rich new pastureland is created.

So will you be able to see the state animal on your visit to the Oregon Coast? Not impossible, but you will need to watch carefully. Beavers like to work in the dark in order to avoid predation by cougars, bobcats, and bears – but being crepuscular animals, they can sometimes be seen working in the dawn and dusk hours as well. After all, the phrase *busy as a beaver* had to have come from some-where! It is in the fresh-water marshes like on the aptly-named Beaver Creek you are most likely to see one, especially where willow shrubs, a favorite food and building material, are becoming es-tablished. Recently they have been seen in salt marshes as well – perhaps they are spreading into that environment, where they can swim in the channels and feast on the roots of marsh sedges. Don't look for the traditional beaver lodges there. They are more likely to live in bank burrows, as stick lodges don't work well in tidal zones.

Chapter 13

Newport and Yaquina Bay

South Beach State Park: Rest stop, beach hike, stroll, refreshments. Located 11.5 miles north of Alsea River Bridge and 1.3 miles south of Yaquina Bay Bridge. Turn west on S. Beach State Park Road, proceed a third of a mile to the day use area parking lot and modern restroom. You will pass the entrance to the extensive campground which includes a hospitality center and three sets of modern restrooms with showers.

South Beach State Park is a large and well-appointed campground. From the north end of the day-use parking lot a paved trail runs nearly a mile through the scrub forest and coastal meadow, with abundant huckleberry and salal berry bushes. You will also see twinberry bushes, but the berries aren't edible. The trail ends at the south jetty of Yaquina Bay and the 500 foot-wide harbor entrance. You are likely to see commercial, recreational, and even research boat traffic, as Yaquina Bay is the busiest harbor on the central Oregon Coast. NOAA, Oregon State University ship operations, and the U.S. Coast Guard are stationed in Yaquina Bay. Other paved

NOAA, Oregon State University ship operations, and the U.S. Coast Guard are all stationed in Yaquina Bay.

trails branch into the campground to the east; the first one ends just north of the hospitality center where refreshments are available. From the day-use parking lot, it is only 300 feet past a picnic area and modern restroom to a broad beach. You can hike along the beach three fourths of a mile north to the south jetty of Yaquina Bay, or five miles south to Beaver Creek – even a couple of miles farther if you choose to wade Beaver Creek. But beware the waxing tide.

Wildlife habitats: Open ocean, sandy beach, vegetated sand dunes, rock jetty, estuary, scrub conifer forest, coastal meadow.

South Bay Complex: Side trip, rest stop, stroll, museums. Accessed from SE Pacific Way at the south end of Yaquina Bay Bridge or SE 32nd Street a thousand feet farther south.

This is complex of government, commercial, research, and visitor-oriented facilities located on a peninsula across from the old town of Newport. It includes the commercial and recreational boat harbor, Oregon State University Hatfield Marine Science Center, Oregon Coast Aquarium, Oregon Department of Fish and Wildlife, Oregon Coast National Wildlife Refuge Complex, NOAA, OSU Ship Operations, along with restaurants and lodging. The Oregon Coast Aquarium (aquarium.org) and the Hatfield Marine Science Center (hmsc.oregonstate.edu) are expensive but professionally done and definitely worth a visit, but reservations are required. Plan to spend half a day visiting them: they provide a good introduction to future careers in oceanography. The half-mile Yaquina Bay Estuary Trail

The Oregon Coast Aquarium and the Hatfield Marine Science Center are expensive but professionally done and worth a visit.

runs along the estuary on the east side of the peninsula and is a good place to observe the shorebirds that live there. Public restrooms that are not within the aquarium and science centers can be found at the commercial harbor docks next to the fish-cleaning facilities. When I visited in June, they were fileting tubs of halibut; in other seasons, it will be Chinook salmon, ling cod, flounders, or various species of rockfish. All the floating public docks are open for strolling, but during neap tide the ramps are steep. It is a busy harbor; parking in the large lot is free but hard to find.

Wildlife habitats: Estuary, harbor.

Yaquina Bay Bridge. This high bridge over Yaquina Bay at Newport is one of the finest and most photographed accomplishments of the bridge engineer Conde B. McCullough from the 1930s. The illustration shows work on replacing the zinc cathodic corrosion protection for the concrete rebar, which was initially applied in 1990. Seismic upgrades are also being added, as seismic danger has been recognized on the Oregon Coast. Broad mudflats in the foreground indicate low tide. A project is ongoing to encourage the growth of eelgrass (Zostera marina) on the tidal mudflats, which are an important part of the estuarine food chain. Zostera largely died out in the 1930s on both the West and East Coasts. Why? A good project for future marine biologists?

Port of Newport/Old Town: Side trip, rest stop, stroll, restaurants. At the north end of Yaquina Bay Bridge, exit Hwy 101 on SW Naterlin Dr., follow around the curves and turn right on SW Bay Street by the U.S. Coast Guard Station, which becomes SW Bay Blvd. This is the main street of the Old Town, running for several blocks along the waterfront.

Newport, like Florence, is one of the port towns with a well-preserved historic district now dominated by restaurants and shops.

There is abundant parking along SW Bay Blvd. and in several parking lots, but on a weekend day they may be crowded. A modern public restroom is located at the foot of SW Lea Street on the left. A few hundred feet past the shops you will find the dock of the Port of Newport Commercial Marina, which extends 500 feet into Yaquina Bay and provides a short stroller walk with a nice view of a breakwater which is frequently a resting spot for pelicans and other seabirds.

Like it namesakes in Rhode Island, Wales, and New South Wales, Newport Oregon is an important seaport. It is just a few centuries younger than the original. The town was actually named for Newport, Rhode Island. Importantly, it is the home port for Oregon State University ship operations. Oregon State is one of the original sea grant universities in the United States and has become well-known for oceanographic research over the last sixty years. Despite the high arch of the magnificent Hwy 101 bridge, larger ships don't often arrive here; ports along the Columbia River estuary with its regional railroad access attract most of the ocean freighters.

A marine stranding was important in early Newport history.

A marine stranding was important in early Newport history. In 1852, a January storm forced ashore the schooner Juliet near Yaquina Bay. Apparently relations between the European Americans and the local Yacona people had not yet turned sour, as they sent a messenger to the Willamette Valley to initiate a rescue with horses. I have traveled that route across the Coast Range many times; even today it takes an hour by car. Stranded in the area for two months before being rescued, the crew and passengers found that the estuary held a rich supply of oysters and clams. It must have been quite a survival experience – I wonder if they ever ate oysters again!

Following on this discovery, by the early 1860s two commercial oyster firms had been established. A town named Oysterville was founded on the south bank, but there is little there today. Because by that time the whole area had been placed within the new Coast Indian Reservation, the Indian agent required a fee of 15 cents per bushel to be paid to the Yacona people who still lived there. When in 1966 the federal government removed the coastal area from the reservation, extensive oyster harvesting and homesteading quickly followed. After a few years, the stock of native Yaquina Bay oysters being greatly depleted, attempts were made to grow East Coast oysters, but they didn't do well, probably due to the colder water. Finally, in the early 1900s, the proprietors of a Portland oyster bar founded an oyster farm in the bay to supply their restaurant. In 1918, the larger Pacific oyster (Magallana gigas, also Crassostrea gigas) was introduced along the coast of Oregon, Washington, and British Columbia. This oyster grows well along the coasts of Japan and Kamchatka. The species was clearly named for the explorer Ferdinand Magellan, the first European explorer to cross the Pacific, but I can find no evidence that he would have eaten one. (Magellan did not survive his attempt to circumnavigate the world, dying in a battle in the Philippines in 1521. Of the 5 ships that left Spain in 1519, only one ship and 18 of the original 270 sailors returned to Seville, although with a heavy load of valuable spices. Shipwrecks and mutinies claimed the other four. It was a heavy price to pay for discovering a very long new route from Spain to the Spice Islands. And naming an oyster.)

Unfortunately, although the Pacific oysters grew well in the Yaquina estuary, they were unable to reproduce successfully in the upwelling-influenced cold water of Oregon, although they did better in the warmer waters of British Columbia. For years the spat supply was imported from Japan. This of course was interrupted by WWII; since then oyster farms have taken over this critical job. In 1968, marine scientists from Oceanography School at Oregon State University along with local Newport entrepreneurs built facilities at the Oregon State Marine Science Center to farm the Pacific oysters, and the Yaquina Bay oyster industry was born again. Now the West Coast has surpassed the East and Gulf coasts in oyster production, with farms from Drake's Bay, California, to Puget Sound, Washington.

The town itself didn't really get going until the railroad from the Willamette Valley was built. At the height of construction in 1881, more than 2000 men and 250 horses were working on the mountainous route. It reached Yaquina in 1885; passengers disembarked there and continued via ferryboat down the estuary to Newport and the coast. No other Oregon Coast town at the time had a rail connection to the interior, so tourism became an important industry – as it remains today. Because of the railroad the town of Toledo, also on the upper bay, became a major lumber town. During the First World War, the world's largest spruce mill was built there to produce spruce lumber for war planes.

On a peninsula across the bay from the old town of Newport, you will find the modern commercial and recreational boat harbor, Oregon State University's Hatfield Marine Science Center, Oregon Coast Aquarium, Oregon Department of Fish and Wildlife, Oregon Coast National Wildlife Refuge Complex, NOAA, and OSU Ship Operations.

Wildlife habitats: Harbor, estuary.

Library: Newport Public Library, 35 NW Nye Street, (541) 265-2153.

Playground: Best choice is Children's Park, south of the bridge, at South Beach State Park.

Future Geographer - Entrenched Meanders

When you look closely at the highway map covering the Oregon Coast Range you will notice many of the rivers are highly sinuous, winding like a snake on their way to the sea. The Umpqua, Siletz, and Yaquina rivers on the central coast are good examples; you can find several others. The Yaquina River even has a winding estuary. Such meandering river patterns are common on flat flood plains, but not in rivers that drain mountain uplifts. One might normally expect straighter stream courses like those draining other mountain ranges like the Cascades and Sierra Nevada. These crooked mountain streams are telling us an interesting story about the geologic history of the Oregon Coast Range.

The term "meander", used both in the English language and in the science of geomorphology to describe a wandering path, actually derives from the ancient Greek river of that name. That river is now in western Turkey and is called the "Buyuk Menderes". It winds its way westward through a flat sedimentary floodplain on its way to the Aegean Sea, exhibiting a classic meander pattern. The term came into English and other western languages from the original Greek. Many rivers in the United States display a similar meandering pattern. They are frequently seen on the broad Atlantic coastal plain of Georgia and the Carolinas. The Mississippi River in Mississippi and Louisiana is famously meandering. In Europe, the Mosel River displays entrenched meanders where it flows through western Germany to the Rhine. The physics behind the process is quite complicated, but meanders are characteristic of rivers that have a very low gradient.

The Coast Range rivers are older than the mountains they drain!

What we learn from these meandering river courses in the Coast Range is that the rivers must be older than the mountains they drain! In the Oligocene epoch, some 30 million years ago, a broad coastal plain stretched all the way from approximately the present coastline to the ancestral Cascade Mountains. Rivers flowing across this nearly flat coastal plain developed typical meandering courses, the same ones we see today. When the Coast Range suddenly began to be pushed up, the meandering rivers didn't have time to change their courses, so they just dug straight down. But the mountains rose even faster, and the river beds were lifted with them. The original meanders became entrenched and were preserved just as we see them.

Rivers like the Yaquina and Siletz once flowed all the way to headwaters in the ancestral Cascades. During the rapid uplift of the

Coast Range, the upstream ends got abandoned. Only the larger Umpqua and Rogue rivers were able to maintain courses all the way to the Cascades. A geography thesis at Oregon State University by Wendy Adams Niem points out that the Yaquina and Siletz rivers once continued eastward in what are now the canyons of the Mary's and Lukiamute rivers. These rivers turned around and now drain toward the east, flowing into the Willamette River. The paths of the eastward continuations of the ancient rivers are now buried beneath the broad floodplain of the Willamette River – which is also younger than the Coast Range. Ms. Niem doesn't speculate in her thesis what rivers in the Cascades might be the upstream parts of the ancestral Yaquina and Siletz rivers, as she had no data on possible river courses buried in the Willamette Valley.

Other Coast Range rivers show the same sinuous pattern of entrenched meanders. Perhaps a correlation between the Coast Range rivers and their ancient headwaters in the Cascades could be made. At Oregon State University on Corvallis there is a college of atmospheric, earth, and oceanographic sciences where this might be done. Anyone interested?

Future Oceanographer – Wave and Wind Energy

You will have noticed the strong winds coming off the Pacific, especially on summer afternoons. Not only that, the seemingly constant wind drives an unending train of waves before it. Oceanographers at Oregon State University see the waves as a source of green energy – one of the more promising in the United States. In 2018 they partnered with the U.S. Department of Energy to build a wave energy test facility between Newport and Waldport, a few miles south of Oregon State's Hatfield Marine Science Center on Yaquina Bay. At the time of publication, the project is seeking to raise $10M in research funding. You may be able to see a model of the project at the Marine Science Center.

At the same time, feasibility studies are being done on floating offshore wind turbines, as the average wind speeds off Oregon are among the highest in the United States. Because the water depth increases rapidly along the Oregon coast, the turbine platforms cannot readily be mounted on the sea floor as is practiced on our eastern seaboard and in the North Sea. Consequently, studies must be done regarding the effects platforms and their mooring cables on fisheries, whales, and sea birds.

Energy from offshore wind, waves, and tides has been harvested in Europe for decades. We need to get going on it on the west coast where there is such strong wind and wave energy. At Oregon State University on Corvallis there is a College of Atmospheric, Earth, and Ocean Sciences where this is being investigated. Anyone interested?

Yaquina Bay State Park: Rest stop, beach hike, stroll. Immediately north of Yaquina Bay Bridge, turn east on SW Naterlin Drive. Curl around beneath the bridge and head west on Yaquina Bay State Park to the viewpoint and a small parking lot.

A hard-surface trail leads from the parking lot to the old lighthouse, built in 1871 soon after the town of Newport was founded. It was turned off after only three years when the taller light was constructed on Yaquina Head, then relighted in 1996. A modern restroom is located to the west of the lighthouse. Sandy trails lead to the beach, where you will find tide pools when the tide is out, the north jetty, and a 3.5 mile beach hike north to Yaquina Head. Yaquina Bay State Park is a great place to see and photograph the iconic Yaquina Bay Bridge, especially in the afternoon light. This is one of the most impressive of the twelve historic coastal bridges designed by Conde B. McCullough and built during the Great Depression to complete the "Roosevelt Highway", now Highway 101.

Yaquina Head Lighthouse: Side trip, rest stop, hikes, stroll, visitor center. Enter the federally-operated Yaquina Head Outstanding Natural Area at NW Lighthouse Drive, 2.75 miles north of the

Hwy 101-Hwy 20 intersection in Newport and 10.0 miles south of Depoe Bay Bridge. There is a $7 per car entry fee, but it is well worth it; a senior national park pass is accepted.

Yaquina Head Lighthouse Natural Area is one of the star natural attractions along the Oregon coast, featuring an interpretation center, a lighthouse, a marine garden, several pocket beaches, bluffs and offshore rocks with nesting seabirds, and unlimited coastal views to the north and south. The pocket beaches (some accessible by trail) are made up of black sand and gravel eroded from the basaltic lava that holds up the promontory. The whole area is laced with hard-surface trails, some steeper than others. The easiest extends 400 feet from the westernmost parking area to the lighthouse, which can be climbed via a steep 93 ft staircase. The lighthouse has been operating since 1873, a useful beacon for ships seeking refuge in Yaquina Bay, a busy harbor just three miles to the south. Modern restrooms are available at the interpretation center, which is located in an old quarry for jetty rock. Primitive restrooms are located at parking lots on the south flank of Yaquina Head and at the lighthouse. Colony rock, a large seastack less than 300 feet offshore from the lighthouse, and the seacliffs and a smaller seastack just to the south offer prime viewing for seabirds. Puffins, murres, guillemots, and cormorants may be spotted there at fairly close range. Again, bring your binoculars.

Unlike so many promontories along the Oregon Coast, Yaquina Head, Yaquina Bay, the Yaquina River, and even the small town of Yaquina are all named for the original inhabitants of the area. The Yaquina (also spelled Yacona) people lived in some 56 villages along the estuary, the river and the surrounding area, harvesting the abundant fish and shellfish found there. Wikipedia tells us that there were only nineteen surviving Yaquina in 1910, only sixty years after the European Americans began to colonize the coast. The tribe was merged into the Native American population in the Siletz Indian Reservation. Today, a century later, perhaps only their name survives.

Wildlife habitats: Open ocean, seastacks and seacliffs with nesting seabirds, rocky shore, sandy beach, coastal meadow, brushy bluff, shore pine thickets.

Devil's Punch Bowl State Natural Area: Side trip, beach hike, stroll, refreshments. Located in the town of Otter Rock. Northbound travelers exit on Otter Crest Loop, 7.4 miles north of the Hwy 101-Hwy 20 intersection in Newport. Proceed 0.3 miles north to 1ˢᵗ Street, turn west and continue 0.4 miles to the parking lot. There is an overflow parking lot and modern restroom at C Avenue. If you are traveling from the north, exit on Otter Crest Loop 4.8 miles south of Depoe Bay Bridge, proceed west 0.1 mile, turn south also on Otter Crest Loop, continue 1.2 miles to 1ˢᵗ Street, then west 0.4 miles to the main parking lot.

Devil's Punch Bowl State Natural Area is a great family side trip, with a flat 900 foot loop strolling trail on the point with a panoramic view of the ocean and coastline. Down the stairs there is the broad Otter Rock beach, somewhat protected from the north wind, with a few tide pools around the point. A 4.5 mile beach hike extends southward to Yaquina Head, but Hwy 101 runs right along the beach for most of the way. Gull rock, a seastack only 3000 feet offshore to the northwest is frequented by a wide assortment of seabirds including brown pelicans, common murres, and pigeon guillemots, so bring binoculars. Seabirds sometimes may also be seen on the rocks of the promontory. Devil's Punchbowl itself is most impressive at higher tides, especially when there is a strong surf running.

As the natural area borders the tiny town of Otter Rock, there is a restaurant, a winery, an ice cream shop, and a coffee bar all conveniently located near the main parking lot.

Wildlife habitats: Open ocean, seastacks, seacliffs, sandy beach, rocky shore, brushy bluff, coastal conifer forest.

Beverly Beach State Park: Rest stop, beach hike, stroll. Entrance at sign on NE 123rd Street, 6.32 miles north of the Hwy 101-Hwy 20 intersection in Newport or 6.5 miles south of Depoe Bay. Turn east off Hwy 101, then left immediately on NE Beverly Drive and proceed 500 feet to the parking lot.

From the parking lot there is a 300 foot paved trail past a modern restroom to the broad sand beach. From there, hikers can cross Spencer Creek and continue along the beach 1.3 miles north to Otter Rock or 3.8 miles south to Yaquina Head, but a couple of small creeks will need to be waded during the rainy season. Just 0.6 miles offshore lies Otter Rock – seemingly named long ago when sea otters still lived in the area – which is frequented by a variety of seabirds. Smaller rocks to the north and south appear to be wave-washed and may be less used by seabirds. Strollers will find Spencer Creek Nature Trail just 600 feet to the east on the main park road, Beverly Beach State Park road. This 0.4 mile nature trail follows Spencer Creek, then rejoins Beverly Beach State Park road; strollers can return via the trail or on the road. Roads through the campground are also fine for strolling.

Wildlife habitats: Open ocean, seastack, sandy beach, brushy creek, tiny estuary, coastal conifer forest.

Marine Reserves on the Oregon Coast

Because of the growing recognition of the importance of protecting the world ocean from overfishing, a number of marine protected areas have been set up off maritime countries around the world. These are areas designed to protect the ocean ecosystems; fishing and other marine harvesting is generally banned, although rules vary, in order to allow fish and invertebrate stocks to replenish. Some are very large, such as the Galapagos Islands Marine Reserve with 51,000 square miles of protected area and the even larger Palau Marine Protected Area with over 190,000 square miles. On our own West Coast, the Channel Island Marine Protected Area off-shore southern California is the largest, at 318 square miles. According to the Seattle-based Marine Conservation Institute, the world needs to conserve 30% of the ocean by year 2030. As of 2020, only around 7% have any protection, and only half of that is well monitored and enforced. It is not at all clear how marine protected areas can be set up, monitored, and protected in the vast areas of the world ocean that lie outside of national maritime boundaries.

A successful effort to protect more of the world's ocean could bolster marine biodiversity and productivity

Oceanographic research suggests that a successful effort to protect more of the world's ocean could not only bolster marine biodiversity but significantly increase the number of fish available for harvest worldwide. Along the Oregon Coast, five small marine protected areas have been designated. They are, from south to north:

Redfish Rock Marine Reserve, near Port Orford
Cape Perpetua Marine Reserve, near Yachats
Otter Rock Marine Reserve, north of Newport
Cascade Head Marine Reserve, near Lincoln city
Cape Falcon Marine Reserve, south of Cannon Beach.

They all lie within Oregon state water within the three-mile zone, where water depths are generally less than around 200 feet. These reserves, although small, are more important than it might seem, as the shallow continental shelves are both more heavily fished and usually have a richer, more varied biological environment than the open seas farther from land. Sediment maps of the sea floor show a large variety of substrates, from bare rock outcrops to sand and gravel to mud. My MS thesis at Oregon State University covered such an area offshore Newport, where I discovered submerged Pleistocene sandy beaches. Farther offshore in deeper water, the seafloor is mainly covered by mud. The Oregon continental shelf is also an important focus of upwelling, leading to cold, nutrient-rich water with high concentrations of plankton, the base of the marine food chain. Each of the marine protected areas covers a few square miles of ocean and is dedicated to both conservation and research. They are managed and monitored by the Oregon Department of Fish and Game. You can find maps, images, and detailed descriptions of each of these marine reserves online at http://oregon-marinereserves.com/.

Fishing rules vary by area. Salmon trolling is allowed in some areas, as salmon are not considered indigenous to the protection areas. Some allow the setting of crab pots. Bottom-trawling, a particularly destructive fishing practice that involves dragging a net across the sea floor, has been banned. Similar to how plowing a field releases carbon that has been stored in the soil, bottom trawling tosses buried organic material up into the water column where it is decomposed by bacteria and turned into carbon dioxide.

Unfortunately, our ocean has problems that cannot be mitigated simply by the establishment of marine protected areas. Other means will need to be employed. Global warming affects the sea, with effects that are only beginning to be understood. For instance, as the surface water warms, the more mobile life forms can move poleward to temperatures more to their liking, but their food supply may not move with them. Ocean mercury pollution, contributed by various industrial processes such as burning coal in electrical power plants, is increasing. Mercury compounds enter the food chain and become concentrated near the top in desirable fish like tuna and swordfish, where they can reach a dangerous level for humans. Most insidious but poorly understood is ocean acidification and its effect on shell-building organisms such as corals and shellfish. Some 30% of the carbon dioxide we pump into the atmosphere becomes dissolved in the ocean, where it lowers the pH slightly and makes shell building more difficult. Although Oregon's marine protected areas cannot begin to solve all of these problems, they at least offer zones where important fish species can recover, protected from overfishing and environmental degradation.

*Oregon's marine protected areas offer zones
where important fish species can recover*

A main problem may be inadequate enforcement. Oregon doesn't
have a navy. The United States Coast Guard generally has other
things to do, but some joint surveys with a Coast Guard helicopter
have been carried out. Citizen reporting has been effective, as fishing boats and crab pot buoys can be seen from shore. Aerial surveillance by the Oregon State Police Marine Fisheries Team is
occasionally employed, but their seven troopers have the entire 350-
mile Oregon Coast to monitor. At the Cascade Head Marine Protection Area, a live-feed surveillance camera is being tried out.
Fortunately, Oregon is an environmentally conscious state and compliance by the fishing industry is relatively high, especially when
compared with illegal fishing on the open seas. Fishers in Oregon
are understandably concerned about the future of their livelihoods
and are generally willing to accept the existence of areas where they
cannot fish.

We clearly need careful studies on how effective the sanctuaries
are in protecting the coastal fish populations, but it would certainly
take some snorkel or even scuba diving with wet suits. They would
be great places to experiment on possible solutions to the purple sea
urchin invasion. Anyone interested? Several universities in coastal
states have oceanography and marine biology departments.

Chapter 14

Depoe Bay, World's Smallest Harbor

Rocky Creek State Scenic Viewpoint: Rest stop, woodland hike, stroll. Located off Hwy 101 10.8 miles north of the Hwy 101-Hwy 20 intersection in Newport, or 1.86 miles south of Depoe Bay Bridge; turn west at the sign.

Rocky Creek State Scenic Viewpoint is good stop for watchers of seabirds and whales, with rocky cliffs all around and deep water just offshore. A variety of seabirds have been spotted there, including common murre, pigeon guillemot, and white-winged scoter. Off the hard-surface trail into the trees just to the north of the parking strip there is a modern restroom. The trail continues some 800 feet through a coastal conifer forest to Whale Cove Vista Point, a nice viewing platform for Whale Cove Habitat Refuge, but it quickly turns into an earthen path. It is definitely worth the short hike, but the trail is muddy, brushy, poorly maintained, and impassable for strollers. Expanses of salal and false lily-of-the-valley line the trail. The small marine refuge is probably too shallow for whales but great for seabirds; along the shore you will see a rocky stretch, some seacliffs, a couple of little waterfalls and the only sandy beach for miles – but none are accessible from the viewpoint. Some say Whale Cove fits the description of the cove where Sir Francis Drake landed in 1569 to do some repairs on his ship. Or it might have been somewhere else along the Oregon Coast. Or in California. There appears to be no hard evidence, which makes the honor easier to claim.

Whale Cove fits the description of the cove where
Sir Francis Drake landed in 1569 to do some repairs on his ship

The black rock formation under the scenic viewpoint and Whale Cove Vista Point appears to be a basaltic mudflow deposit, most likely related to the basaltic lava flows that snuck through from eastern Washington and Oregon during the Miocene epoch.

Wildlife habitats: Open ocean, seacliffs, rocky shore, brushy bluff, coastal conifer forest, sandy beach, and coastal meadow.

Depoe Bay

The town of Depoe Bay is an interesting travel stop, with its claim to have the smallest navigable harbor in the world: the *Guinness Book of World Records* agrees. The harbor entrance is spanned by a 200 foot bridge, but the basalt-lined channel itself is only 50 feet wide below the water surface, having been widened from the original 35 feet. More than a hundred fishing boats, pleasure craft, and three Coast Guard vessels share the six-acre harbor during the summer. Sidewalks line the bridge on both sides, so you can watch the boats go in and out just below your feet. If they are fishing boats, seagulls are likely to be following them into the harbor. It does not seem likely that Depoe Bay could have been used by the sailing ships of

Depoe Bay entrance difficult for sailing ships

previous centuries, as one wayward wind gust through the gap would have put the craft onto the basaltic rocks alongside the narrow channel with disastrous results.

According to one online bathymetric chart, a deep submarine canyon cuts across the continental shelf starting at the harbor entrance, deepening to over 90 feet only a third of a mile offshore. (The canyon does not appear on all online bathymetric charts.) Assuming the one chart is accurate, how might such a canyon have been eroded? It is appears to be a relic of the lower sea level of the Pleistocene epoch, but the amount of water flowing today through the Depoe Bay harbor entrance seems clearly inadequate to have done the job. Only the tiny North and South Depoe Bay Creeks dump into the harbor.

A possibility, however speculative, might be sought in the far larger Siletz River, which has a western loop only two and a half miles east of Depoe Bay and now enters the Pacific some six miles to the north. The mountain pass between the Siletz River and South Depot Bay Creek is currently less than 360 feet in elevation. Could they have been connected at some previous time, perhaps during the 2.2 million years of the Pleistocene Era, with the Siletz flowing through Depot Bay? Or even before the Coast Range rose to its present height? It would require some tectonic activity, but it is well known that the meanders you see in Siletz River on the highway map were eroded down from a flat floodplain that preceded the uplift of the Coast Range. And how else could such a notch in the hard basalt at the entrance to Depoe Bay have been cut? It presents a nice puzzle for a future geologist. Anyone interested?

Library: Go to Newport or Lincoln City.

Playground: Depoe Bay City Park, 135 SE S 40 Lane, southeast of the bay.

Depoe Bay Sidewalks and Bridge: Rest stop, stroll.

Depoe Bay is a one-sided town: shops on one side of Hwy 101 and the Pacific Ocean on the other. You can stroll across the short bridge with sidewalks on either side, returning on the other side, and watch the boat traffic. There is a crosswalk on the south end. You can choose which side you want to walk – there is a crosswalk at the traffic light at Bay Street just north of the bridge. No beach hiking trails here, but a nice sidewalk for strolling runs along the west side of the highway and parking strip just north of the bridge for a third of a mile, just above the crashing surf. It ends in the Depoe Bay Scenic Park, which currently has a bench and good views but no other facilities. The city of Depoe Bay maintains a modern restroom 200 feet north of the bridge, on the east side of the highway amongst the shops. You will find street parking on both sides of Hwy 101, near the restaurants and shops. Boat tours and fishing charters are available at the harbor, on coast Guard Drive off Bay Street or on SE Shell Street. Local charter boats have two advantages over those at most Oregon ports: the offshore weather and sea state can be readily observed from town, and they are only a few minutes away from active fishing.

Wildlife habitats: Open ocean, seacliffs, rocky shore, harbor.

Boiler Bay State Scenic Viewpoint: Rest stop, stroll. Located off Hwy 101, 1.1 miles north of Depoe Bay Bridge and 5.9 miles south of Siletz River Bridge.

Boiler Bay State Scenic Viewpoint, just north of Depoe Bay, is a good promontory wayside for watching the waves as they crash against the black basaltic lava and for looking for seabirds on the rocks. There is neither beach access nor hiking trails, as the low cliffs are treacherous and sneaker waves are an ever-present danger there. One can walk or drive a stroller a couple hundred feet out onto the point across the coastal meadow, with full views and sounds of the sea. In the meadow there are several picnic tables, but in full sun and wind. A modern restroom has been installed in the meadow within the arc of the parking strip.

Wildlife habitats: Open ocean, sea cliffs, rocky shore, coastal meadow. A large assortment of sea birds has been spotted here, species changing with the season; I saw an oystercatcher on my last visit. It is also a good location for watching gray whales, with an un-interrupted 180 degree view. At 40 feet elevation, the viewpoint is high enough above the water for you to see the water surface and spouting whales a few miles out to sea.

Fogarty Creek State Park: Rest stop, beach walk, stroll. Entrance on east side Hwy 101 at the sign (not Fogarty Avenue), 2.7 miles north of Depoe Bay Bridge or 4.4 miles south of Siletz River Bridge. Proceed 0.25 miles south to the large parking lot.

This large tree-covered state park is laced with paved strolling trails. One of them runs down the north bank of Fogarty Creek to a small sandy beach. A modern restroom is located in the trees just south of the main parking lot. A wooden bridge takes you across Fogarty Creek to the south parking lot, which is also accessed by the south park entrance. A half-mile walk to the north along the beach brings you to a small promontory called Fishing Rock, a state recreation site at the south end of the town of Lincoln Beach.

Although much of the next twelve miles of coast to the north is developed, you will first cross Siletz Bay and the salt marsh of Siletz Bay National Wildlife Refuge. Waterfowl are often abundant there. However, parking is limited to the roadside of the high-speed highway.

Wildlife habitats: Open ocean, sandy beach, rocky shore, coastal conifer forest, tiny estuary.

Gleneden Beach State Recreation Site: Rest stop, beach hike, limited strolls. Located in the town of Gleneden Beach. Turn west on Wesler Street, 5.1 miles north of Depoe Bay Bridge and 2.1 miles south of Siletz River Bridge. Proceed 800 feet to the parking lot on your right.

Gleneden Beach State Recreation Site serves as the town park and beach access for Gleneden Beach, with picnic tables and a modern restroom. A beach hike to the north takes you 3.5 miles past Salishan to a sand spit at the mouth of Siletz Bay, where you get a good view of the tidal currents flowing in and out of a natural river mouth and the shorebirds that frequent that habitat. There are no jetties protecting the entrance. To the south, 2.2 miles along the beach reaches Fishing Rock in Lincoln Beach. These beach hikes are not remote; except for the north end of the Siletz River sand spit. The entire length is lined with homes.

Wildlife habitats: Open ocean, sandy beach, coastal meadow, park; estuary and estuary mouth at the north end of the beach hike.

Alder Island Nature Trail: Rest stop, stroll. Located on the south shore of the Siletz River, in Siletz Bay National Wildlife Refuge. From the south, turn east on Millport Slough Lane, just opposite the more prominent Keys Place, 7.0 miles north of Depoe Bay Bridge and just past Salishan. From the north, 0.25 miles south of Siletz River Bridge. Proceed 250 feet into the parking lot.

Alder Island Nature Trail is a new addition to Siletz Bay National Wildlife Reserve, which previously had little public access. The reserve itself is fairly new, established in 1991 to preserve what remains of the saltmarsh of the Siletz River. A flat, 0.8 mile gravel and earthen trail takes you through a red alder grove along Millport Slough, a minor abandoned channel of the Siletz River. Red elderberry bushes are also present; with luck, you may see wild bandtail pigeons and other birds feasting on them. The slough drains a restored saltmarsh, an estuarine habitat that is important to young salmon and steelhead as they make their way to the ocean from the headwaters of the river. Long ago the area had been 'reclaimed' to become rich pastureland for dairy cows, a fate that has befallen too many salt marshes along the coast of the Pacific Northwest and other coasts worldwide. The nature trail leads to the south bank of the main Siletz River, here a tidal estuary 350 feet wide. You are likely to see herons, egrets, cormorants, a variety of ducks, and other waterfowl. There are well-designed information kiosks and a primitive restroom. Unfortunately, the trail is quite close to the highway and its traffic sounds.

Wildlife habitats: Salt marsh, estuary, riparian forest.

Future Oceanographer – Winter Sea Level

One might think that sea level doesn't change over the seasons. This is generally true on an oceanwide basis. But along the Oregon Coast and similar coastlines there are special phenomena that can make sea level quite a bit higher in the winter than in the summer. The result can be to bring the wave swash much farther up the beach. This can potentially cause erosion of the bank, or even flooding of low-elevation towns, especially during storms. That is partly why the driftwood on a summer beach seems so far away from the surf. Four factors contribute:

That is partly why the driftwood on a summer beach seems so far away from the surf.

1. Water Temperature: Oregon coastal water temperature is generally several degrees higher in the winter because upwelling has ceased bringing cold, deep water to the nearshore. As warm water is slightly less dense than cold water, it takes up more space, contributing a small portion of winter sea level increase. The effect is variable both in time and location. For example, a five degree Fahrenheit increase from 40 to 45 degrees over a 300 foot water column would lead to a little less than two inches sea level rise.

2. Coriolis Effect: During the Oregon summer, the coastal longshore current generally flows from north to south. The Coriolis effect, related to the rotation of the Earth, pushes flowing water to the right in the northern hemisphere. The result is slightly lower water level nearer the coast. During wintertime, the opposite is true. South and southwest winds related to winter storms can cause a north-flowing coastal current. As the Coriolis Effect pushes the flowing water to the right, water level near the shore is slightly elevated.

3. Storm Surge: Because of its Mediterranean climate, severe storms occur almost exclusively in the winter months, or at least in

the winter-half of the year. Because of the low-pressure nature of the North Pacific storms, they can bring with them a storm surge of that can exceed four feet.

4. <u>Wave Transport</u>: When surface waves are being created at the ocean surface by the wind, there is a small component of mass transport in the direction of the wind and waves. Therefore, when a winter storm blows in bringing a strong west or southwest wind, sea water can pile up against the shore.

For these reasons, when a winter storm blows in from the west, sea level can be raised quite a bit. When the storm peaks during a high tide, especially a king tide, local coastal flooding can occur and wave damage in low-lying areas becomes likely. Sneaker waves are also more common in the winter. Sea level measurements made over a fifty-year period in Yaquina Bay showed winter sea level to average just under a foot higher than summer sea level. However, during a 1997-98 El Nino event, sea level peaked nearly two feet above summer sea level in January and February. When an El Nino-inspired, higher-than-normal sea level is combined with a winter storm surge and a king tide, coastal flooding can occur. For sure this explains how the piles of driftwood we see can be washed so far up the beach. We are looking at an example of a sea level that might be common some decades into the future – perhaps sooner than we think.

We need to be able to predict variations in sea level along shorelines where people live and where they recreate, and what global warming might bring. It seems like a combination oceanography and climatology problem. At Oregon State University on Corvallis there is a College of Earth, Ocean, and Atmospheric sciences where these things are studied. Anyone interested?

Steller's Jay – The Pacific Northwest Blue Jay

Growing up on the Oregon Coast, my favorite bird was the blue jay. This stately dark blue-and-black jay is formally known as the Steller's jay after the explorer who first described it. Steller's jays have a varied diet, from acorns and seeds to lizards and bird eggs. And of course anything they can steal around a forest campground. I have watched blue jays collecting acorns from tanoak trees and storing them for the winter in holes in dead trees that had been dug out by downy woodpeckers. I don't know that the woodpeckers got anything out of the deal, but it worked out well for the blue jays. My favorite memory of blue jays is from our campsite the Medicine Bow Mountains of Wyoming. We got to watch a spirited territorial battle between a jay and his reflection on our shiny portable barbecue.

Steller's jays (Cyanocitta stelleri) are the handsome species of jay that is found in conifer forests in all of our western states. They range as far north as the Kenai Peninsula of Alaska, as far south as Nicaragua, and occasionally even up to the tree line on the mountain ranges of the Rockies and the Cascades. Along the Oregon Coast you will see them mainly in forested areas, especially in the few remaining patches of virgin forest, but they venture out into other habitats. You may also see the scrub jay in the more open areas along the southern Oregon Coast. These also have blue plumage, but have no crest. They are not classified as jays by ornithologists, and don't tend to be found in the forests.

The discovery and naming of the Steller's jay is an interesting story in itself. In 1738, the German scientist Georg Wilhelm Steller left St. Petersburg to join Vitus Bering as the Russian expedition's naturalist on his second Kamchatka expedition, part of the massive eastern exploration campaign started by Emperor Peter the Great. Leaving his wife behind in Moscow, he reached in the small town of Okhotsk on the Sea of Okhotsk in March, 1740, after an arduous 3400 mile winter journey across Siberia, a trek I cannot even imagine. When he arrived, two ships, the St. Peter and the St. Paul, were being completed for the expedition. The ships departed Okhotsk in September, sailing around the southern tip of the Kamchatka, then northward to Avacha Bay, roughly opposite the Aleutian Islands, where they spent the winter. The following spring the expedition continued eastward in search of America. The St. Peter reached

Kayak Island, east of Prince William Sound, Alaska, in July, where they stopped for fresh water. Steller was allowed ashore to explore – but was only allowed ten hours to do so!

Steller's jay was first described by the German naturalist Georg Wilhelm Steller on an 18th century Russian exploration campaign

The crew of the St. Peter never set foot on the Alaska mainland, only a few miles away. But they could see Alaska's Mt. St. Elias in the distance to the northeast. It was on Kayak Island that Steller found and described the blue jay that was later named in his honor. Recognizing the similarity to the familiar blue jay inhabiting the eastern American colonies, Steller correctly surmised that the expedition had indeed reached America.

On their return journey to Okhotsk, the St. Peter became shipwrecked on what is now called Bering Island, the easternmost island of the Aleutian chain and still owned by Russia. The crew spent the winter on the island, living on what they could hunt and gather. Quite amazingly, in the spring they were able to construct a small sailing vessel from the wreckage of the St. Peter and sailed on to Kamchatka and eventually to Okhotsk. Georg Wilhelm Steller never made it back to St. Petersburg or to his wife in Moscow, having died of a fever in transit at Tyumen, Siberia. Fortunately, his journals eventually reached the Imperial Saint Petersburg Academy of Sciences. And that is why we have a Steller's jay (Cyanocitta stelleri) in both English and Latin.

A full account in English of the Bering expedition entitled *The American Expedition* can sometimes be found in used book stores and makes fascinating reading. The original was written by the expedition's Swedish navigator, Sven Waxell. Sven was sailing aboard the sister ship St. Paul, which had become separated from the St. Peter in a storm early in the voyage but eventually reached the islands of southeastern Alaska before turning back to Russia.

CHAPTER 14   265

The blue jay is not really blue at all

Did you know that blue jays and other blue-feathered birds are not really blue at all – they only appear that way? Jays and other blue-plumaged bird species aren't able to find blue pigments in their diet. Beyond blueberries, Oregon grape, some huckleberries, and a few unappetizing flower petals, there really isn't much available, and even these blue pigments are unstable. Instead, they make use of a structural trick, an exceptional feat of evolution that has been repeated independently by several unrelated blue-feathered birds. The blue color we see results from a special interaction of light waves with the feathers and the arrangement of keratin protein molecules within them. Other colors seen in bird plumage generally come from pigments in the food they eat.

Steller's Jays are an easily recognizable bird with a historically wide distribution in western North America. Is climate warming changing their range or that of their feed, in latitude or in elevation? Anyone interested in this environmental study?

Chapter 15

Lincoln City and D River

Taft Waterfront Park: Rest stop, meadow hike, stroll. Exit Hwy 101 on Southwest 51st Street in Taft, 0.13 miles north of Siletz River Bridge. Taft is now near the southern end of Lincoln City. Proceed 0.25 miles west to the large parking lot opposite the public fishing pier.

Taft Waterfront Park provides a wonderful opportunity to watch the tide ebb and flow through the unimproved mouth of the fairly large Siletz River, with no Army Corp of Engineer's improvements on the estuary outlet. There is a great close-up view of bay and the ever-changing sand spits. A four to eight foot tidal range leaves the public fishing pier sometimes totally out of the water. Strolling is limited to the 700 foot long parking lot, sidewalks into the residential area to the north, and the 200 foot fishing pier – which should be quite active with fishers and crabbers when the tide is in, especially in the fall when Chinook salmon are running. You will need to watch out for errant back-casting, as salmon lures are quite large. You may see seals following the salmon into the estuary. For longer beach walks, the sandy beach is open all the way to D River, three miles to the north. A modern restroom is located at the landward end of the fishing pier next to the parking lot. The Siletz River is the largest river

Taft Waterfront Park provides an opportunity to watch the tide ebb and flow through the unimproved mouth of the Siletz River

on the Oregon Coast with neither a historic town along its estuary nor a set of jetties to protect the harbor. Kernville, now just a few old buildings and empty lots by the north end of the highway bridge, once had a fishing port and salmon cannery; you can see the old wooden pilings along the river there, often with gulls or cormorants perching on them. Although the Siletz has a fairly large estuary lagoon which you see before you, tidewater extends some fourteen crooked miles up the river beyond the Hwy 101 bridge. Like the Yaquina River and estuary just to the south, the Siletz displays many entrenched meanders. It hosts runs of Chinook salmon in both summer and fall, along with coho salmon, steelhead, and cutthroat trout.

Wildlife habitats: Estuary, sandy beach.

Lincoln City

Lincoln City is the quintessential beach town – seven miles long, about a mile wide, and a broad, sandy, ocean beach from one end to the other. Sort of like Atlantic City, but flanked by forested mountains instead of swamps, a lot fewer people, and no casinos. The Lincoln City economy grew up around tourism and the automobile, beginning in the 1920s. In 1855, much of the Oregon central coast around the present Lincoln City was made part of the Coast Indian Reservation, where members of a number of different Oregon and northern California tribes were forcibly settled. Due to displacement from their home lands, mistreatment, disease, starvation, and eventually the loss of the more valuable areas of the reservation around the rivers, the Native Americans that had been relocated into the reservation did poorly and most died. By the end of the century much of the area had been taken away from them and opened up for homesteading. Some of their lands were later sold to new arrivals from elsewhere in the United States and northern European countries. Still, a few succeeded. Jacob and Sissy Johnson, both Native Americans, managed to hold on to their land near the mouth of Siletz Bay where they operated a passenger ferry across the bay.

*Many homesteaders came from
Finland and the Scandinavian countries.*

Because the Lincoln City area was some distance from the roads
and railroads that were reaching the coast in the latter half of the
nineteenth century, most of the colonization came later. Homesteaders were invited with offers of 160 acres of free land, mainly around
Devil's Lake and Salmon River just to the north. Along with Orego-
nians and other Americans, many settlers from Finland and the
Scandinavian countries answered the call. "To someone born in Finland, a country where only the wealthy owned land, the opportunity to get free land seemed like a dream. The Oregon Coast, with
its many rivers, lakes and trees, also promised a familiar way of
life", according to Ann Hall. One should remember that between
1809 and 1917, Finland was under Russian control; it was likely
Russian overlords that the Finnish immigrants were escaping. At
the same time, many Scandinavians and other northern Europeans
homesteaded along the southwestern Washington coast. A few surviving Native Americans from the Coast Indian Reservation also
homesteaded, but were allotted only 80 acres per family. Not having
a tradition of farming they didn't thrive.

Turning hilly, forested land into farmland that satisfied the Homestead Act rules was not an easy task. For a homestead to meet federal
regulations, a pioneer had to live on the property for three years and
build a home. Farmed land and an orchard provided evidence that
the homesteader planned to make a life there. Much of the acreage
was hilly, not like the flat American Midwestern prairies where homesteading was more successful. For many, it was too much. It was not
until the 1920s and 1930s when the Roosevelt Military Highway, now
Highway 101, was being constructed that the area became extensively
developed, mainly as a vacation destination.

The Roosevelt Military Highway brought in travelers and settlers
from afar. When the estuaries were bridged during the 1930s, ocean

shore developments became very popular. Modern Lincoln City has only been incorporated since 1965, when five small beach towns merged so as to share the construction and maintenance of water projects and sanitary facilities. Only Cutler City, the southernmost town of the original five, is located on an estuary, but the fish processing industry had peaked much earlier and farther up Siletz Bay at Kernville, where a salmon cannery had been constructed some seventeen years earlier.

Traveling north, Taft is the next town of the original five. Located at the mouth of Siletz Bay, it was built on a site where Native Americans had been living for centuries, or even millenia. Enormous shell middens, piles of mainly oyster shells harvested from Siletz Bay, were found in the area. Similar shell middens are located up and down the Oregon Coast, mainly near estuaries where fishing and clamming were extensively practiced.

An early twentieth century vacation property development originally called Nelscott or Nelscott Beach comes next. It got its unusual name from the property developers Charles Nelson and W. G. Scott, who combined their names when forming their company "Nelscott Land Company". The next former town to the north along the beach was the former Delake, centered on D River and Devil's Lake. Today Devil's Lake is open for fishing for planted rainbow trout in season. Oceanlake is the northernmost of the towns making up Lincoln City, so named because of its location between Devil's Lake and the Pacific Ocean. It was homesteaded in the early 1900s, but like the other towns, its development is mainly tied to tourism.

Library: Driftwood Public Library, 801 SE Hwy 101, #201.

Playground: Regatta Park, 2700 NE 14th Street.

D River State Recreation Area: Rest stop, beach hike, stroll. Entrance to parking lot west of Hwy 101, 200 feet south of D River Bridge in Lincoln City.

D River State Recreation Area is the main beach park for Lincoln

City, a popular vacation destination on the Oregon Coast. It fronts on a really nice wide beach but it can be crowded. A modern restroom is located at the south end of parking lot. Strolls are limited to the parking lot and sidewalks along Hwy 101, north or south. Hikers can take a sandy beach hike 3 miles south to Siletz River, or 3.8 miles north to Roads End – but first you must cross D River Bridge to the north side and enter the beach at NW 2nd Drive and NW Inlet Avenue. More secluded strolls and additional modern restrooms are found along the access roads in the associated campground in Devil's Lake State Recreation Area, just across the highway, with a walk to the lakeshore and dock. Enter at NE 6th Drive, 600 feet north of D River Bridge and proceed 350ft east to E. Devils Lake State Park road. Farther into town, there is another modern public restroom by the public parking lot at Hwy 101 and 17th Street.

D River is proclaimed by signs in the town as the shortest river in the world, but the claim has been disputed in favor of even shorter rivers in Indonesia, Democratic Republic of Georgia, Croatia,

The shortest river in the world?

and Montana, all of which are at least as large as D River and are sourced by huge springs – not unlike the headwaters of the Metolius River near Bend, Oregon. But is it the shortest river in the United States? Sometimes that may be true. The length of the D River depends on the phase of the moon. At a very low tide, it may have to run more than 1100 feet from Devil's Lake across the rather flat beach to the edge of the breakers, and sea gulls can be seen taking a fresh water bath. But at high tide later the same day, the distance from Devil's Lake to the edge of the sea may be only 440 feet, and during a spring tide even shorter at 120 feet. It is under those conditions that the coho salmon are likely to be seen coming up the river and beneath the Hwy 101 bridge, and in that hour or two it may be the shortest river in the country. It is then just shorter than the stated 201 feet length of the Roe River, near Great Falls,

Montana, its only real competitor. The publishers of Guinness Book of World Records seem to have backed away from the debate. So you decide. But we can be sure it has the shortest name! You can find an interesting 120 page history of Delake at the following link: http://lincolncityor.govoffice3.com/vertical/sites/%7BDDC39B4D-9F7A-4251-AEA0-F594E7F89DDB%7D/uploads/ Delake_Context_Statement_2009_NEWtoPrint_small.pdf

Wildlife habitats: Open ocean, sandy beach, estuary outlet – often with numerous seagulls or other shore birds – lake, park. The area offshore is protected from some commercial fishing in Cascade Head South Marine Protected Area. At the campground, park and lake habitats host abundant waterfowl. Bald eagles and ospreys have been spotted nesting in the trees that border Devil's Lake.

Roads End State Recreation Site: Side trip, beach hike. Drive north 2.1 miles from the D River Bridge to NW Logan Road. Turn left and continue one mile past the shopping center and casino to the parking lot entrance on your left. From the north, the turnoff is 2.1 miles south of Otis junction.

This is a less crowded beach compared to the D River State Recreation Site. There are no stroller trails here, but beach hikers can walk a mile and a quarter along the built-up shore to rock outcrops at Roads End Point. From there, Rock Island lies only 2000 feet offshore and hosts many seabirds. To the south you can walk 2.8 miles along the built-up shore to D River. Neither walk is a wilderness experience, but the beach is several hundred feet wide, depending on the tide, and there is a modern restroom at the parking lot. Immediately offshore is Cascade Head Marine Reserve.

Wildlife habitats: Open ocean, sandy beach.

Cascade Head Scenic Research Area: Side trip, rest stop, meadow hike, stroll. From Hwy 101, turn west on N 3 Rocks Road, 1.1 miles north of the junction of State Hwy 38 and Hwy 101 and 0.8 miles

north of the Salmon River bridge. From the north, the junction is 10 miles south of Neskowin. Proceed 2.3 miles to Knight County Park.

This side trip doesn't take you inland like many of the others, but instead introduces you to the small but splendid, totally unimproved estuary of the Salmon River, a rarity on the Oregon Coast. Knight County Park has a parking lot, boat ramp, and a primitive restroom. It has no running water, but there is a small creek just down the slope to the east. The park is noted on maps as a trailhead; some of the "trails" are access roads to research facilities and to the few homes on Cascade Head: they may work as stroller trails. The main Cascade Head Trail starts along Savage Road, at the corner of the park, then branches off and eventually reaches an altitude of over 1100 feet. Continuing on Old Ranch Road takes you to the edge of a coastal conifer forest and coastal meadows on Cascade Head, from which you can see the mouth of the Salmon River just below you. However, there is no trail across the lower meadow, which slopes steeply, and there is still a couple hundred feet of elevation loss getting to it. Three Rocks, seastacks 800 to 1400 offshore to the south, are white with guano from the seabirds that frequent them. The estuary is a couple miles long and lined with mud flats, salt marshes, and sand bars: birding should be excellent. Some dikes have been breached to allow the salt marshes to return to previously "reclaimed" land.

Cascade Head Scenic Research Area is a Nature Conservancy property; they have preserved critical environments all over the world. Cascade Head, acquired in 1966 to protect it from further development, is listed as a "haven for rare plants, wildlife, and grassland communities". The 270 acres of meadows at Cascade Head are part of a UNESCO Biosphere Reserve and is carefully managed to keep invasive plants out. Offshore, the marine life is similarly protected in the Cascade Head North Marine Protected Area. With these three levels of protection, the coastal meadows at Cascade

Head must be among the most protected areas in the country out-side of the national parks.

Wildlife habitats: Estuary, open ocean, coastal meadow, coastal conifer forest.

Salmon River Hatchery: Side trip, rest stop, stroll. From Hwy 101, take State Hwy 18 east toward Otis; at 1.25 miles turn north on North Old Scenic Hwy 101 and continue 0.35 miles to N. North Bank Road. Turn right and drive 0.6 miles to the hatchery – drive slowly, as the sign comes up quickly.

This hatchery is multi-purpose, raising Chinook salmon, steel-head, and rainbow trout to stock local rivers. Unlike most hatch-eries, Salmon River Hatchery is open dawn to dusk, every day of the week. The facilities and helpful staff get good reviews from vis-itors; fish food is provided so the youngsters can help out with the feeding. Paved trails lead around the fish tanks; the one on the river side leads past Sitka spruce and western redcedar to one of the largest red alder trees you will ever see. A beautiful trail runs along the Salmon River; you should check with the onsite host to see if it

One of the largest red alder trees you will ever see

is ready for strollers, as it gets quickly overgrown each spring. Only four miles from the ocean, visitors might not escape the coastal fog, but the inside displays describing the operations of the hatchery can provide a welcome and educational escape from misty or rainy weather. Modern restrooms are provided.

Wildlife habitats: Meadows with many horses, river.

Neskowin Ghost Forest (Neskowin Beach State Recreation Site): Rest stop, beach hike stroll. Located 12.0 miles north of D River Bridge, 5.0 miles south of Little Nestucca River Bridge. Enter from Hwy 101 at the sign at Salem Avenue in Neskowin. Proceed 150 feet straight into the parking lot.

The parking lot and modern restroom are a little distance from the beach. The easy connection is by a 500 foot paved trail from the south end of the lot, running down Neskowin Creek. It ends at the broad sandy beach, and a little farther along you can see the "ghost forest". There are no facilities on the beach. Hikers can continue up to a mile farther south along the beach through the ghost forest, which consists of a few dozen ancient Sitka spruce tree stumps sticking out of the sand, some with sea life encrusted on them. You can wander among them, but you will need to wade Neskowin Creek in order to do this. The crossing is easy enough during low tide in the summer, but during the rainy season when the creek is high, take caution. Swift-flowing water that is only knee-deep can be treacherous, especially for children. When the tide is in, running into the tiny Neskowin Creek estuary, you don't want to go there anyway because the Ghost Forest will be largely submerged. Unfortunately, there is no ready access to the beach on the south side of Neskowin Creek, as all the land fronting the beach is private.

The "ghost forest" consists of Sitka spruce tree stumps emerging from the sand – after being buried for nearly three centuries

At Ghost Forest, you are seeing the remains of a Sitka spruce forest that became flooded and silted in because of sudden land subsidence during an epic earthquake on January 26, 1700. We can be precise about the date because the huge tsunami it generated was recorded in Japan. Both radio-carbon dating and tree-ring analysis back this up. Because of the size of the "orphan" tsunami in Japan, it can even be estimated that the earthquake had a magnitude in the range of 8.7 to 9.2 – comparable to the 2011 Tohoku earthquake in Japan and the Alaska earthquake of 1964. The subject is covered in fine detail by Brian Atwater and several Japanese scientists in USGS Professional Paper 1707. Both of these modern earthquakes unleashed tsunamis that damaged coastal facilities in Oregon and California.

Neskowin Ghost Forest. *These Sitka spruce stumps are sticking up from the beach at Neskowin. The stumps are relict from earthquake-related ground subsidence and burial in the year 1700, which caused the trees to die. For much of two centuries they remained buried in the beach sand, finally becoming re-exposed in 1997 – possibly related in part to tectonic uplift along the coast. Radiocarbon dating of wood from the stumps confirms that their age matches that of a mysterious tsunami recorded in Japan in that year.*

Of course the towering spruce trees are gone now; it is quite remarkable that so many stumps have survived for nearly three centuries. Perhaps this is a testament to the strength of the spruce wood that was harvested along the Oregon Coast and extensively used during the first world war to build fighter planes. Apparently the stumps were buried for much or even most of their history, which helped to preserve them. They finally became exposed in a winter storm in 1997. Coastal uplift may have been a factor. Wave action working on the local sand supply could bury them again, especially as relative sea level continues to rise. Interestingly, barnacles encrusting the stumps can give them some protection from erosion by wind and waves carrying abrasive beach sand. However, other organisms that are known to burrow holes in piers and bridge abutments may eventually lead to the stump's demise. If you are traveling farther north on the Washington coast, you might want to visit the Copalis Ghost Forest. There, the cedar stumps are larger and "live" in a tidal marsh.

Sandi Doughton's informative book *Full Rip 9.0: The Next Big Earthquake in the Pacific Northwest* provides excellent background on the 1700 earthquake – as well as a warning that it is likely to happen again. That is one reason the USGS is working so hard to find a way to predict earthquakes. You will have noted the tsunami evacuation route signs along the highway. The short story is: If you feel a strong earthquake or see the sea acting strangely, head for high ground and stay there for an hour or two. You can learn more online at the following link: https://en.wikipedia.org/wiki/1700_Cascadia_earthquake.

Wildlife habitats: Open ocean, seacliffs, very small estuary, sandy beach.

Nestucca Bay National Wildlife Refuge: Side trip, rest stop, woodland hike, meadow stroll. Turn west on Christiansen Road, 4.3 miles north of Neskowin, and drive 0.43 miles to a parking lot on the right for the salt marsh overlook. An additional 0.4 miles on a gravel road reaches the parking lot for the wildflower meadow. From the north, the turnoff is 0.7 miles south of Little Nestucca River Bridge.

There are two worthwhile destinations in the wildlife refuge. The first is an overlook above a 100-acre marsh along the Little Nestucca River estuary. During spring and fall migrations, the marsh is visited by thousands of Canada geese. Educational displays teach us all about these familiar honkers – did you know they comprise two

species and six subspecies? All may be seen here as they pass
through, but identifying them all correctly seems like a real challenge, especially from a few hundred yards. No trails start at this
parking area, but there is a primitive restroom.

*Wildflower Meadow in Nestucca Bay Wildlife Reserve. This sixty-
acre meadow displays a profusion of wildflowers and native grasses. It has
probably never been either plowed or grazed. A paved trail winding through
the meadow takes you to the lookout platform visible at top center, from
which you have a fine view of the meadow, the Pacific Ocean, Nestucca
Bay, and the Coast Range beyond.*

For traveling families, the real attraction of Nestucca Bay National
Wildlife Refuge is the 60-acre meadow farther up the road. The profusion of wildflowers and wild grasses shows no sign of having been
plowed, planted, or grazed by livestock. There are no signs of human
habitation at all. Such large pristine meadows are rare indeed in the
rainforest environment, but they can be a delight where they occur.
At the meadow parking lot there is second primitive restroom. Along

the paved 0.6 mile trail climbing gently up to a viewing platform, I counted 26 species of wildflowers on a mid-June afternoon and startled numerous small meadow birds. Expanses of purple lupines were

I counted 26 species of wildflowers on a June afternoon

in full bloom. Sharp-eyed youngsters may find wild strawberries and wild mountain blackberries along the trail. Three deer were grazing contentedly near the edge of the woods when I was there, and the people before me saw two elk. For hikers, there are two one-mile trails leading through the woods to the north bend of Nestucca Bay, which can make a two-mile loop.

How does such meadow originate and become preserved in a rainforest environment? Most likely by wildfires, originally, then by repeated wildfires that remove the snags and stumps. They are not a permanent feature. The Nestucca Bay meadow and the few others I have seen along the Oregon Coast are all being encroached from the sides by shrubs and trees and will eventually be gone.

Wildlife habitats: Marsh, meadow, conifer forest; the hikes add sandy beach and estuary.

Chapter 16

Pacific City and Cape Meares

Pacific City

For Pacific City and the next few rest stops, one must leave Hwy 101 1.4 miles north of Little Nestucca River Bridge and drive up the coast toward Cape Mears, returning to Hwy 101 at Tillamook on State Highway 131 south of Cape Mears. Southbound travelers can take State Highway 131 west from central Tillamook to Cape Mears, then south toward Pacific City and Hwy 101.

Although Pacific City even today is only a small unincorporated town, it boasts an unusual dory fishing fleet with an interesting history. It should be noted that Pacific City lies within the 66 mile stretch from Tillamook Bay to Yaquina Bay with no improved harbors, the longest distance on the Oregon Coast without a safe harbor for small craft. The estuaries at Netarts Bay, Sand Lake, Nestucca Bay, and Siletz Bay are still without jetty protection. It is 24 miles from Pacific City to Tillamook Bay to the north, the closest jettied harbor.

Early in the last century, the Nehalem River at Pacific City was an important commercial salmon fishing port, and many were caught and canned there. The first cannery was built on Nehalem Bay in 1886. By 1926 the salmon runs were declining; the state banned commercial fishing in the river and estuary the following year. But the fishermen were still there and schools of salmon still swam offshore. The Nehalem River being difficult to enter safely except at high tide, the fishermen designed and built dories that could be launched from the beach directly

The fishermen designed and built dories that could be
launched from the beach directly through the surf

through the surf. These craft are flat-bottomed, around 20 feet in
length, and double-ended – much like the smaller float boats still in
use on the McKenzie River. They were specifically designed to han-
dle breakers without being swamped. Originally oar-powered, the
few still in use today have small outboard motors. It looks like a
dangerous job, but only six deaths have been recorded in over a century of their use. To reach the Dory Port, turn west on Hungry Harbor Road, 3.8 miles from Hwy 101. This leads directly to the parking
lot for Pacific City Beach, with modern restroom facilities at the NE
corner of the parking lot.

The beach is popular and can be crowded during the summer.
No strolling trails originate here but one can hike along the beach
nearly four miles south to the sand spit at the unimproved entrance
to Nestucca Bay, where you can watch the tides flow in and out of
a natural harbor. The last half of the hike is within Nestucca Bay National Wildlife Refuge, with excellent opportunities to view shorebirds in Nestucca Bay and on the open ocean.

Pacific City had more than salmon. We have all heard of the curative mineral baths all around the world, especially in Europe, some
dating back to Roman times. In the early 1900s, Pacific City had their
own unique mud called "kelp ore". It was a locally-mined mudstone, bluish in color, which assayed to contain potash, iodine, marine microfossils, and particularly fossilized kelp – possibly making
it unique in the world of mud. In 1904, an entrepreneur named Hans
Brooten, a Norwegian immigrant, found a deposit of this kelp ore
on his property near Pacific City. Believing the substance to have
curative properties, Brooten started an industry based on his special
mud, making such products as liniments, tinctures, poultices, and
even additives for livestock feed. Most importantly for Pacific City,
Brooten built a 54-tub bath house with steam heating, along with

facilities for the patients, bringing many visitors to town. Unfortunately, lawsuits with competitors and negative findings by the Oregon Medical Board that questioned the medical benefits of kelp ore took their toll, and the facilities were closed in 1940. You can find an article on the kelp ore muds online at: https://www.ore-gonencyclopedia.org/articles/brooten-kelp-ore-resort/.

Library: South Tillamook Library, 6200 Camp Street

Playground: No playgrounds with equipment.

Kelp Forests in Peril

In 2019, Josie Iselin published *The Curious World of Seaweeds*. As an artist-turned-botanist, she saw the unique beauty of the seaweeds she photographed and wrote about. Although her investigations were focused on the California coast, many of the seaweeds she studied range up the West Coast to Oregon, Washington, and even Alaska. It is a beautiful book, lovingly illustrated. Unfortunately for the present-day visitors to the Oregon Coast, the photographs in Iselin's book are almost all we have left to enjoy of the kelp forests and the seaweed pastures that once grew on the rocky sea floor. They are now almost totally absent in the Oregon offshore. Some marine biologists worry that they may never return.

What we are witnessing amounts to the loss of a critical coastal biosphere, and it occurred in just a few years. The interrelated causes of this tragedy are just beginning to be understood. The effects are profound, as the forests of seaweeds played critical roles in the life cycles of many commercially and recreationally important fish, and to the larval stages of other marine species. Josie Iselin watched the calamity unfold as she researched her book and wrote about what she was observing. It is an important story for coastal marine ecologies all around the world, so I will briefly summarize below what I have learned as it applies to the Oregon Coast.

Total and irreparable loss of a critical coastal biosphere?

A key factor appears to be global warming and the oceans' responses to changes in the Earth's atmosphere. Most of the heat being trapped in the atmosphere ends up warming the shallow water layer of the ocean – if it were not for that, the atmosphere would be far warmer than it is today. Eventually the deep water masses will be heated as well, but their exposure to the atmosphere is limited, and deep ocean circulation is very slow. In addition, immense quantities of carbon dioxide have been absorbed in the sea from the air above it – an important mitigating factor in the atmospheric heat-trapping effect. The dissolved carbon dioxide forms carbonic acid, resulting in the acidification of the shallow seas. Because the shell material of mollusks and many other marine organisms is composed of calcium carbonate, which is soluble in acidic conditions, this makes it more difficult for shell-secreting organisms such as clams, corals, and various larvae to make shells. If they cannot do so, even in the larval stages, they will not survive. Will there be tipping points, after which one shellfish species after another gives up the fight against the worsening conditions?

The troubles were first observed in 2014, when a giant mass of warm, low-density, surface water began to dominate the northeast Pacific, offshore U.S. and Canada. The warm water mass was locally called the "blob". It dissipated after a year or two, but had lasting effects. Blob conditions recurred in 2019, and again in 2020, continuing into 2021 when this book was being researched. The last incursion was designated by NOAA as the "Northeast Pacific Marine Heatwave of 2019".

One effect of this warm surface water has been to stifle upwelling strength, thereby reducing the nutrient richness of the shallow coastal water on which seaweeds depend. It is important to note here that seaweeds are classed as algae rather than plants. As such they have no root system, only holdfasts that glue them to the rocks on the sea floor. They must get all their nutrients from the seawater. As some of the seaweed varieties require cold water conditions for their survival, warmer conditions make it more difficult for them to thrive.

Sea star wasting syndrome

Even before the ocean warming event became evident, a mysterious ailment called sea star wasting syndrome began to affect the sea star population from California to British Columbia. By 2014, the syndrome had reached northern California and Oregon, and the sunflower sea star began to disappear. Sunflower sea stars in those areas now appear to be nearly extinct. Importantly, sunflower sea stars are currently the chief predator of sea urchins, so the purple sea urchins have multiplied exponentially. The cause or causes of the sea star wasting syndrome are not yet understood. Treatment of sea stars in a tank with an antibiotic proved effective, but the pathogen has not yet been identified, and treating a thousand miles of coastline with antibiotics is clearly neither feasible nor desirable. An ecological study led by Oregon State University found that more than 90 percent of the seaweed species in the kelp forests have been lost to the urchin invasion, and there is no evidence of recovery. Dr. Steve Rumrill, a prominent Oregon marine biologist, has been quoted saying "It's like we are caught up in a vortex of abnormal ocean events and it's scary."

Another key factor is the absence of sea otters. Sea otters live in the kelp forests, where they can hide from killer whales and sea lions. Sea otters love to eat the soft-shelled sea urchins and therefore protect the kelp forests from being overrun by them. Since the sea otters were hunted to extinction in Oregon over a century ago, the sunflower sea star had become the only remaining major predator of purple sea urchins. It had assumed the role of the keystone species, the apex predator keeping the biological system in balance. With the sunflower sea stars gone, the sea urchins have multiplied unchecked. They have eaten the kelp forests and seaweed pastures right down to the holdfasts on rocks. Even the hard coralline algae that coats the rocks is being devoured. There is nothing left for the abalones, snails, limpets, and other invertebrates to eat. As seaweeds have no roots, they cannot regrow from the soil like a land plant. What once were kelp forests have become "sea urchin barrens", covered with millions of purple sea urchins that can live many years, even decades.

Kelp forests had provided important three-dimensional, underwater habitat that was home to hundreds of species of invertebrates, fish and other algae. Some species aggregate to spawn in kelp forests or utilize these areas as juvenile nursery habitat, where they are safe from predation by seals and sea lions. It is feared by some ocean scientists that unless the sunflower sea star population recovers, the disruption of the coastal ecology may be permanent. The full extent and importance of this change will probably not be fully known for years as the standing crops of fish and shellfish are harvested, perhaps not to be replaced.

So What Does the Future Hold for the Kelp Forests?

So what does the future hold for the kelp forests? We don't yet know. After previous die-offs of sea stars, the species recovered. Perhaps a similar wasting disease will strike the hungry and weakened purple sea urchin population. Possibly a few remaining sunflower sea stars have natural immunity to the wasting disease and will propagate. Purple sea urchins are also eaten by crabs and some fish, particularly wolf eels. Wolf eels are scary-looking creatures that can be more than seven feet long, but they are not common. They live all around the North Pacific, including off Oregon and California. They are not true eels, but a large, super-long fish. With strong jaws, they can consume hard-shelled crustaceans, even mussels. Sheepshead fish, a sea urchin predator living south of Monterey Bay, may migrate north as the sea warms. Maybe acidification of the ocean will affect the sea urchins or their larvae, as like mollusks, they build their shells with calcium carbonate. But for the foreseeable future the kelp forests and seaweed pastures covering the rocks are gone along the Oregon Coast. Sea urchin barrens may be an alternate stable state of low primary productivity that makes no use of the nutrients in the water as the seaweeds have done.

If we are to fully understand what has happened, with the intent of effecting a solution, numerous factors will need to be studied. Time is of the essence, and it is not only an Oregon problem. Direct ocean water measurements focused on currents, temperature, chemistry, and nutrient supply; biological oceanographic studies; satellite measurements of surface conditions; local and regional meteorology; all need to be analyzed and compared over space and time. We can be sure such studies are currently being done in many university laboratories, particularly on the West Coast of the United States. Marine protected areas, where no fishing or collecting is allowed, may be key. It is an awesome but critically important task. The future of the oceanic coastal biological community is at stake, and it may already have been damaged beyond repair. Even if kelp forests recover, it may be decades before the complex web of biological communities dependent on them attain their former glory.

What is to be done? Efforts have been made to remove the sea urchins, either by harvesting them or smashing them in place. Some sea urchins have been harvested for roe for the Japanese culinary market, but that effort is but a drop in the bucket. There are simply too many; hundreds of thousands have been counted living on a single reef. An encouraging sign involves sunflower sea stars from the San Juan Islands of Washington that so far appear to be immune to the sea star wasting disease. A few sea stars can produce millions of larvae, so propagation of a new population seems possible.

The problem is worldwide

It is not only in the Pacific Northwest that coastal biospheres are experiencing trouble. In eastern Australia and Tasmania, the kelp forests are being decimated by a different species of sea urchin, the long-spined sea urchin. Nova Scotia is experiencing loss of their magnificent kelp forests, yet there are no purple sea urchins to blame – increasing water temperature is a likely culprit. Bleaching of the corals on tropical reefs has been widely noted; it is also related to rising water temperature and its effect on algae growth in the coral polyps. While this is not in itself fatal to the coral, as only the symbiotic algae are lost, the corals are weakened. Even coastal water contamination by sewage and agricultural runoff may be a contributing factor. These are just a few of many signs that we are destroying the biosphere of the Earth we live on, and its ability to keep us fed.

At Oregon State University on Corvallis there is a College of Atmospheric, Earth, and Ocean sciences. They are studying the problem. Anyone interested in helping?

Future Chef – Edible Seaweed

Eating seaweed? That stuff that washes up on the beach? How gross! But you have probably been doing just that all of your life. Ice cream, for instance, often contains either agar or carrageenan as a gelling agent to improve its texture. Just look at the list of ingredients. The word "agar" means "red algae" in the Japanese language, and is mostly derived from two seaweed genera: *Gelidium* and *Gracilaria*. It is said to have been discovered in 1658 by a Japanese innkeeper who left extra seaweed soup outside overnight. It was winter, and the substance froze. When the innkeeper thawed the soup in the morning, he noted that it had turned into a kind of a gel. Today, agar is used in a variety of processed foods as an emulsifier or binding agent. It has a host of other uses as well, and contains some important trace minerals.

You have probably been eating seaweed all of your life!

But agar comes only from some species of red algae in the North Pacific Ocean. Not every country or company uses agar; some use carrageenan, which is made from *Chondrus crispus,* a red seaweed variety found in the northern North Atlantic and popularly known as Irish moss. In the United States, substituting carrageenan for agar dates back to the WWII campaign in the Pacific, when Japanese-sourced agar was understandably difficult to obtain. Carrageenan has no food value and can be considered as organic content in the foods. You will see it in many dairy products such as cottage cheese and yogurt.

But seaweed by itself can also be eaten. Japanese restaurants often feature seaweed as a delicious salad, often dressed with sesame oil, sesame seeds, and other tasty ingredients. I suggest you try it. They also commonly wrap sushi in a thin seaweed frond. Seaweed also made up part of the varied diet of the Native Americans who lived along the Oregon Coast. Perhaps they knew that seaweed is an excellent source of iodine. Many years ago on the beach in southern Oregon I once encountered an aged Chetco man harvesting a specific seaweed variety from what had washed up in a storm. He was forming it into plate-sized disks and leaving it to dry in the sun on driftwood logs. I wish I had inquired further about how he was planning to use it.

Seaweed on the Oregon Coast is in dire trouble because of the marauding purple sea urchins, an invasion that must somehow be stopped. At Oregon State University on Corvallis there is a College of Earth, Oceanographic, and Atmospheric Sciences. They are studying the problem. Anyone interested in helping them?

Sand Lake Recreation Area: Rest stop, beach and woodland hikes, stroll. From Hwy 101 traveling north, turn west on Brooten Road, 1.4 miles north of -Little Nestucca River Bridge, following signs to Pacific City, where you will turn west on Pacific Avenue at the traffic light. Cross the bridge and turn right on Cape Kiwanda Drive, which becomes, then McPhillips Drive, and finally Sandlake Road. Turn west on Galloway Drive, 10.7 miles north of the Hwy 101 intersection, and drive 2.37 miles to East Dunes Campground. Traveling south on Hwy 101 from Tillamook, take Sandlake Road west 5.3 miles to the campground. That junction is 8.8 miles south of Trask River Bridge.

Sand Lake Recreation Area consists of a large campground situated on a sandy peninsula between Sand Lake and the Pacific Ocean. It is partly forested, with broad sandy beaches to the west and north and on the sand spit to the south. Seabirds can be seen offshore on the west side, and various shorebirds frequent the estuary and mud flats on the east side. The parking lot at East Dunes Campground has a modern restroom at the south end near the road, and there are others scattered through the campground. Paved campground-access roads offer stroller trails largely protected from the wind in the coastal conifer forest. Beach hikers can take a four-mile walk north to Cape Lookout, a basaltic lava promontory. (There is also a fine trail along Cape Lookout, accessible from a pullout on Cape Lookout Road some seven miles farther north. It is described as a smooth, broad trail, but it has 900 feet of up and down elevation gain/loss and only a primitive restroom facility at the parking lot. Distance to the cape and back is about five miles, but the view from the end is spectacular.)

Wildlife habitats: Open ocean, sandy beach, coastal conifer forest, estuary with mud flats at low tide.

Cape Lookout State Park Campground: Rest stop, beach hike, stroll. Located on Cape Lookout Road 9.5 miles north of the junction with Sandlake Road, that being 7.5 miles north of Pacific City. Turn west at the sign and proceed 0.6 miles to the day-use area next to the beach.

For the adventurous hiker, there is an almost five-mile one-way beach trek to the tip of Netarts Spit, where the estuary entrance has never been altered by the Corp of Engineers. This should be a great trek for birders, with the ocean and seabirds to the west, a long beach with low dunes with seagulls and sanderlings, the estuary mud flats which should be great for shorebirds, and extensive coastal conifer forests and coastal meadows for a few terrestrial bird species. One could walk one way on the beach and return along the estuary, in places more than a quarter mile away. There is a sandy trail along the peninsula for the first mile behind the low dunes; after that you and the waterfowl are likely to be quite alone. You might check the tide tables to see when the mud flats and beach are best exposed. Take water, as there are no facilities north of the campground. Campground access roads offer shaded strolling opportunities.

You and the waterfowl are likely to be quite alone.

Note that Netarts Bay is not a drowned river valley like the many estuaries on the Oregon Coast. It is simply a shallow coastal embayment that got closed off by a sand spit – nature's way of making the coastline straighter. It is fed only by several small creeks, each no more than a mile or two long. Consequently, the water salinity is the same as the ocean that ebbs and flows in and out each day. But the birds don't seem to mind. Hiking south along the beach from the campground quickly brings you to the bluffs of Cape Lookout. From there, the Oregon Coast Trail will take you up the hill to the parking lot and primitive restroom at the Cape Lookout trailhead for the five-mile round-trip hike to the cape.

Mouth of Netarts Bay during Rising Tide. *This long sand bar separates Netarts Bay from the ocean. Cape Lookout is seen in the distance. The point can be reached along the beach from Cape Lookout State Park at the base of the cape: it is several miles away but can be a rewarding hike for birders, with the Pacific on the west and Netarts Bay on the east.*

At first glance, it would seem like Cape Lookout would be an ideal location for a lighthouse. However, a study by the U.S. Coast and Geodetic Survey found the elevation to be higher than ideal – on a clear day the light would be visible far out to sea, but on foggy or cloudy days, it might be lost in the clouds and not visible at all. And it is on those days, and particularly nights, that the lighthouse is most needed. So the lighthouse was built instead on Cape Meares, 10.4 miles farther north as the seagull flies, closer to the harbor at Tillamook Bay, and at a lower elevation.

A per-car entrance fee is requested; recreation passes are accepted.

Wildlife habitats: Open ocean, sandy beach, low dunes with dune grass, estuary with tidal mudflats, salt marsh, coastal conifer forest.

Whiskey Creek Fish Hatchery: Side trip, rest stop. Located at 7660 Whiskey Creek Road. Turn west at the sign 2.4 miles north of Cape Lookout State Park Campground. From the north, the hatchery is 2.9 miles south of Netarts.

Whiskey Creek Fish Hatchery is the one you don't have to drive up a river into the Coast Range to visit – it is right on Netarts Bay and Whiskey Creek Road south of Netarts. Since the late 1980s the hatchery has been owned and operated by volunteers from the Tillamook Anglers Association, the only such fish hatchery in Oregon of its kind. What devoted fishermen and women! Our country needs more of these kinds of citizens. The Oregon Department of Fish and Wildlife supplies the baby fish – a quarter million Chinook salmon each year, to be raised for release into local streams. There are five small rivers that empty into Tillamook Bay. The hatchery

ODFW supplies the baby fish – a quarter million Chinook salmon each year, to be raised for release into local streams.

even has a small trout pond where you can feed some really big rainbow trout – but bring some quarters to buy fish food from the gumball machines next to the hatchery tanks. A modern restroom is located on the premises. The hatchery borders on Netarts Bay, where you will be able to observe shorebirds on the water or on the mudflats, depending on the tide. But there aren't any hikes or strolls originating here, except the 300 feet of paved parking lot and trail to the trout pond. Unless you are inclined to walk out on the mud flat with your bucket and shovel and dig some clams!

Wildlife habitats: Estuary, estuary mudflat, coastal evergreen forest.

Cape Meares State Park: Side trip, beach hike, woodland hike, stroll. Location: From the junction of Hwy 131 and Netarts Bay Road in Netarts, drive 4.9 miles north on Hwy 131, which is also Cape Meares Loop and Bayshore Drive, to Cape Meares Lighthouse Drive. Turn west and proceed for 0.5 mile down the hill through a dense Sitka spruce forest and the campground to a large loop parking lot.

Cape Meares Lighthouse: Here at last is your opportunity to look at a classic Fresnel lens without climbing a couple hundred steep stairs in a stone tower. Because the bluff it is standing on is so tall, sometimes extending into the clouds and fog, the lighthouse was designed to be only 38 feet tall – but it was still visible 21 miles out to sea. You can examine the lens at eye level from a viewing platform only 40 feet away. The light shone from 1890 until 2014 when it was de-activated by the Coast Guard. Since then, it has been lovingly cared for by the Oregon Department of Parks and Recreation, helped out by the volunteer organization Friends of the Cape Meares Lighthouse in Tillamook. During more than a century of operation, the lighthouse was instrumental in warning mariners of a collection of seastack hazards: Pillar Rock, 800 feet from the cape, Pyramid Rock, 2700 feet from the cape, and Three Arches Rocks, 1.6 miles to the south.

How many things can you think of that have been in operation for more than a century? The Fresnel lens, invented by Augustin-Jean Fresnel in the early 1800s but based on earlier optical inventions, has been used in lighthouses for nearly two centuries all over the world! As you can see, it is constructed with multiple prisms to make a light-weight lens with a large diameter to focus a small light source into a beam. According to an article in the Oregon Encyclopedia by Cameron La Folette, (https://www.oregonencyclopedia.org/articles/cape-meares-lighthouse/), the ruby-red lens elements allowed a flash of red light every minute as the lens rotated – originally on carriage wheels!

The seacliffs around Cape Meares are nearly vertical, more than 200 feet high. Why so steep? It is often the case for both vertical cliffs and waterfalls that the hard rock of the cliff face lies on a softer rock formation beneath. As the softer rock is eroded away by the sea or a river, the hard rock of the cliff face breaks off and falls. That is probably the case here. Niagara Falls is a classic example, where hard, flat-lying carbonate rocks at the top of the falls overlie softer shales at the base. In the case of the basalts at Cape Meares, vertical cliffs are encouraged to form because of vertical fractures, a common feature of basalt flows. These are formed during the shrinking of the lava as it cools. Waterfalls you may have seen in western Oregon tumble over similarly vertical cliff faces of ancient basalt flows: Multnomah Falls, in the Columbia Gorge, and Silver Falls, east of Salem are classic examples.

Fresnel Lens on the Lighthouse at Cape Meares. When viewed in the sunlight, the red lens is brilliantly illuminated: at night it flashed red every sixty seconds, but Cape Meares lighthouse is no longer in operation. The lighthouse tower is so short because the cape is so high, as it is important that it be seen beneath a fog or cloud layer. This is one of a string of lighthouses built in the second half of the nineteenth century up and down the Oregon Coast so that one was always in view of coastal ship traffic. Modern navigational aids have made them obsolete so they have been mostly shut down.

Pigeon guillemots and cormorants take advantage of the safety of the vertical cliffs to build nests on impossibly precarious ledges

Seabirds such as pigeon guillemots and cormorants are taking advantage of the safety of the vertical cliffs to build nests on impossibly precarious ledges. You can see them from the parking lot overlook and from the trail to the lighthouse, but binoculars will be useful. The initial flights of the fledglings must be quite an experience! They are unlikely to see their nests again.

Basalt Seacliff at Cape Meares. *This cape is one of several basaltic rock promontories along the Oregon Coast. You can make out at least half a dozen individual lava flows with rubbly zones in between. Three of the flows display columnar jointing caused by contraction during cooling.*

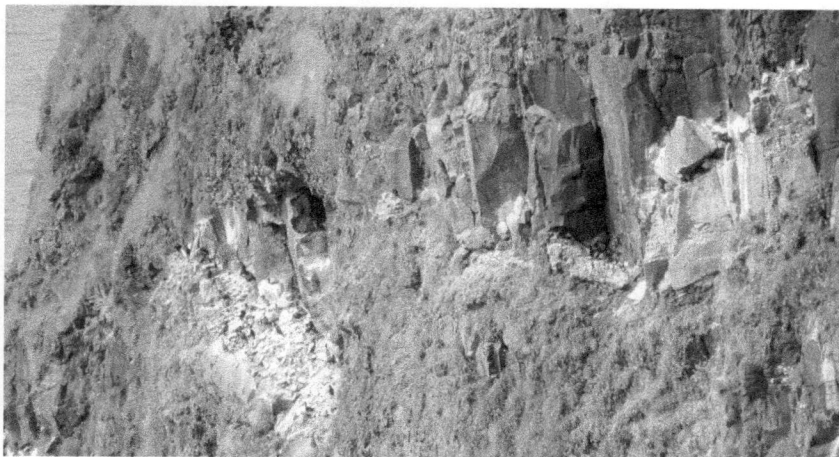

Close-up View of the Vertical Basalt Seacliff at Cape Meares. White areas of guano left by pelagic seabirds show where they make their nests on tiny ledges, totally safe from any land-based predators. At least ten cormorants can be counted in the lowest guano patch. The fledging cormorant's first flight must be a harrowing experience! Fortunately, they will land in the water for their first swim.

From the parking lot, an easy 950-foot asphalt path leads to the lighthouse, but it can be very windy. Additional hard-surface paths run through the old growth spruce forest and campground just to the east, which also has a modern restroom located just above the parking lot. A harder hike goes almost a mile from the park entrance down to the rocky shore and sandy beach to the north, with over 400 feet elevation loss; one can continue for five miles along the beach to the opening of Tillamook Bay. Another hiking trail starting there leads through the old forest to the largest Sitka spruce in Oregon, said to be 850 years old and 144 feet tall.

Wildlife habitats: Open ocean, seastacks, sea cliffs, coastal meadow, coastal evergreen forest, rocky shore, sandy beach.

Chapter 17

Tillamook and Nehalem Bays

Tillamook

Approaching Tillamook along Hwy101 from the south, north, or even across the hills, it becomes immediately obvious that the town sits on a special piece of landscape: a delta plain of 30 square miles extent. Nowhere in coastal Oregon is there another valley so broad and fertile. Five small rivers coalesced to form this fertile plain, all trying to fill in Tillamook Bay from the south and east. Settlers as early as the 1850s recognized its unique value as farmland: deep rich soil, mild climate, plenty of rain, and numerous rivers for irrigation when needed. Ideal for dairy farming. By 1909, ten local dairy farmers had gotten together and founded the Tillamook County Creamery Association and began producing high-quality cheese. Today it is a co-op with some 80 dairy farmer members, making and selling multiple-award-winning cheeses all

By 1909, ten dairy farmers had founded the Tillamook County Creamery Association and began producing cheese.

over the country. In 1947 they began making ice cream and now produce a full suite of dairy products. (I particularly recommend Marionberry pie flavor ice cream, made with a blackberry developed at Oregon State University. One its ancestors is the sweet, wild mountain blackberry you may have picked.) You can visit the creamery just north of town along Hwy 101. How often do you have an opportunity to visit the facility where the food you buy is actually produced?

Tillamook history goes farther back, but with a seventy-year time gap. In the summer of 1788, Captain Robert Gray arrived in Tillamook

Bay on the sloop *Lady Washington* and spent a week renewing supplies while exploring the area. Note the year of his voyage, only a few years after our Declaration of Independence was written. Starting out the previous year in Boston, Captain Gray carried a Massachusetts passport. As possibly the first European American to make landfall on the Oregon shore, Captain Gray apparently didn't make a favorable impression on the local Tillamook tribes. In a fight, one of his ship crew members and several Tillamooks were killed. It was not until seventeen years later, in 1805, that President Thomas Jefferson's Lewis and Clark expedition reached the Oregon Coast.

Although Gray's voyage was primarily a business venture with the objective of collecting of sea otter pelts to sell in China, Gray was also looking for the mouth of the legendary "Great river of the West", of which he undoubtedly had learned from earlier accounts by fur traders. This he found and entered in 1792 on his second voyage, naming it the *Columbia River* after the second ship under his command, the *Columbia Rediviva*. Appropriately, the ship was named for an earlier explorer, Christopher Columbus – the *Rediviva* part is Latin for revived, referring to ship's reconstruction in 1787.

Library: Tillamook County Library, 1716 3rd Street.

Playground: Coatsville Park, 1404 9th Street.

Cedar Creek Fish Hatchery: Side trip, rest stop, stroll. Located off State Hwy 22, 1.45 miles southeast of the village of Hebo. The junction with Hwy 101 is 19.3 miles south of Tillamook.

The Cedar Creek Fish Hatchery is another good family stop. Located six miles from the Pacific and behind some coastal hills, it is likely to be sunny and warm when the weather is cold or windy along the coast. There are modern restrooms and short walks for strollers. When I was last there they had tanks of really large steelhead; children are encouraged to help out with the feeding with fish food supplied by the hatchery. Note that just southeast of Hebo there is a ranger station for Siuslaw National Forest. At the end of the parking lot you will see a fairly large sequoia tree, a conifer native to the Sierra Nevada Mountains in California.

Wildlife habitats: Brushy creek, evergreen forest.

Future Fisheries Biologist – Anadromous Fish

The most important fish species in the rivers along the Oregon Coast are anadromous: they live most of their lives at sea and come back to the rivers to spawn. Each of these species lays its eggs to be fertilized in rivers or their tributaries. The young fish live and grow in the river systems for up to a year or two before migrating back through the estuaries and out to sea. Lampreys stay in the rivers even longer.

Salmon and Steelhead

Salmon and steelhead are endemic to all the Oregon coastal rivers and larger creeks. To learn where to catch the sea-run salmon and steelhead, you should refer to Frank Amato's *Oregon River Maps & Fishing Guide*. This over-sized paperback volume covers twenty of the larger rivers in detail. You will find that there is a run of salmon or steelhead almost any month of the year in one river or another.

In centuries past, runs of salmon in the rivers were legendary and supported numerous salmon canneries

In centuries past, runs of salmon were legendary and supported salmon canneries on several of the larger rivers. Since then, a combination of factors has tragically reduced the runs to small fractions of their former glory. Overfishing, first in the rivers and estuaries and happening in the ocean even today, has been the principal cause. But our poor management of the rivers and their watersheds has contributed. On the Columbia and Snake rivers, several hydroelectric dams disastrously impacted the ability of salmon and steelhead to migrate upstream to their traditional spawning beds. On the lower Snake River, it has been recommended that the dams be breached. On the Klamath River, this has recently been done, at least in part due to urging by several Native American tribes that traditionally harvest the salmon from the river.

Other factors, mainly affecting the smaller coastal streams which have no dams, include logging the forests in the watersheds, resulting in silting of the gravelly spawning beds. Clearing the shade-producing stream-side riparian vegetation that overhangs the tributary creeks is another factor, as that allows the water to warm to lethal temperatures during the summer, as well as removing an important food supply of falling insects and larvae. Logging practice in the national forests no longer allows that. Many of the floodplain wetlands and estuary salt marshes have been converted to pastureland, thus taking away valuable feeding and nursing areas for the juvenile fish as they return to the sea and gradually become accustomed to salt water. The importance of these factors is becoming understood, but much of the damage cannot be reversed.

Cutthroat Trout

It is these fine game fish with the characteristic red mark on their throat that you are likely to catch if you fish in the smaller coastal rivers and creeks. They may be sea-run or resident; however, the resident cutthroat trout in many smaller streams never seem to reach the eight-inch legal minimum size for keeping.

Sturgeon

These primitive fish have been around at least since the Late Cretaceous, more than 65 million years ago. Two of the many species, the huge white sturgeon and the smaller green sturgeon, are found in the Columbia River and in the larger estuaries up and down the West Coast. They are extremely long-lived, but don't begin to reproduce until they are fifteen or twenty years old. White sturgeons more than ten feet long have occasionally been caught in the Columbia River, but as they are breeding size they must be released.

As sturgeons are not important commercial fish species, and are not as common, their life cycles are not so well understood as those of salmon. Sturgeons are rather fussy about water conditions for spawning – clear flowing water, gravel substrate, and proper water temperature. They migrate through the estuaries far into the interior to find these conditions. A sturgeon may lay hundreds of thousands of eggs at one time. They don't dig redds like salmon, but allow the sticky eggs to adhere to the gravel, where they hatch after one or two weeks. The embryos then drift downstream to areas of slack water, where they live for a year or so before returning to the flowing stream. Many species worldwide are becoming endangered as stream conditions deteriorate

Surprisingly, green sturgeons spend most of their time at sea in the coastal waters. They return to rivers to spawn, but unlike salmon don't seem to be choosy about which one. It would appear that they seek fresh water input into the sea rather than a specific scent. Important food items include benthic prey, especially burrowing shrimp.

Shad

Not a native species, this Atlantic coast fish was transplanted into the Columbia River system around 1885 and have since proliferated spectacularly. They have since spread to some other rivers along the Oregon Coast, particularly the Umpqua, Siuslaw, and Coquille rivers. Unfortunately, as large members of the herring family, shad are oily and bony – many anglers catch-and-release these feisty fish. Cooks say that baking shad softens the bones, but I have never tried it. Shad roe is quite good though. Unlike salmon, shad release their eggs into the flowing stream, where they drift suspended in the water and hatch after a few days.

Pacific Lampreys

These primitive eel-like fish are also anadromous in the Oregon Coast rivers. Like sharks and some other primitive fish, lampreys have only a cartilaginous skeleton. As adult lampreys are only 15 to 25 inches long and pretty skinny, you probably won't notice them as they come through the estuaries unless they are attached to a salmon or steelhead you have caught. Lampreys spawn in gravelly stretches of the rivers in redds just like salmon, but they lack the salmon's famous stream-specific "homing" instinct. From there, the similarities cease. Lamprey eggs hatch into larvae, which may live for years as filter feeders living in still, muddy areas of the stream bed. Finally the larvae metamorphose into adult lampreys and migrate to the sea. There they become carnivorous for a year or so, attaching themselves with their sucker mouths to anything they can catch up to: fish, seals, marine mammals, and occasionally even whales. They use their teeth to hang on and a raspy tongue to cut a hole through the victim's skin. You have seen movies of whales breaching: perhaps they do that to rid themselves of lampreys; the process must be painful. Finally they swim back to a river to spawn and the cycle starts anew.

Hideous and slimy as they are, lampreys are actually edible and are considered a delicacy in Europe and Japan. Native Americans who lived in coastal Oregon are reported to have caught lampreys and preserved them by drying.

Effects of Global Warming

Global warming has become a major factor in the health of the Oregon rivers and the fish that live in them. Rainfall has diminished and the rainy season has become shorter, particularly in southern Oregon and northern California. This has led to smaller river flows in the summer, with the danger of exposing gravel beds in which fish have laid their eggs. The warming climate has led to increased stream temperatures, sometimes too high for the salmonids to live comfortably. Salmonid species have thrived in the streams of the Pacific Northwest because the cool water supports their requirements.

Even forest fires have a deleterious effect on fish habitat. As the forests dry out in the longer, warmer, dry seasons, fires in the western forests have become larger, hotter and more frequent. Shade-producing streamside vegetation is consumed and may take decades to grow back, so water temperature rises in the summer. Bare hillsides yield sediment into the streams, clogging the gravel beds where salmon like to spawn, and reduced winter floods may be insufficient to wash them clean again.

Nutrient Recycling

One value of the anadromous fish runs that receives little attention is the nutrients that they bring to the streams and the lands that border them. When the migrating fish die in the streams, they decay and enrich the water with the nutrients they bring from the ocean. Additionally, many of the fish are predated upon by bears, ospreys, eagles, otters, and other animals. Their remains in the form of skeletons and droppings then fertilize the surrounding forests and bottom lands, replacing critical nutrients that get washed away in the winter rains. If the fish no longer run up the rivers, the recycling of nutrients ceases.

This aspect of salmon runs in the streams was recently demonstrated by Allison Dennert, working on a graduate degree in British Columbia. She found that if she laid a salmon carcass in a field of wildflowers in the floodplain of a small stream, the plants in the immediate vicinity grew larger flowers and leaves. Fortunately, at least for rivers in the Oregon Coast Range, nitrogen-fixing red alders are common along streams, but potassium and phosphorus are still needed nutrients that fish carcasses can supply. Similar agro-environmental studies could be done on Oregon streams; maybe the loss of nutrients could be estimated and along with it the fertility of the forest lands along the streams. Anyone interested? You will find excellent forestry and agriculture schools at Oregon State University in Corvallis.

Tillamook River Rest Area: Rest stop. Located off Hwy 101 6.25 miles north of the intersection with Sand Lake Road, north of Hebo and Beaver. Southbound, the rest area is 4.8 miles south of central Tillamook.

Tillamook River Rest Area is just that, providing a modern restroom along the highway but no trail access. A picnic table is set up in the grassy area under the trees. A couple hundred feet through the trees to the west is the small Tillamook River, where you are likely to see waterfowl. When the flow is stronger during the fall and winter, salmon and steelhead will be running up this river to spawn, but by then the water is likely to be turbid so they will be hard to see.

Wildlife habitats: Park, river.

Trask River Fish Hatchery: Side trip, rest stop, stroll. Turn east on long Prairie Road at the Air Museum sign, 8.7 miles north of the Hwy 101-Sandlake Road intersection, north of Hebo and Beaver. From the North, the turnoff is 2.4 miles south of central Tillamook. Proceed 2.5 miles through the dairy farms; turn east on Chance Road; continue 2.6 miles to the hatchery driveway with a sign, and finally 600 feet down the hill to the hatchery.

Trask River Fish Hatchery is a century-old fish hatchery with multiple tanks for hatching and rearing salmon and steelhead. It even offers a one-day-a-week fishing experience for youngsters, but I suggest you call to make sure which day it is ((503) 842-4090). Guided tours can also be arranged, but you need to call in advance. The hatchery lies in forested valley with large western hemlocks

The hatchery offers a one-day-a-week
fishing experience for youngsters.

and bigleaf maples. In the adjacent Trask River you may see herons, other waterfowl, and even birds of prey. A modern restroom is available, and there is a pleasant five-minute stroll along the river. An interesting forestry point: The slope above the top of the driveway was logged in 2017 and is now re-growing with young western hemlock trees, which are doing well. This is unusual, as cutover land is usually planted to Douglas-fir, a more valuable crop.

Wildlife habitats: Farmland, cutover land, river.

Garibaldi

How many towns in the U.S. are named for Italian patriots? Not many. But Oregon has one: Garibaldi, named by the town founder Daniel Dodge Bayley for his Italian hero Giuseppe Garibaldi. Giuseppe Maria Garibaldi was an Italian general, patriot, revolutionary, and republican who contributed to the unification of Italy in the middle 1800s. Garibaldi is considered by many as the George Washington of Italy. Bayley had apparently followed and admired Garibaldi's exploits in the newspapers in his native New Hampshire before travelling to Oregon Territory on a wagon train in the 1840s.

How many towns in the U.S. are named for Italian patriots?

According to an article in the *The Munson Records* (Genealogy website) in 1895 based on letters from Bayley's intrepid wife Elizabeth Munson, the trip was arduous, guided by an inexperienced mountaineer. At one point, Elizabeth was offered six horses for one of her daughters, but declined the offer. It took the Bayley's and their six wagons nine months to complete the journey, as chronicled in the fascinating account told in the following link: https://www.genealogy.com/forum/surnames/topics/bayley/177/.

Eventually finding the Willamette Valley too crowded for his taste, Bayley crossed the Coast Range to Tillamook Bay in the 1860s. He founded a town with a hotel and general store on the north shore and named it Garibaldi. In 1870 Bayley was appointed the area's first postmaster by President Grant.

Fun for the family: Garibaldi may not have hiking opportunities, but it is the southern terminus of the Oregon Coast Scenic Railroad. The tourist train runs 46 miles along Tillamook Bay and the coast to the northern station at Rockaway, using vintage engines and rail cars. You can reach them at (503) 842-7972 for schedules and reservations. A meal is provided.

Library: Garibaldi Library, 107 6th Street.

Playground: Lumberman's Memorial Park, Third Street and American Avenue

Garibaldi Boat Basin: Rest stop, stroll.
In Garibaldi, turn south on Third Street or Seventh Street.

You will find a small-boat harbor with restaurants, businesses, and several floating docks accessible to strollers, but no hiking trails. There is a modern restroom on American Avenue just west of Third Street and the Scenic Railroad office. Charter fishing boats are available here. Besides abundant gulls, you may see brown pelicans, guillemots, and oystercatchers around the harbor. Miami River cove just to the east of town is a good birding destination, especially during low tide.

Wildlife habitats: Estuary, harbor.

Rockaway Big Tree Trail: Side trip, stroll. Watch for the sign 4.0 miles north of central Garibaldi, just past E. Washington Street in Rockaway Beach; turn east into the parking lot. From the north, 10.2 miles south of Nehalem River Bridge.

Another ancient rainforest trail starts here: 1.2 miles out-and-back on a recently-built boardwalk along marshy Saltair Creek. Your destination is a truly enormous western redcedar, 154 feet tall and estimated to be between 500 and 900 years old, surviving in a tiny patch of old-growth western redcedar, western hemlock, Sitka spruce, and red alder. Please stay on the boardwalk that rings the

A truly enormous western redcedar,
154 feet tall and estimated to be between 500 and 900 years old

famous cedar, as it was constructed to prevent soil compaction around the roots and prolong its life. Edible berries grow in the shade – salal, salmonberry, huckleberry, and red huckleberry – but you might get your feet wet and muddy in the Saltair Creek marsh if you step off the boardwalk to pick them. A patch of skunk cabbage decorates a section of the boardwalk with its giant leaves and bright yellow, calla lily-like flowers. A picnic table beckons at the far end of the walk.

At the small parking lot you will find only a primitive restroom, but a modern restroom is located just 0.8 miles to the north, across 1st Avenue from the visitor center parking lot. At the north edge of that parking lot, youngsters will find *Pirate Ship Playground,* a fine climbing structure. From here you can hike three miles south along the beach to the north jetty and entrance of Tillamook Bay or north the same distance to the south jetty of the Nehalem River. During the wet season you will need to wade a small creek or two.

Manhattan Beach State Recreation Site: Rest stop, beach hike, stroll. Located just south of Nedonna Beach, 16.8 miles north of junction Hwy 101 and Hwy 6 in Tillamook, or 7.3 miles south of Nehalem River Bridge. Turn west on Beach Street, cross the railroad tracks, and turn immediately left at the park sign. Proceed 0.2 miles to a large parking lot.

Manhattan Beach State Recreation Site has a 500 foot long parking lot somewhat protected from the wind and suitable for strollers, with a modern restroom at the north end. At the south end of the parking lot beyond a low gate a 400 foot maintained earthen trail extends the stroll through the shore pines to a small stream crossing the beach. There are sandy trails to the beach by restroom and near south end of the parking lot. A short beach walk takes you a mile north to the natural ocean outlet of the Nehalem River. A longer beach walk takes you 5.0 miles south to the jettied entrance to Tillamook Bay, but during the wet season you will need to wade a few small streams. Shorebirds are often seen at both hike destinations.

Wildlife habitats: Open ocean, sandy beach, low vegetated sand dunes, coastal conifer forest.

Nehalem Fish Hatchery: Side trip, rest stop, stroll. Located on State Hwy 53, 11.2 miles east of the junction with Hwy 101, which is just north of Wheeler and south of Nehalem. It is immediately south of North Fork Nehalem River Bridge.

Nehalem Fish Hatchery is a nice family stop, nine miles into the Coast Range from the ocean and most days out of the coastal fog and wind, and open from dawn to dusk. For the young fishers, fish food can be purchased from a dispenser for 25 cents for feeding the young trout and salmon – some of them larger than you might expect – so bring some quarters. For hyperactive youngsters, they have a field where they can run or play catch. For the whole family, on the south end of the field there is a trail through a riverine alder forest to Umbrella Falls, where a small tributary cascades 30 feet down to a pool in the river. Although the trail is in good shape for strollers,

A small tributary cascades 30 feet down to a pool in the river.

you have to get across the grassy field first. The forest understory consists of vine maple, thimbleberry, elderberry, and swordfern. The last time I visited, a fisherman was catching coho salmon from the pool – perhaps they were returning to the hatchery. A modern restroom with public access is located in the hatchery building.

Wildlife habitats: River, mixed riverine forest, field. I saw Steller's blue jays.

Nehalem Bay State Park: Rest stop, beach hike, stroll, playground. Located next to the town of Manzanita. Exit Hwy 101 on Laneda Avenue, 2.4 miles north of Nehalem River Bridge and 13.8 miles south of the Cannon Beach interchange. Proceed west 0.5 miles, then south on Carmel Avenue, which becomes Tie Lane, Beach Street, Sunset Lane, and finally Necarney Lane, for 1.1 miles. Turn left on Horizon Lane to the park entrance and turn right.

Nehalem Bay State Park serves as the city park for the town of Manzanita, with campgrounds, several modern restrooms, and playgrounds. The best set of playgrounds is 0.6 miles south of the entrance station, to the right of the road. Stretches of paved access roads through the campground are great for strollers and are somewhat protected from the wind. A sandy trail leads to the beach just west of the playground. Hikers can trek three miles north to a rocky point or 2.7 miles south to the north jetty of Nehalem Bay. You will see abundant shorebirds on the mud flats, if the tide isn't too high. The peninsula is a sand spit that is only a couple thousand feet wide at the widest point.

Recent press releases have documented the discovery of ancient ship timbers in caves along the coast near Manzanita.

Recent press releases have documented the discovery of ancient ship timbers in caves along the coast near Manzanita. The exact locations were not revealed, but they must have been in the rocky coast just to the north in Oswald West State Park. A dozen of these timbers have been attributed to the Spanish Galleon *Santos Cristos de Burgos,* which went missing in 1693 on the regular voyage from the Manila to Mexico. The unfortunate galleon must have been several hundred miles off course, as they usually made landfall in northern California. Perhaps she was avoiding a storm. Chinese silk, porcelain, and blocks of beeswax were the main cargo; beeswax and bits of porcelain have been found along the Oregon coast over the centuries. According to a July10, 2022, Washington Post news article, the Chinese porcelain provides an important clue, as the designs changed every few years. It has been dated to the late sixteenth century, which helps to date the year of the shipwreck. Oral histories of the native tribes also included accounts of such a shipwreck, more than a century and a half before the tales might have been documented in writing. One can wonder if they rescued the sailors.

Except for Astoria, the Oregon Coast didn't really get settled until after 1850. There was simply too much good rich land available in the Willamette Valley for the early settlers to claim, based on the Oregon *Donation Land Act* of 1843. Perhaps reports of the Lewis and Clark expedition of 1805 got it all started. This is quite surprising, as many ships from a number of nations plied the waters just offshore for 240 years before Lewis and Clark reached the Pacific by land. Most were commercial ventures, some were pirates or explorers, and more than a few just drifted in from the Orient. Theodore Schellhase in his well-researched volume *Lost Treasure Ships of the Oregon Coast* includes two appendices compiled by Herbert Howe Bancroft. The first, entitled *Vessels to the Northwest Coast 1819-1840,* is an annotated list of 68 sailing ships, not including Russian visits to Fort Ross or Spanish ships on the run from Manila to Acapulco. The second is more expansive: *Japanese wrecks on the Pacific coast / European and American,* which includes 49 Japanese vessels that either wrecked or were found adrift and 29 British or American shipwrecks. These appendices were apparently taken from Bancroft's 1884 publication *History of the Northwest Coast.*

Wildlife habitats: Open ocean, sandy beach, estuary, jetty, coastal conifer forest, coastal meadow, vegetated low sand dunes.

Chapter 18

Cannon Beach to the Columbia

Oswald West State Park: Rest stop, woodland hike, stroll. Located at a large trailhead parking lot on the east side of Hwy 101, 6.4 miles north of Nehalem River Bridge, 9.8 miles south of Cannon Beach interchange.

If you are staying in Cannon Beach or Manzanita, here is a nearby place to experience some nature. Oswald West State Park has preserved a great piece of the Pacific Northwest rainforest, perhaps the finest example south of Olympic National Park in Washington. The large parking lot serves as trailhead parking for a network of stroller-ready trails through a mixed conifer forest to Short Sand Beach, half a mile down the slope. There is a modern restroom at the north end of the parking lot. A second trailhead is located at the subsidiary parking lot just to the south on the west side of the highway. The trails are sloping but not steep, a little rocky in places but passable, a little muddy during the rainy season. You will see giant hemlocks near the road, huge western redcedars along the trail, and enormous Sitka spruce trees closer the beach – some of them six feet in diameter and well over a hundred feet tall. It is a stunning rainforest experience, with sword ferns, lady ferns, and maidenhair ferns lining the trail. The understory has lots of red huckleberry bushes – try a few of the bright red berries if they are ripe – along with evergreen huckleberry, salal, salmonberry, and rhododendron. Leave the red elderberries for the wild bandtail pigeons. A shorter, gentler, but equally beautiful walk starts behind the restroom and runs up Short Sand Creek for a ways to a wooden bridge, returning to the highway

*Oswald West State Park has preserved a great piece
of the Pacific Northwest rainforest.*

and crossing the highway bridge back to the parking lot. Rougher hiking trails to Cape Falcon and Cape Falcon Lookout, a couple miles distant, originate at the trailhead parking just to the north of the main parking lot, part of the Oregon Coast Trail. That trail also continues to the south to Neahkahnie Mountain. It is most likely that caves in the seacliffs around Short Sand Beach or Cape Falcon are where the 18th century Spanish galleon timbers were found. (See discussion above at Nehalem Bay State Park.)

Oswald West State Park. *This photo shows the undisturbed primeval forest at Oswald West State Park south of Cannon Beach. Much of the Oregon Coast must once have looked like this. Here it is a "climax forest", in which western redcedar and western hemlock have replaced Douglas-fir, a conifer that doesn't grow well in the shade. The understory here is largely sword ferns and red huckleberry bushes. Closer to the beach, large Sitka spruce trees dominate the forest.*

Short Sand Creek at Oswald West State Park. *The scene well illustrates how the shade that creek-side vegetation provides can keep the water cool. The bushes are also a source for falling insects and caterpillars for young fish. Cutthroat trout are likely to live here, as they do in small streams all along the coast. Toss in a caterpillar and watch what happens to it.*

Lady Ferns at Oswald West State Park. These delicate lady ferns (Athyrium filix-femina) line the park trails and streams in this large wilderness park south of Cannon Beach. Smaller deer ferns (Blechnum spicant) can be seen just above. Several varieties of ferns grow well in the Pacific Northwest rainforest, enjoying the cool and moist climate.

Wildlife habitats: At the parking lot and on the trails, coastal conifer forest and brushy stream. Along the shore, open ocean, sandy beach, seacliffs. Offshore are the Cape Falcon Marine Reserve and the Cape Falcon West Marine Protected Area. These adjoining marine reserves have different degrees of protection for sea life.

Arcadia Beach State Recreation Site: Rest stop, beach hike. Located 6.6 miles north of Short Sand Creek Bridge in Oswald West State Park, or 1.75 miles south of Tolovana exit.

Arcadia Beach State Recreation Site is another access point for the broad beach of Cannon Beach and Tolovana, probably less crowded on a summer afternoon. The small parking lot with a primitive restroom provides beach access via a trail with stairs at the north end – don't be fooled by the primitive trail at the south end of the lot, as it doesn't go anywhere. There are no strolling opportunities here, but beach hikes take you 4.6 miles south to the bluffs at Oswald West State Park and Cape Falcon or 3.7 miles north past Cannon Beach to Ecola Creek – even a little farther if you want to wade the creek.

Wildlife habitats: Open ocean, sandy beach, coastal conifer forest.

Tolovana Beach State Recreation Site: Rest stop, beach hike, short stroll. Located 14.9 miles north of Nehalem River Bridge. Exit Hwy 101 at the Tolovana sign to Warren Beach Road, circle around under the highway to West Warren Way. Continue three blocks to a large parking lot on your right. From the north, the exit is signed Tolovana Park and is just south of Cannon Beach.

Tolovana Beach State Recreation Area serves the neighborhood of Tolovana Park, on the southern end of Cannon Beach. It mostly comprises a large parking lot with adjacent beach access and a modern restroom. On the east side it borders South Hemlock Street, which a mile farther north becomes the main street of Cannon Beach. Strolling opportunities are largely limited to the 1200 foot sidewalk around the parking lot; streets through the neighborhood immediately to the north have no sidewalks. Beach hikers can explore a broad extent of the ocean beach, extending 5 miles to Arch Cape in the south or 2.5 miles north past Cannon Beach and Ecola Creek to Chapman Point. Haystack Rock, the famous seastack on the edge of the beach, is visible less than a mile to the north.

Wildlife habitats: Open ocean, sandy beach, park.

Cannon Beach

You might expect a town with a name like Cannon Beach to have been involved in a significant war – or at least prepared for coastal defense. That is not at all the case. The three cannons found on the beach south of town had a far more interesting history. All were mounted on the USS Shark, a naval vessel that was once used in the suppression of the slave trade and piracy offshore West Africa, in the Mediterranean, and in the Caribbean Sea! Were they actually used in fighting pirate ships? It seems likely, but proof might only be found in the ship's log, which hasn't yet been found, or possibly

Three cannons found on the beach south of town
had a far more interesting history

in nineteenth century U.S. Navy files in Washington DC. Here is the story of the USS Shark:

The USS Shark, a two-mast schooner, was built for United States Navy in the Washington Navy Yard and launched in 1821. It was the first of seven naval vessels given that name over the years, including two schooners, four submarines, and a patrol vessel. None are currently afloat. Being only 86 feet in length and displacing 198 tons, the USS Shark was lightly armed with ten 18 pound carronades and two smaller guns. (Note: the 18 pound caliber refers to the weight of the cannonball; the carronades weigh in at 1100 pounds each.) The carronade was a small cannon developed around 1869 and initially manufactured by the Carron Company iron foundry in Scotland. An 18 pound carronade was typically just over three feet long and was normally carried on the ship's deck, bolted to a wooden carriage. Shot for the carronade was quite varied. Carron supplied their carronade orders with cannonballs, bar shots, chain shots, and canister shots. Each had its uses in naval warfare. Chain shots, which were two halves of a cannonball connected by a strong chain up to six feet in length, were effective at destroying the rigging of an enemy sailing ship. Bar shots, essentially two cannonballs connected by an iron bar, could spin through the air and sever a mast. Canister shots, basically a cannon-sized shotgun shell, were devastatingly effectively against enemy personnel on deck.

After more than 20 years of active duty in and around the Atlantic Ocean, the USS Shark was dispatched to the Pacific via the Straits of Magellan, being the first U.S. naval vessel to make that voyage. She patrolled the coast of Peru, went to Honolulu for repairs, then in 1846 sailed up the Columbia River as a show of American force in the Fort Vancouver-Willamette Valley area. On September 10 of that year as she attempted to re-cross the bar at the mouth of the Columbia River she struck an uncharted shoal and was swept into the breakers, eventually grounding on Clatsop Spit just south of Cannon Beach. It should be noted that sand bars at the mouth of the Columbia were ever-changing, and today even with the jetties can still be hazardous to boat traffic. Although the crew was saved, the USS Shark was a total loss.

That is not the end of the story of the USS Shark. Some 52 years after she ran aground, one of her 18-pound carronades was discovered on the beach south of what is now the town of Cannon Beach.

That cannonade is now proudly displayed in the Cannon Beach History Center, along with a capstan that is also apparently from the same vessel. More than a century later two more 18-pound carronades were found in the same area. These were lovingly restored by the Center for Maritime Archaeology and Conservation at Texas A&M University, and are now on display in the Columbia River Maritime Museum in Astoria. Certainly there must be more cannon and other munitions waiting to be discovered in the same area, or possibly along the coast between Arch Cape and the Columbia River, but none have been found since 2008. It also seems possible that the members of the local Clatsop tribe saw the schooner wash ashore and might have salvaged materials from it, but I have found no record of that. The Clatsops, who had a village at the mouth of what is now named Ecola Creek, apparently kept watch on the local beaches for dead sea mammals, from which they harvested blubber and possibly meat. Unfortunately, the Clatsops were early victims of European diseases, from which they had no defense. You can read more about the Shark in the following link: https://cbhistory.org /blog/what-about-the-shark/

Of course it was the discovery of the Shark's carronade that led to the town name Cannon Beach, but not exactly how one might think. The original community, established in the 1850s, was named Elk Creek after the creek and shallow estuary that reach the ocean there. Roosevelt elk can still be seen in the area, even occasionally on the beach. But the local history goes even farther back than that. In 1806 the first colonists to visit were a party that included Lieutenant William Clark and Sacajawea of the Lewis and Clark Expedition. They encountered a group of Native Americans rendering blubber from a whale that had washed ashore, and were able to barter for 300 pounds of whale blubber and some whale oil. Lieutenant Clark gave the name "Ekoli" to the creek that crosses the beach there, after the Chinook language word for whale. But that name didn't stick for long – homesteaders in the 1850s initially preferred the name "Elk Creek" over an Indian name, naming their growing community after the creek. Only later was the name "Ecola" re-adopted, perhaps because there are towns named "Elk Creek" in several other states.

But the naming wasn't done. A post office was established in 1910, called the Ecola Post after Lieutenant Clark's original name for the creek. In 1922 the US Post Office Department insisted they change their name once again because of confusion with the town of Eola, located in what is now the Eola-Amity Hills wine region just west of Salem. The community wisely chose "Cannon Beach", after the beach south of town where the first USS Shark's first carronade was found.

In 1964, a tsunami caused by the Good Friday earthquake near Anchorage, Alaska, flooded the town and destroyed the highway bridge across the Ecola Creek estuary. Episodes of strong west winds coinciding with king tides have also periodically flooded the low-level downtown area – a phenomenon that is likely to become more common as sea level rises. Although Cannon Beach avoided damage by the 2011 Tohoku earthquake in Japan, the low-lying town is still vulnerable to seismic sea waves generated by earthquakes around the North Pacific. As much of the Cannon Beach lies within an earthquake and tsunami evacuation zone, visitors should pay heed to posted signs noting escape routes to use if an earthquake occurs, as a tidal wave may soon follow.

As tiny Ecola Creek didn't provide a big salmon run like many of the larger rivers, the town got a slow start, mainly as a tourist destination for Portlanders. Even that wasn't easy, as access was very difficult. Although a toll road through the rugged coastal hills from Seaside to Cannon Beach was built in 1890, it was only gravel and boasted 111 hairpin curves! Tourists then could travel by train from Portland to Astoria, then on another train to Seaside. A stagecoach was offered for the rest of the journey. Altogether the trip took over seven hours. A traveler could get seasick before reaching the sea! The toll road wasn't replaced by the modern Hwy 101 until 1950. But the toll road allowed permanent settlers to come in, and the town began to grow – 40 years later than most other Oregon coastal towns, and more than 80 years after the beach and its whale was first visited by Lieutenant William Clark and Sacajawea.

There is little to be said about Ecola Creek and its estuary. Ecola Creek drains only 22 square miles of mountainous terrain. The estuary becomes blocked from the ocean during low water periods in the summer, and there has never been a local fishing fleet. Yet small Coho salmon and steelhead runs come in the fall and winter. A few Chinook salmon have been caught, but they may have strayed in from neighboring rivers.

A more important landmark – should I say seamark? – is Haystack Rock, located on the edge of the beach and extending into the ocean. Puffins can be seen nesting this protected seastack, especially on the seaward side. The rock is included in the Oregon Islands National Wildlife Refuge; at low tide, there are tide pools around the base that are protected as well. Haystack Rock is composed of basaltic lava which flowed down the Columbia River Canyon from eastern Washington during the Miocene, some 17 million years ago.

Library: Cannon Beach Library, 131 N Hemlock Street.

Playground: Cannon Beach Playground, 244 N Spruce Street

Ecola State Park: Side trip, rest stop, woodland hike, stroll. Located at the north end of Cannon Beach. To access from the south, exit Hwy 101 on E. Sunset Drive, which is the main offramp for Cannon Beach. Follow it around under the highway to S. Hemlock Street, the main drag of Cannon beach. Follow Hemlock Street north 0.9 miles, where it curves east on Third Street. Continue on a short zig zag route, left on N. Spruce Street, right on East Third Street, left on Fir Street, crossing Ecola Creek Bridge, and left on East Fifth Street, all of which are the main road. Follow East Fifth Street 0.15 mile to Ecola State Park Road and turn right. Proceed 1.7 miles to Ecola Park Road and turn left 0.1 miles into the parking lot. The route from Cannon Beach is paved, but it is narrow,

curvy, hilly, and in places has poor visibility, so please drive slowly and carefully. You are likely to encounter bicycle and foot traffic. This is the same route you would take from downtown Cannon Beach. From the north, the Ecola State Park exit is 2.8 miles south of the Hwy 26 interchange; follow Fir Street west 0.15 miles to Ecola State Park Road, turn right and follow the directions above.

The Ecola State Park parking lot is situated in a high coastal meadow on Ecola Point. There is a modern restroom in the trees just to the south. From the west end, a paved trail leads 600 feet to a spectacular viewpoint nearly 200 feet above the beach and rocky shore, but there is no beach access here. Other shorter trails branch off but are not paved. The viewpoint provides an excellent perch for observing seabirds, possibly sea lions as well, on Sea Lion Rock and several closer rocks. One can also see Tillamook Rock Lighthouse, two and a half miles to the northwest and a mile offshore. Decommissioned in 1957, it earned the title of Terrible Tilly during its 76 years of operation with absolutely no protection from the stormy sea. If you want to live in absolute privacy, a 2022 edition of the Lincoln City News Guard points out that Terrible Tilly is for sale for $6.5 million.

The viewpoint provides an excellent perch for observing seabirds

Hikers can take the one-mile Indian Beach trail from the west end of the parking lot north to the Indian Beach Day use area. Some climbing is involved, but the trail has been under repair. Watch for signs. More hiking trails extend another mile to the north from Indian Beach, which is also accessible by Ecola Park Road; these are part of the Oregon Coast Trail. South of the main parking area, the Oregon Coast Trail follows the access road to Cannon Beach. There is a primitive trail to Indian Beach at the Indian Beach Day Use Area.

Seaside. A convenient exit from Hwy 101 is Broadway which, except for the last block, is one-way west. Broadway exit is 4.1 miles north of the Hwy 101 – Hwy 26 interchange and 12.7 miles south of Youngs Bay Bridge.

Seaside is famous for its beachside promenade. It extends from U Street, 0.9 miles south of Broadway, to 12th Avenue, 0.6 miles north of Broadway, with hotels on one side and the beach and vegetated low dunes on the ocean side. Ideal for stroller walks if the wind is calm. A nice aquarium is located near the north end. You will find modern restrooms located beneath the Broadway turnaround at the beach. The walk was built more than a century ago to protect the businesses from the ocean, which has retreated beyond the vegetated sand dunes way to the west. Oceanway Public Parking Lot, covering an entire city block, is located a block to the north of Broadway between North Columbia Street and North Edgewood Street. There is also abundant street parking: Seaside has many visitors in the summer.

Seaside is famous for its beachside promenade

Broadway is the main commercial street for the Seaside tourist trade, and is also inviting for strollers. Hikers can go south 1.9 miles along the beach to the rocky point at Tillamook Head or 1.2 miles north to the mouth of the small Necanicum River estuary, beyond which the beach is open 16 miles to the Columbia River. That beach hike is best accessed from Lesley Miller Dunes Meadow Park at the foot of Pacific Way in Gearhart, the next town to the north. Although the beach hike constitutes the northernmost section of the Oregon Coast Trail, it is open to motor vehicles, so beware. At the other end of Broadway, 0.8 miles east of the beach, you come to Broadway Park on the north side. The park features ball fields, a skate park, playground equipment, a modern restroom, and a kayak launch into Neawanna Creek. This creek is a tributary of the Necanicum River, which it joins near the mouth of the estuary. Although the creek is mostly within the city limits of Seaside, it runs through a couple miles of salt marsh with abundant shore birds.

Library: Seaside Library, 1130 Broadway.

Playground: Broadway Park, 1300 Broadway Street.

Cullaby Lake Wetlands Interpretive Trail: Side trip, rest stop, marsh hike, stroll. Exit Hwy 101 at Cullaby Lake Lane, 5.95 miles north of Neawanna Creek Bridge in Seaside and 6.5 miles south of Youngs Bay Bridge. Turn right on Hawkins Road at 0.2 miles and proceed 0.7 miles to a large parking lot with a fee station and a modern restroom.

This excellent paved trail starts at the southwest corner of the main parking lot near the host's residence and takes you more than a mile through a fresh-water marsh – the interpretive signs call it a "fen", which is a more common feature in the Upper Midwest states. Several commercial cranberry bogs are located just south of the trail, but they are not visible through the vegetation. At the south end, the trail runs into another parking lot, also with a modern restroom, lake access, and a beach volley ball court – but you need to bring your own net. You can return to the first parking lot on a continuation of the loop trail, but the return trail is not as stroller-ready as the main part of the loop through the fen. A better choice might be the paved park road, but you will need to watch for vehicular traffic.

Along the trail there are a few benches and an elevated platform with information signs describing the animal life of the fen. You will see a wealth of plants that grow well in a marshy environment. Trees and bushes include Sitka spruce, alder, willow, cascara, red elderberry, twinberry, and wax myrtle. There is a patch of the swamp-loving skunk cabbage, displaying big yellow flowers in the early spring. Because the blooms exude a carrion smell, they don't attract bees but are fertilized instead by flies. In season you will find

edible berries along the trail: huckleberry, salmon berry, wild blackberry, and a few canes of evergreen blackberry, a commercial variety
introduced from Europe and gone wild. Ferns are abundant, especially lady fern, a species that thrives in swampy ground. Cullaby
Lake is home to a resident population of ducks and geese, and many
more pass through during the spring and fall migrations. If you are
lucky, you may see beavers, bobcats, raccoons, and, according to the
host, even a bear or a cougar, although neither have been seen in recent years

*If you are lucky, you may see beavers, bobcats, raccoons,
and, according to the host, even a bear or a cougar,
although neither have been seen in recent years*

Kayaks can be launched from either parking lot in the county park
for exploring this two-mile long scenic lake; the northern lot has a
dock. Only a small portion of the shoreline near the park entrance
has been developed. It is drained to the north by the tiny Skipanon
River, which may be kayak navigable in parts of the year as it flows
toward Young's Bay and the Columbia River. Fishing for bass and
pan fish can be good, especially in the summer, and rainbow trout
are planted in the lake. However, the lake is shallow and the shoreline is weedy, so a boat is useful for fishing.

Wildlife habitats: Lake, freshwater marsh, coastal coniferous forest.

**Sunset Beach State Recreation Area: Side trip, rest stop, beach
hike, stroll. From Neawanna Creek Bridge in Seaside, drive 6.3
miles north to Sunset Beach Road and turn west. Proceed 0.9 miles
west, crossing Sunset Lake, to a parking lot on the right. From the
north, Sunset Beach Road is 4.9 miles south of Youngs Bay Bridge.**

The paved parking lot and modern restroom for Sunset Beach State
Recreation Area are 500 feet from the beach, which is accessible farther
along the road. The lot serves as the southwestern trailhead for the

historic Fort-to-Sea Trail, which runs five miles to Lewis and Clark National Historic Park. This long section of the trail is overgrown at the margins and too narrow for strollers, at least near the parking lot, but it is a fine hiking trail. The continuation to the beach is a broad, delightful trail that runs a quarter mile through an open conifer forest to a broad expanse of beach-grass vegetated dunes – quite beautiful, especially in a breeze. At that point the trail becomes narrower and sandier and you may eventually want to turn around before reaching the beach. The trail crosses some swampy areas on wooden bridges.

*A broad expanse of beach-grass vegetated dunes
is quite beautiful, especially in a breeze*

From the beach access at the end of the road, hikers can walk five miles south to the Neawanna Creek estuary at Seaside or nine miles north past Fort Stevens State Park to the south jetty of the Columbia River. Watch out for the motor vehicles, which frequently access the beach at the same entry point. Of course you can do this too, just don't get stuck in the soft sand when the tide is coming in! AAA doesn't have a tugboat.

European Beachgrass at Sunset Beach State Recreation Site.
European beachgrass (Ammophila arenaria) blankets the low sand dunes
at Sunset Beach near Astoria, at the southwestern end of the Lewis and
Clark Fort-to-Sea Trail. Unlike most plants, European beachgrass seems
to get all the nutrition it needs from the seemingly sterile sand: few will
grow on sand dunes. The variety was imported from Europe specifically to
stabilize sand dunes, but is now invasive, especially on the northern Ore-
gon Coast. The species has been able to out-compete American dunegrass
in many areas.

Wildlife habitats: Ocean, sandy beach, coastal meadow, coastal
conifer forest, fresh water marsh.

**Fort Stevens State Park: Side trip, rest stop, beach and woodland
hikes, stroll. From Neawanna Creek Bridge in Seaside, drive 8.26
miles north to Fort Stevens Highway, State Hwy 104 just south of
Warrenton, turn west, then north. Proceed 2.1m to SW 9th Street, turn
left, proceed 1.0 mile to NW Ridge Road, and turn right. Drive 1.8m
north to Peter Iredale Road, turn left 0.8 miles to a pair of beachfront
parking lots with a modern restroom between them. Coming south
from Astoria, turn west on East Harbor Drive at the southwest end
of Youngs Bay Bridge. Drive west into Warrenton, turn south on
Hwy 104 which is South Main Avenue. Continue south 0.6 miles to
SW 9th Street, turn west, and follow directions as above.**

You are now within the large Fort Stevens State Park. The park
to the north is laced with miles of trails through coastal meadows,
marshes and coastal conifer forests, but mainly too sandy for
small-wheeled strollers. Beach hikers can trek 3.6 miles north to
the south jetty of the Columbia River or 11.5 miles south to the
town of Seaside and the Necanicum River, all on the Oregon Coast
Trail, but watch out for vehicular traffic. From the beach parking
lot you can see what is left of the skeleton of the Peter Iredale, a
four-masted British barque that ran aground here in 1906. The

Peter Iredale is just one of many ships that have foundered trying to cross the treacherous Columbia River bar, and many lives have been lost. Even today, there is a cadre of fifteen bar pilots stationed in Astoria to help ships navigate in and out of the Columbia.

The Peter Iredale is just one of more than 2000 ships that have foundered trying to cross the treacherous Columbia River bar

From the parking lot you can return 0.4 miles to Burma Road, turn north to Jetty Road, and drive another 3.5 miles to a lookout tower near the end of Clatsop Spit, where you will be at the shore end of the south jetty of the Columbia River. The jetty is not designed for foot traffic; you should stay off. Logs on the jetty top show what a sneaker wave can do. This is parking lot D on the park map and there is a primitive restroom. Another half mile on Jetty Road brings you to Jetty Road at the Beach, where you can drive or walk onto the estuary beach for splendid shorebird viewing to the north on the Columbia River. You can see the Washington shore 3.7 miles across the estuary. However, there are no facilities here. Along Jetty Road you will have passed access to other parking lots with ocean beach access but no restroom facilities. From these lots you can walk across Jetty Road to the salt marsh bordering Jetty Lagoon for shorebird viewing.

Near the south end of the park, off Peter Iredale road, there is a large parking lot in a grassy meadow setting with a modern restroom at the north end of Coffenbury Lake. Just beyond the restroom is the trailhead for a fine 2.2-mile strolling trail with a packed earth surface, running all the way around the lake. You will find it quite secluded, as most of the visitors seem to stay around the parking lot and grassy field. This is the best strolling trail in the park, running through a dense conifer forest most of the way but with views of the lake.

Wildlife habitats: Open ocean, jetty, sandy beach, estuary, coastal meadow, lake, fresh water marsh, coastal conifer forest.

Chapter 19

Astoria

Astoria

When Astoria was founded in 1811 as a fur trading post, it was the first American town west of the Rocky Mountains, predating the other Oregon coastal towns by almost forty years. Some California towns are a bit older, especially those built around the Catholic missions, but they remained under Spanish rule until 1822, then under Mexican rule until 1848 when California was ceded to the United States. San Diego is the oldest of them, founded in 1769.

There were earlier visitors to the lower Columbia region, but they didn't stick around. Captain Robert Gray sailed into the river in 1792 on the three-masted sailing ship *Columbia Rediviva* and named the river after his ship. During the winter of 1805-1806, the Lewis and Clark expedition wintered nearby in log structures at Fort Clatsop, but in the spring they abandoned camp and commenced on the arduous journey back to St. Louis. There may have been early visits to the area by fur trappers, as suggested by a devastating small pox epidemic amongst the local Clatsop people around 1802. Of course the exact cause is lost to history. There are records of 95 ship visits to the Pacific Coast between 1788 and 1802. When Captain Robert Gray encountered the Clatsops in his visit in 1792, he found them already depleted by European diseases. An earlier sailing ship must have landed, bringing the disease ashore. However, small pox may have been carried to the coast by Native Americans traveling along trading routes from farther inland. Consequently, the local Clatsop population had been greatly diminished by the time Lewis and Clark arrived, from perhaps more than 1,500 to fewer than 200 individuals.

Small pox was not the only European disease to affect the vulnerable Native American populations of Northern Oregon. Beginning in 1830, a malaria epidemic decimated the vulnerable local tribes, possibly brought in by sailing vessels – or even by traders from the Mississippi Valley, where malaria was rampant at the time. The spreading of lethal European diseases amongst the Native Americans became an important factor in the American colonization of western Oregon – there were simply too few surviving Native Americans in their scattered tribes to put up much of a resistance.

For more than a century after Fort Astoria's founding in 1811 by John Jacob Aster for the American Fur Company, harvesting of natural resources dominated the Astoria economy. As the supply of furs declined, the fish canning and forest products industries took over. By the mid-1900s, those natural resources had dwindled as well. Unlike the inland towns in the Willamette Valley, the lower Columbia region has little fertile farmland. But a colorful historic old town had been built and has largely been preserved; since around 1980, tourism has been the economic stalwart. Astoria is the only coastal town north of San Francisco with a street car. After Lewis and Clark left for home, Fort Clatsop subsequently fell into decay, but in 1955 it was rebuilt as a fine state park, located south of town.

The most impressive engineering marvel in Astoria is the Astoria-Megler Bridge, crossing the Columbia River estuary to Washington. Finished in 1966 to finally complete the Mexico to Canada highway you have been traveling, the bridge boasts the longest truss span in the United States at 1232 feet, standing nearly 200 feet above the main channel of the river. It still ranks

The longest truss span in the United States at 1232 feet

number two in the world, surpassed only by the Ikitsuki Bridge, built 25 years later to connect two islands in Japan. And that bridge has a continuous truss span only 80 feet longer.

The Astoria-Megler Bridge is just over four miles long. Many long crossings, like the Golden Gate, use suspension or cable-stayed technology and can have individual spans that are much longer. Initially charging tolls, the Astoria-Megler Bridge crossing was paid off in 1993 and is now free – in stark contrast to the bridges crossing San Francisco Bay, where tolls continue to increase. The bridge is a little scary at 20 stories above the river, but it was designed to withstand 150 mph winds. The seabirds like it. From Astoria you can see dozens of them perching on the pile caps just above the water where they are safe from predation.

The Columbia estuary badly needed a bridge. During stormy weather, it was not a pleasant crossing for a ferry boat. The Columbia bar is much worse, especially during winter storms. Over the last two and a half centuries more than 2000 ships have foundered attempting to cross into or out of the Columbia, starting with the U.S. Navy's schooner *Shark* in 1746. Hundreds of lives have been lost, rightfully earning the Columbia Bar the name *"Graveyard of the Pacific"*. Even today, with jetty protection, the crossing can be perilous, with storm waves, strong tides, river currents, and migrating sand bars all leading to hazardous turbulence and unexpected waves that might be 40 feet tall. And it doesn't help that the river mouth is often shrouded in dense fog. At Cape Disappointment, on the Washington shore, the U.S. Coast Guard runs water rescue programs during the late fall and winter when conditions are at their roughest. Their National Motor Lifeboat School is based here because the danger of the Columbia Bar is so extreme that it is perfect for training. Not a school I would care to attend!

One might wonder why the exploration and settlement of the rest of the Oregon Coast came so much later than the founding of Astoria in 1711 and even after the opening of the Oregon Trail in the 1830s. There are at least three reasons: first, when settlers in their covered wagons on the Oregon Trail finally reached the Willamette Valley after a long and difficult journey across the country, they found a large valley with mild weather and fertile soil. Why should they have gone farther? Their numbers were not large. It took decades for the Willamette Valley to feel population pressure that might encourage settlers to go farther west to the coast. Second, potential farmland was limited in the coastal valleys – only Tillamook boasted a real agriculture valley, and it is far smaller than the Willamette and Rogue River valleys. Finally, the coastal weather is not nearly as favorable for farming, with the infamous 80 to 120 inches of annual rainfall drenching the area. It was not until the 1850s, twenty years later, that colonization along the coast really got started.

Library: Astoria Public Library, 450 10th Street.

Playground: Tapiola Park, 900 W Marine Drive

Astoria River Walk: Side trip, rest stop, sidewalk hike, stroll. Located along the Astoria waterfront. A good access point is on 36th Street at Leif Erikson Drive, which is U.S. Highway 30, the Columbia River Highway. The exit is about a mile east of the old town and 2.3 miles east of the Astoria-Megler Bridge that crosses the Columbia River estuary.

The Astoria River Walk runs for nearly five miles along a railroad right-of-way, fronting the entire Columbia River waterfront of the town: some is industrial, some commercial, some even rural where it crosses small bays on dikes and bridges. It is quite popular with townspeople and tourists alike, shared by joggers, bicyclists, dog walkers, and strollers on foot and even wheelchairs. For the almost the whole length there is a fine view across the Columbia River

A fine view across the Columbia River estuary to Washington

estuary to Washington, more than three miles away. You are likely to see ship traffic coming in to Portland and other port cities along the Columbia, as well as numerous small craft. The large public parking lot at the foot of 36th street has a modern restroom. In the downtown area all the streets reach the River Walk. Toward the west end you will find the Columbia River Maritime Museum at 1792 Maritime Drive, a highly recommended stop. Much history of Astoria and the Columbia River port are covered there. There is no public restroom, but one is available a short distance away at the Astoria Nordic Heritage Park at the foot of 16th Street on Marine Drive. For a dollar, you can take a trolley ride on the old tracks along the side of the River Walk.

Wildlife habitats: Estuary, coastal meadow, harbor, urban, industrial.

Chapter 20

Wild Berries along the Oregon Coast

One of the joys or growing up in a rural part of the Oregon Coast was the profusion of wild berries ripening in the summer. We ate them off the bush and picked them by the bucketful for jams, jellies, and pies. As you explore the Oregon Coast, you will find them growing wild at most places you stop, often right next to the parking lots. Finding berries can be the high point of a scenic vista stop for travelers who are too young to appreciate the scenery. Some berries, of course, are better than others, some aren't much good at all, and some of the prettiest berries can be mildly toxic to humans. So I cover the more common berries in the paragraphs below, in alphabetical order. The Audubon field Guide to the Pacific Northwest provides excellent color photographs of the blooms, the foliage, and the berries. I recommend taking a copy with you. You can also find acceptable images online, but you have to know what you are looking for. Watch out for poison oak – it has small white berries and often grows among other berry bushes. You and your children need to learn to recognize it, as the berries are toxic and the leaves cause a nasty rash.

The author also wishes to point out that people occasionally have allergic reactions to berries, with multiple symptoms that range from hives, itching, and swelling to difficulty breathing or a drop in blood pressure; other symptoms can be found online. Those who are susceptible to berry allergies might consider carrying a doctor-prescribed emergency allergy medicine such as epinephrine.

*Watch out for poison oak – it has small white berries
and often grows among other berry bushes*

Blackcap Raspberry *(Rubus leucodermis).* Rubus is simply the Latin word for blackberry. More interesting is the species name *leucodermis,* which refers to the powdery white skin of the blackcap cane. The English term *raspberry* is quite descriptive of the fine thorns on the canes.

Along the southern Oregon Coast you may be fortunate enough to find wild blackcap raspberries growing wild. I have been that lucky only a few times. The canes are similar to those of the familiar raspberry, except that they arch like a Himalaya blackberry and take root where the cane touches the ground.

Blueberry *(Vaccinium caespitosum or uliginosum).* Caespitosum simply means growing in clumps, and uliginosum refers to the marshy habitat.

There are two varieties of blueberry that are found mainly the northern Oregon Coast and in Washington: the dwarf blueberry and the bog blueberry. Both are most likely to be found in bogs and are easily recognizable by the familiar blue berries with a pale gray bloom, and both are juicy and delicious. The Willamette Valley just over the Coast Range to the east is an important commercial berry-growing region for blueberries, raspberries, and marionberries. See my blueberry pancake recipe below at *evergreen huckleberry.*

Interestingly, recent research has shown that blueberries are not actually blue at all, but only seem that way. The main pigments are anthocyanins, which are dark red. There are tiny structures in the waxy coating that alter the wavelength of the reflected light that we see, making the berries appear blue.

Blue Elderberry *(Sambucus cerulea). Sambucus* is a Latin word for a player of the sambuca, an ancient harp-like musical instrument.

Perhaps it refers to the pinnate leaf of the elderberry. (I am sure it is unrelated to the Italian anise-flavored liquor of that name, but the origin of its Latin name might be interesting to explore further.) Cerulea comes from the Latin word caeruleus, meaning dark blue.

The blue elderberry is more common east of the coast mountain ranges, but may occasionally be found along the northern Oregon Coast. The birds seem to like them. Because elderberries are so prolific on the bush, elderberry wine has been made. However, it is a tricky process as the seeds are poisonous to humans. One also hears of elderberry blossom wine, more common in Appalachia than in Oregon.

Evergreen Huckleberry *(Vaccinium ovatum)*. The origin of *vaccinium* in Latin is somewhat obscure. It is <u>not</u> the same as *vaccinia*, pertaining to the cowpox virus that led to the vaccine for small pox, but may have a related origin in the Indo-European language family. Huckleberry is a corruption of the Old English hurtle berry or whortleberry.

If you like blueberry pancakes, you will *love* huckleberry pancakes, as huckleberries have a more intense flavor. Huckleberry bushes bear well in open forests, where they get some shade, or in forest openings. Bushes under dense forest cover tend to have few berries. But they thrive in open areas as well, especially in the coastal fog belt. On the southern Oregon Coast, seemingly identical bushes may bear small black huckleberries or larger blue huckleberries, which are milder, juicier, and easier to pick. The berries tend to last on the bush well into the fall; you may still be able to find some on a late October trip. Like blueberries, huckleberries are rich in powerful phytochemicals and antioxidants.

My recipe for the best pancakes
you will ever bake over your campfire:

Here is my recipe for the best pancakes you will ever bake over your campfire. For a larger family, you can double the recipe; any leftover pancakes can be saved for a few days in refrigeration for future breakfasts or snacks – cold huckleberry pancakes rolled up with powdered sugar or marionberry jam are really tasty.

<u>Huckleberry or Blueberry Pancakes</u>

Whole wheat flour	1/4 cup	(For healthy fiber)
Cornmeal	1/4 cup	(For crunchy texture)
White flour	1/4 cup	(For necessary gluten)
Buckwheat flour	1/4 cup	(For extra flavor)
Huckleberries*	1 cup	(For flavor and antioxidants)
Egg	1	
Buttermilk**	1 cup	
Baking powder	3/4 tsp	
Baking soda	1/2 tsp	
Salt	1/2 tsp or less	
Vegetable oil***	1-2 tablespoons	

Beat the egg, add the buttermilk and mix together. (If you are making pancakes at home, you can separate the egg and beat the white to fold in at the end for fluffier pancakes.) In a separate bowl, combine the dry ingredients, mixing well. If you are camping, it might be easiest to pre-mix a recipe of the dry ingredients at home, but keep the container well sealed. Note that this recipe has no added sugar.

Pour the liquids into the dry ingredients and mix sparingly; too much mixing affects the gluten and leads to a tough pancake. A few lumps are ok, they will disappear during baking. Correct the texture if needed with buttermilk or flour so you have a batter, not a dough or a liquid. Lastly, add the oil and huckleberries and fold them in quickly. Bake to a golden brown on medium heat, turning when bubbles reach the surface. Serve with butter, chopped and toasted pecans, crushed strawberries, and maple syrup. (You may have seen huckleberry syrup in shops: that is also a good choice.)

*Huckleberries and blueberries are interchangeable in this recipe. Pick the largest and ripest huckleberries you can find; the larger blue ones are best. Other kinds of berries are too squishy and will fall apart in the batter and stain it purple. If you use frozen blueberries from the store, it is best to thaw them first in warm water: otherwise you will end up with raw batter next to the berries in the pancake. If you can't find a whole cup of huckleberries, toss them in anyway.

**It should be buttermilk: low-fat is fine. Milk just doesn't give the right texture or flavor. A mixture of plain yoghurt and milk will work also, but not quite as well.

***More oil for a metal pan, less for non-stick pan or griddle.

Himalayan Blackberry (*Rubus armeniacus*). The Latin species name clearly relates to the plant's origin in Armenia, where it is native: apparently the plants were originally imported into the United States from India.

These are the blackberries you will see in dense thickets alongside the roads, in fields, and even in park settings. Since their introduction a century and a half ago, they have become highly invasive, and are extremely difficult to eradicate. That said, they do provide both food and protective thickets for wildlife. Arching blackberry canes can grow 10 to 20 feet in a year and take root wherever they touch the ground. Himalayas are large, tasty blackberries that make excellent blackberry jelly, but are too soft and too seedy for a good pie. Just be careful not to stumble into the briar patch, as you will need a friend to pull you out.

Oregon Grape *(Mahonia aquafilium)*. Mahonia may sound Latin, but the name simply honors Bernard McMahon, one of the scientists on the Lewis and Clark expedition. *Aquifoliaceae* is the Latin term for the holly family, although they are not related.

There are three varieties of the Oregon grape, the Oregon state flower. Where ranges overlap they tend to hybridize, so they are hard to tell apart. *Mahonia aquafolium* is the "tall Oregon grape", which I have mainly seen along the coast. It has a beautiful yellow flower in the spring, which produces clusters of small, blue, grape-like berries on a bush with holly-like leaves. It seems that prickly leaves provide good protection from browsing animals both in Europe and America. They are said to be edible, but all you get is a skin, a little tart juice, and a lot of seeds that aren't good for you anyway. So leave them to the birds.

Pacific Yew *(Taxus brevifolia.)* Taxus goes at as far back as the Ancient Greek word for bow; brevifolia refers to the short needles.

The yew is the only conifer with a red berry fruit. Stay away from them. You may see birds eating them, but the seeds inside are very toxic to humans, especially children. Apparently birds that eat them are able to spit out the poisonous seeds or pass them through, whereas humans are likely to chew them up and release the poison. Unfortunately, the bright red berry looks a bit like the red huckleberry, and the plants may be found together.

Pacific yew – a highly toxic red berry to avoid

Pacific yew is a stunted needle-bearing tree that grows mainly in the understory, like the red huckleberry. It has become famous in recent years because of the cancer-fighting chemical taxol, found in the bark. Fortunately for the sparse yew tree population, taxol has been successfully simulated in the lab.

Poison Oak (Pacific poison oak), *(Toxicodendron diversilobum).*
Here the full Latin name says it all: a poisonous plant with lobed
leaves.

Both the leaves and the small, white berry of the poison oak bush
or vine are contact poisonous and must be not be touched. I include
it here just as a warning to parents of foraging children, as poison
oak often grows right along with edible berries. All parts of the
plant, even the gray stem, carry the toxic oil urushiol that causes a
severe skin rash. Keep your dog away from infested areas, as they
can carry the toxin on their fur. Some people are immune to the
toxin, but the immunity may wear off with age. Remember the old
adage: *Leaves of three, let it be.* On the Oregon Coast, poison oak
grows either as a bush or as a trailing vine. The leaves are shiny and
green, sometimes reddish. Unfortunately, poison oak can be a very
pretty vine as it climbs in trees and shrubs. I encourage taking a
good illustrated field guide along if you aren't familiar with the
plant, or look up an image on your cell phone. If you think you may
have brushed against some poison oak plants, it is best to wash the
affected area immediately with soap and water. If you do get a poison oak rash, the doctor might recommend a soothing lotion. For a
severe rash, doctors can prescribe more effective treatments.

Red Elderberry *(Sambucus racemosa).* *Sambucus* is a Latin word
for a player of the sambuca, an ancient harp-like musical instrument.
Perhaps the pinnate leaf of the elderberry bush reminded the namer
of that instrument. Or not. *Racemosa* comes from Latin *racemose* "of
a flower cluster", which in this case is descriptive as the white flowers are quite showy.

A favorite food of the wild bandtail pigeons and other birds, the
red elderberry has a bitter taste and is mildly toxic to humans. It is
said that red elderberries can be used for jelly, but I have tried it and
found the jelly to be bitter and not worth making. The bushes contain
cyanide-producing toxins; perhaps that is the reason. But it is great
fun to see a flock of bandtail pigeons attack a loaded elderberry bush.

Red Huckleberry *(Vaccinium parvifolium)*. *Parvifolium* is from Latin *parvifolius* meaning small leaf.

Commonly found in the understory in shady, forested areas, this delicious, tart berry is extremely high in vitamin C. The berry looks like a large salmon egg and might even be used as bait for the cut-throat trout in the small coastal streams, or you can just toss them in and watch for the trout rise to take them. Red huckleberry leaves are small, light green, flat and fuzzy, rather than shiny and curved like the evergreen huckleberry.

Redflower Currant *(Ribes sanguineum)*. *Sanguineum* is the Latin word for blood-red – obviously describing the flower, not the fruit.

The currant of western Oregon is a small bush with a lovely red flower, but the blue-black berry is seedy, rather tasteless and hardly worth eating. This currant is not the source of the dried currants you buy for fruitcake – those are actually tiny raisins. That name came from the Greek "Corinth", an area west of Athens from where the tiny raisins were once imported.

Salal *(Gaultheria shallon)*. The genus name Gaultheria honors the 18th century Quebecois physician Jean Francois Gaultier. *Shallon* was derived from the Chinook word for salal.

You may recognize the salal brush from the florist shops, where it may be sold as lemon leaf, which it closely resembles, and added to floral bouquets. It is very common all along the Oregon Coast and Coast Range, in both sunny and shady areas. The berry is juicy but rather bland. As they ripen late and hang on the bush into the fall, they were an important addition to the Native American diet, both fresh and as component of pemmican. Unlike so many of the Oregon berries, the salal bush is not thorny.

Salmon Berry *(Rubus spectabilus)*. Spectabilis is Latin for (1) visible or (2) notable, admirable, worth seeing. In my opinion, not very descriptive of the rather ordinary salmon berry – but you don't see many orange berries. Perhaps the namer was referring to the red blossoms.

You will find salmon berries in many moist, shady coastal locations and along streams, as they prefer wet soils. The berries grow on a cane very similar to raspberries, to which they must be closely related. Whether orange (salmon-egg colored) or red, they make a sweet, juicy snack, but don't cook well.

Snowberry *(Symphoricarpus albus)*. Symphoricarpus is derived from the Ancient Greek words sumphorein, to bear together, and karpos, meaning fruit. One Latin meaning of *albus* is "white", as in albino.

This pretty white berry will be found in much of the Pacific Northwest, the Rocky Mountains, and occasionally along the Oregon Coast. You may recognize it as an ornamental shrub; the berries tend to hang on the branches through the winter, hence their common name. Because of their long season, snowberries are eaten by many wild animals and birds. However, snowberries contain saponins and can be mildly toxic to humans. You should leave them on the bush for the birds; they aren't very good anyway.

Thimbleberry *(Rubus parviflorus)*. *Parviflorus*, Latin for having small flowers. Not very imaginative.

This is a delicious, spicy berry that grows in wet, forested areas all over the Western U.S, the Upper Midwest, and western Canada. It actually does look like a small red thimble when it is ripe. Like raspberries and salmonberries, the thimbleberry grows on a vertical cane, but it is thornless. I have seen thimbleberries in several of the scenic vistas along Hwy 101. It is unusual to find enough thimbleberries for the purpose, but they can be cooked with a little water and then strained to make an outstanding syrup to pour over vanilla ice cream.

Trailing Blackberry (*Rubus ursinus*). *Ursinus,* Latin for bear. Presumably a favorite food for the local black bears.

Locally known simply as wild blackberry, this is the king of wild berries along the Oregon Coast. There are subspecies up and down the Pacific coast, from Baja California to British Columbia and inland to Montana that look and taste much alike. The fruit is sparse so it takes an hour or two to pick enough for a pie – if you have a good patch – but it is well worth the effort, especially if you have youngsters to do the picking. Wild blackberries freeze well and also make an excellent jam. Compared to domestic blackberries, the flavor is more intense and the seeds are much smaller. The berries are black when ripe, first going from green through red and purple colors. You will find the unripe red blackberries to have a delightfully tart flavor. (Or maybe you have to grow up eating them!) The wild blackberry is one of the ancestors of the commercial marionberry and boysenberry cultivars, having been interbred with the loganberry, the Himalayan blackberry, and the olallieberry.

Western Wild Cucumber (*Marah oregonus*). Marah comes from the Hebrew word mara, meaning bitter. *Oregonus* of course simply refers to the state of Oregon, where it grows well.

This isn't a berry, of course; I include it here just so you won't be tempted to eat one: <u>the entire plant is toxic</u>. It grows most everywhere where there is good sun and moisture. The small round cucumber looks familiar but it isn't fleshy like the domestic salad cucumber. The fruit is but a prickly skin holding a couple of large seeds. Although unrelated to the domestic cucumber, its leaves and viny growth habit are much the same. The whole plant has a bitter taste, as is suggested by the genus name. Native Americans living along the coast are said to have had medicinal uses for the wild cucumber, mainly as poultices. I don't know how effective it was.

Woodland Strawberry (*Fragaria vesca*). Fragaria comes from the Latin fragans, meaning odorous, apparently referring to the perfumed flesh of the berry. Vesca is Latin for thin or attenuated. The common name strawberry is derived from old English – did they grow them in beds of straw?

You will find the wild strawberry all along the West Coast of the United States and in the mountain meadows. I have picked them on Kayak Island, Alaska; high in the Canadian Rockies; and in the Oregon coastal meadows. They thrive in any grassy area along the coast, even on the exposed bluffs. Don't pass them up, as they are sweet and delicious even though tiny. The term "woodland" is an unfortunate misnomer: they are mainly found in sunny meadows.

Chapter 21

Favorite Wildflowers

There are far too many wildflower varieties along the Oregon coast for me to cover in this book. You can find detailed descriptions and flower identification guides in the *Audubon Field Guide to the Pacific Northwest* and Philip Munz's *Introduction to Shore Wildflowers of California, Oregon, and Washington*. I only wish here to draw attention to a few spectacular local wildflowers you are likely to encounter. These are some of my favorites: one white, one coral, one pink, one blue, one purple, one yellow, one red, and one orange.

These are some of my favorites: one white, one coral, one pink, one blue, one purple, one yellow, one red, and one orange.

Ocean Spray *(Holodiscus discolor)*

Found in forested areas in the all of the western United States, ocean spray is a snow-white flowering bush that really does resemble its name.

Western Azalea *(Rhododendron Occidentale)*

This flowering bush may be found along the coast and coastal mountains in northwestern California and southwestern Oregon, blooming from April to June. The lovely blooms are mainly white, but with reddish buds and a coral-hued center. Unlike the commercial azalea, which is an Asian import, the western azalea has a delightful aroma. Azalea bushes are most likely to be seen in open, brushy areas along the coast. Azalea Park in Brookings features huge azalea bushes said to be 150 years old; it is a place to visit during the spring.

Pacific Rhododendron *(Rhododendron macrophyllum)*

The Pacific rhododendron may be found in both forested and brushy areas along the Pacific coast; it is the state flower of Washington where it grows in abundance. Blooming in the spring, the huge pink flower clusters can be spectacular. It is but one of hundreds of species of rhododendron, most of which are native to southern Asia, where the commercial rhododendron originates.

Ceanothus, or Wild Lilac *(Ceanothus sp.)*

Along the southwestern Oregon coast, wild lilac bushes can blanket entire hillsides with their pale blue, lilac-like flowers. Around Brookings, I have seen the bushes exceeding twenty feet in height, but they more often occur as a smaller shrub. Wild lilac bushes often colonize burnt or logged areas, where their nitrogen-fixing behavior helps to enrich the soil. There are several closely-related species living in the coastal mountain ranges and along the coast, in shades of dark to pale blue.

Oregon Iris *(Iris tenax)*

Wild irises grow all over the United States, and in Europe and Asia as well; each area has its own variety and species name. The iris is mentioned in the Bible, the Torah, and the Quran, and yields girl's names in each culture. Along the Oregon coast a small, purple variety grows abundantly in the coastal meadows.

Oregon Grape *(Mahonia aquifolium)*

Oregon's state flower has beautiful lemon-yellow flowers in the spring and bunches of small grape-like berries in the summer. The small, blue berries are said to be edible, but you probably won't want to eat more than one. Despite its green prickly leaves it is unrelated to English holly.

Salmon Berry *(Rubus spectabilis)*

Except for the European poppy, red wildflowers are not easy to find; salmon berry is one that is found here. It grows as raspberry-like canes in moist, shaded areas, particularly along streams. The berry may also be red, but salmon-egg orange is more common.

Tiger Lily *(Lilium lancifolium)*

The tiger lily is a visitor that has gone wild. Native to China, Korea, and Japan, this beautiful orange lily has been planted in gardens all around our country and has spread as a garden escapee into the surrounding areas and far into the countryside. They prefer sunny to semi-shady areas with moist soil. In the early spring, you may also see brilliant orange California poppies blooming in the coastal meadows, but not in the profusion that occurs in the high deserts of southern California.

Chapter 22

Emergency Care

Astoria: Columbia Memorial Hospital, 2111 Exchange Avenue, Astoria, (503) 325-4321. Emergency room open 24 hours.

Bandon: Southern Coos Hospital and Health Care, 900 11th Street SE, Bandon, (541) 347-2426. Emergency room open 24 hours.

Brookings: Curry Medical Center Emergency Care, 500 5th Street, Brookings, (541) 412-6960. Emergency room open 24 hours.

Cannon Beach: Providence Cannon Beach Clinic, 171 N Larch Street #16, Cannon Beach, (503) 717-7400. Hours M-F 8:00am to 5.30pm. For after-hours care go to Providence Seaside Hospital in Seaside.

Charleston: No local medical services. Go to Bay Area Hospital, 1775 Thomson Road, Coos Bay, (541) 269-8111.

Coos Bay: Bay Area Hospital, 1775 Thomson Road, Coos Bay, (541) 269-8111. Emergency room open 24 hours.

Depoe Bay: No local emergency services. Go to Samaritan North Lincoln Hospital, 3043 NE 28th Street, Lincoln City, (541) 994-3661. Emergency room open 24 hours.

Florence: PeaceHealth Peace Harbor Medical Center, 400 9th St, Florence, (541) 947-8412. Emergency room open 24 hours.

Coquille: Coquille Valley Hospital, 940 E 5th Street, (541) 395-3101. Emergency room open 24 hours.

Gardiner: No local medical services. During business hours, go to Lower Umpqua Hospital, 600 Ranch Road, Reedsport, (541) 271-2171, open M-F 8:00am - 4:00pm

                   For after-hours care, go to PeaceHealth Peace Harbor Medical Center, 400 9th St, Florence, (541) 947-8412. Emergency room open 24 hours.

Garibaldi: No local medical services. Go to Adventist Health Tillamook, 1000 3d Street, Tillamook, (541) 842-4444. Emergency room open 24 hours.

Gearhart: No local medical services. Go to Providence Seaside Hospital, 725 S Wahanna Road, Seaside, (503) 717-7000. Emergency room open 24 hours.

Gold Beach: Curry General Hospital, 94220 4th Street, Gold Beach, (541) 247-3000. Emergency room open 24 hours.

Lakeside: No local medical services. Go to Bay Area Hospital, 1775 Thomson Road, Coos Bay, (541) 269-8111. Emergency room open 24 hours.

Langlois: No local medical services. Go to Southern Coos Hospital and Health Care, 900 11th Street SE, Bandon, (541) 347-2426. Emergency room open 24 hours.

Lincoln City: Samaritan North Lincoln Hospital, 3043 NE 28th Street, Lincoln City, (541) 994-3661. Emergency room open 24 hours.

Neskowin: No local medical services. Go to Samaritan North Lincoln Hospital, 3043 NE 28th Street, Lincoln City, (541) 994-3661. Emergency room open 24 hours.

………

Netarts: No local medical services. Go to Adventist Health Tillamook, 1000 3d Street, Tillamook, (541) 842-4444. Emergency room open 24 hours.

Newport: Samaritan Pacific Community Hospital, 930 SW Abbey Street, (541) 265-2244. Emergency room open 24 hours.

Manhattan Beach: No local medical services. Go to Adventist Health Tillamook, 1000 3d Street, Tillamook, (541) 842-4444. Emergency room open 24 hours.

Manzanita: No local medical services. Go to Adventist Health Tillamook, 1000 3d Street, Tillamook, (541) 842-4444. Emergency room open 24 hours.

North Bend: Bay Area Hospital, 1775 Thomson Road, Coos Bay, (541) 269-8111. Emergency room open 24 hours.

Oceanside: No local medical services. Go to Adventist Health Tillamook, 1000 3d Street, Tillamook, (541) 842-4444. Emergency room open 24 hours.

Otter Rock: No local medical services. Go to Samaritan Pacific Community Hospital, 930 SW Abbey Street, (541) 265-2244. Emergency room open 24 hours.

Pacific City: No local medical services. Go to Adventist Health Tillamook, 1000 3d Street, Tillamook, (541) 842-4444. Emergency room open 24 hours.

Reedsport: Lower Umpqua Hospital, 600 Ranch Road, Reedsport, (541) 271-2171. Open M-F 8:00am - 4:00pm.

For after-hours care go to PeaceHealth Peace Harbor Medical Center, 400 9th Street, Florence, (541) 947-8412. Emergency room open 24 hours.

Rockaway Beach: No local medical services. Go to Adventist Health Tillamook, 1000 3d Street, Tillamook, (541) 842-4444. Emergency room open 24 hours.

Seaside: Providence Seaside Hospital, 725 S Wahanna Road, Seaside, (503) 717-7000. Emergency room open 24 hours.

Tillamook: Adventist Health Tillamook, 1000 3d Street, Tillamook, (541) 842-4444. Emergency room open 24 hours.

Waldport: Samaritan Waldport Clinic, 920 SW Range Drive, (541) 563-2197. Hours M-F 8:30am - 5:00pm

                  For after-hours care go to Samaritan Pacific Community Hospital, 930 SW Abbey Street, Newport, (541) 265-2244. Emergency room open 24 hours.

Warrenton: No local medical services. Go to Columbia Memorial Hospital, 2111 Exchange Avenue, Astoria, (503) 325-4321. Emergency room open 24 hours.

Wheeler: Limited local medical services. Go to Adventist Health Tillamook, 1000 3d Street, Tillamook, (541) 842-4444. Emergency room open 24 hours.

Winchester Bay: No local medical services. During business hours, go to Lower Umpqua Hospital, 600 Ranch Road, Reedsport, (541) 271-2171.

                  For after-hours care, go to PeaceHealth Peace Harbor Medical Center, 400 9th St, Florence, (541) 947-8412. Emergency room open 24 hours.

Yachats: No local medical services. Go to Samaritan Pacific Community Hospital, 930 SW Abbey Street, Newport, (541) 265-2244. Emergency room open 24 hours.

Chapter 23

Oregon Coast Publications

One does not write about the magnificent Oregon Coast in a vacuum. There are many excellent books available in shops, bookstores, or to be found online that deal with various aspects of Oregon's 360 mile coastline. I list a selection of them below from my library shelves, in alphabetical order by title. I have gained valuable insights from each for this volume, and thank the authors, who have invested so much time and energy in their research and documentation. The Oregon Coast is a broad subject, seen differently by different observers. Consequently, there is surprisingly little overlap in these publications. You can purchase a small collection of them that suits your interests for less than the price of a meal for the family, and your small traveling library will enhance any vacation you take in the area. In the summaries that follow, I have suggested whether each book is one to take along, to read beforehand, or to keep at home as reminders of the wonderful memories of your trip. You will find in the following section the formal references you will need to order the books in the library or bookstore.

Here are the books:

1. *Beach Placers on the Oregon Coast* by J. T. Pardee. This 41 page Department of Interior publication from 1934 gives a fascinating account of mining the beaches and sandy marine terraces for gold and platinum. You may have noticed black mineral sand layers on the beaches of the southern coast, especially around the mouth of the Rogue River. They still contain very small amounts of these metals. You can pan the black sands and recover some, but don't expect to pay for your vacation with your earnings. Interestingly, the main minerals in the black sands are magnetite, ilmenite, and chromite –

valuable ores of iron, titanium, and chromium where found in larger quantities. (If you have a gold pan, take this book along.)

2. *Beautiful America's Oregon Coast* by Linda Stirling and Larry Geddis. A fine 80-page full-color pictorial and text tour of the Oregon Coast. (Memories)

3. *Beautiful Oregon Coast* by Paul Lewis and multiple photographers. This thin, magazine-sized volume was published in 1977 in the days of Kodachrome film. A few of the images open up to the full 11 by 16 inch size of the book. It is long out of print, but if you happen to see a copy in a used book store, pick it up and enjoy the glorious scenery photographs. (Memories)

4. *Between Pacific Tides* by Edward F. Rickets and Jack Calvin. This classic 500-page treatise describes and analyzes everything you might find in the tide pools, clinging to the rocks in the surf zone, or hiding in the mud, from San Diego to Cape Flattery. It was published originally in 1939 and revised every few years until 1992, when the fifth edition was published. I own the 1960 third edition with a foreword by John Steinbeck. The book is conveniently organized by environmental zone: protected outer coast, open coast, sandy beaches, bays and estuaries, eelgrass, and mudflats. My 1960 edition has 383 black and white photographs and sketches of seashore life. (Take along especially for tide pool exploration.)

5. *Birds of Oregon, a General Reference* by David Marshall, Matthew Hunter, Alan Contreras, and around 100 contributing authors. For serious birders and amateur ornithologists, this 704 page volume will be very useful with its many line drawings and range maps. It covers the 353 species now known to occur regularly in Oregon and another 133 species that are occasional visitors to the state. (If you are a serious birder, take this volume along with your binoculars. For casual bird identification, the excellent color photographs in the *Audubon Guide* may be more useful.)

6. *Birds of Oregon, a Field Guide* by Stan Tekiela. A somewhat abbreviated field guide to the more common birds you might see. The range maps are quite good. Birds with different-appearing sexes are

illustrated separately, a nice feature. This pocket-sized book has the advantage of sorting the birds by color for ease of identification, but leaves out many key species, especially those living along the shore. For instance, only two of the many gull species are included and the seabirds living on the offshore rocks are given short shrift. Band-tailed pigeons, one of my favorite woodland birds, was left out. (A good general guide to have along.)

7. *Buzz, Sting, Bite* by Ann Sverdrup-Thygeson. Only somewhat focused on her native Norway, Sverdrup-Thygeson's informative book has been expertly translated into English. Of course you can't cover the whole insect world in 200 pages, but this book does a fine job of explaining the importance of insects in our world, the dangers they face, and the role they play at the bottom of the macroscopic food chain we depend on. Her chapter on "insects as janitors" could easily be describing the function of insects in the litter and soil of our own Pacific rainforest, where they help reduce vegetal debris to soil and at the same time provide a juicy meal for those willing to scratch for it: birds, raccoons, skunks, shrews, and many others. (A good read whether or not you visit the Oregon Coast.)

8. *By the Shore* by Nancy Blakey. Although Nancy Blakey is a Washington author living on an island in Puget Sound, her book covers family activities to enjoy all along the coast from Vancouver Island, Canada, to Depoe Bay, Oregon. It is the only book in my collection that contains directions for preparing and cooking the seafood you might be fortunate enough to catch, harvest, or find in the market. Most of the seafood varieties are found in Oregon as well as Washington and British Columbia. She covers the catching and preparation of salmon, squid, clams, oysters, crabs, and shrimp. I have tried some of her 17 tempting recipes and they are really good! Think *Sunday Salmon Chowder* or *Campfire Paella with Squid*. (Take along, especially if you have small children.)

9. *Camping Oregon: A Comprehensive Guide to Public Tent and RV Campgrounds* by Rhonda and George Ostertag. The authors cover 105 campgrounds along the coast and in the nearby Coast Range

and Klamath Mountains. The main campgrounds are also covered in Oregon Camping (below) but each has some campgrounds that the other does not. (Campers will want to take this guide along.)

10. *Celebrating the Siuslaw, a Century of Growth* by Ward Tonsfeldt, PhD. This is an interesting historical review of the Siuslaw National forest area, covering the central Oregon coast from Coos Bay to Tillamook. Its 242 pages discuss not only the early history of the central coast and its colonization but also the various aspects of managing a great national forest. A well-illustrated chapter shows the history of logging practices, from buck saws to chain saws, and from steam donkey engines to modern Caterpillar machinery. (Interesting background reading.)

11. *Chetco* by Michael W. Adams and 39 "principle collaborators". Chetco is a 476-page, 10x12 inch compendium of the history of the Brookings-Harbor and Chetco Valley area and the families who lived there, from the time of the Native Americans to its publication date in 2011. It contains a wonderful collection of archival black-and-white photographs dating to the late nineteenth century, long before the town of Brookings was established. (I haven't found it in book shops, but you can see a copy at the Chetco Valley Museum in Harbor.)

12. *Coastal Oregon* by Judy Jewell and W. C. McRae. This is a fine travel book, covering the towns along the coast. Restaurants, lodging, and activities are covered as in the AAA guide, but in far more detail. For instance, Jewell and McRae's book devotes six pages to the small town of Port Orford, while the AAA TourBook book gives it less than a column. (Take along)

13. *Crossings: McCullough's Coastal Bridges* by Judy Fleagle and Richard Knox Smith. There are three editions of this locally-published book: pocket size, book size, and coffee table size. The bridge engineer Conde B. McCullough designed and oversaw the construction of iconic bridges crossing six of the largest estuaries on the Oregon coast: Rogue River, Coos Bay, Yaquina Bay, Alsea Bay, Siuslaw River, and Umpqua River. As writers and researchers, Fleagle and

Smith have put together a loving account of the planning and construction of these bridges in the 1930s, some ninety years ago. Numerous excellent black-and-white photographs enhance their account. They focus particularly on the Siuslaw River Bridge in Florence, where the authors both live. (Read, take along, and read again.)

14. *Curious Kids Nature Guide* by Fiona Cohen. If you are taking children on a car trip on the Oregon Coast, Fiona Cohen's book provides a great introduction to the wildlife they should be watching for. The thin book is a virtual biology lesson, revealing interesting, little-known facts about the plants and animals they will see. Did you know that some lichens that live on tree branches can take nitrogen from the air, then fertilize the host tree when they fall to the ground and decay? Or that cockles can move with a pole-vaulting like motion when threatened by a sun star? Marni Fylling's numerous wildlife illustrations are both accurate and beautiful. (First read this book to your children, then take it along.)

15. *The Curious World of Seaweeds* by Josie Iselin, 2019. The author is an artist-turned-botanist, and as such sees the beauty of the seaweeds she photographs and writes about. What's more, she is able to describe them in non-scientific terms. As you might expect, her book is lovingly illustrated as well as informative. Of the dozens of seaweeds and sea grasses that grow along the Oregon Coast, Iselin devotes a chapter to each of sixteen you will want to watch for on the beach, on the rocks at low tide, or in the tide pools. This focus allows her to delve into great detail, both of the seaweed species and of seaweed in general. However, she paints a grim picture of the existential problems the seaweeds are facing today, related to overgrazing by purple sea urchins after the loss of their sunflower star predators, and the unfortunate extermination of sea otters that find sea urchins the staff of life. (Read before you go to help appreciate the biology of the eastern Pacific Ocean, but the seaweeds Iselin describes may already be gone.)

16. *Day Hiking Oregon Coast* by Bonnie Henderson. This illustrated

book describes and maps 125 separate hikes. It is devoted exclusively to the hikes, beaches, headlands and the rugged scenery of the Oregon coast. The coastal mountains and rivers are not covered. Difficulty, distance, path surface, and elevation gain are listed for each hike, as well as a paragraph or two describing of the things you are likely to see. A useful table of the 92 hikes shows for each hike distance, difficulty, dog rules, tidepools, whale-watching, notable forests, wildflowers, historical points of interest, and the presence of sand dunes. Maps are included for each hike. (Take along if you are a hiker.)

17. *Full-Rip 9.0* by Sandi Doughton. This volume is a really impressive work of investigative reporting by a science reporter for the Seattle Times. It is well worth reading for its own sake as an important geology lesson. The book documents earthquakes and tsunamis in the fairly recent past in the Pacific Northwest, and tells us (frightenly) what we might expect in the future along the Oregon and Washington coasts. The book investigates in great detail the evidence for a great subduction-fault earthquake along the coastline in January, 1700 – dated to the day and hour by Japanese historical records of the resulting orphan Tsunami! (Read)

18. *Hiking Oregon's Geology* by Ellen Morris Bishop. Although this book covers hikes in the whole state, nine of the hikes are along the coast and three more just a few miles inland, possibly beyond the coastal weather. The rock exposures and geologic history on each hike are nicely explained. From the cover: *"Hiking Oregon's Geology should be in every hiker's backpack – and on the bookshelf or in the glove box of anyone interested in the marvels of Oregon's diverse, colorful landscape."* Hike distance, elevation gain, and degree of difficulty are listed for each hike. A few of the hikes are inland, covering geological outcrops along the coastal rivers and mountains. (Take along if you are a serious hiker.)

19. *History of Fishing on the Siuslaw* by Trygve O. Nordahl. This delightful 24-page pamphlet documents both the history of fishing on the Siuslaw River but also the serial decline of fish populations

over Nordahl's 70-year career. Interestingly, Nordahl never recognizes the role of overfishing in the decline of fish stocks. (Great reading if you are a fisherman.)

20. *Holy Rollers: Murder and Madness in Oregon's Love Cult* by T. McCracken and Robert B. Blodgett. Although only peripherally related to early happenings in Yachats and Waldport, I found it a fascinating and meticulously researched account of the Holy Rollers religious cult and its effects on western Oregon in the first decade of the twentieth century. (Take along for something to read after dinner.)

21. *Indian Life on the Northwest Coast of North America, as Seen by the Early Explorers during the Last Decades of the Eighteenth Century* by Erna Gunther. This well-researched volume, based on ships' logs, museum displays, and early publications, provides the best picture extant of the native societies from Nootka Sound on Vancouver Island south to the Columbia River. This volume is currently available only in libraries. (Read on your return.)

22. *In Search of Ancient Oregon* by Ellen Morris Bishop. This book is a beautifully illustrated journey through 400 million years of Oregon's geologic history. Fully half of the book's 288 pages are devoted to the author's magnificent photographs of the rock formations that were deposited in each of the geologic ages she describes. Although not focused on the Oregon Coast, there are sections on the complex tectonic origin of the Klamath Mountains of southwestern Oregon and the origin of the basalt flows that form many of the coastal promontories. She also covers the ancient history of subduction zone earthquakes along the Oregon and Washington coast, a subject covered more fully in the recent book *Full-Rip 9.0* by Sandi Doughton. (Read)

23. *Insider's Guide to the Oregon Coast, 4th edition*, by Lizann Dunegan. A detailed guide to everything you might want to do on an Oregon Coast vacation: shopping, quaint lodging, restaurants, attractions, golfing, and night life. This 222 page volume covers in more detail what the AAA TourBook mentions so briefly – and goes

well beyond. Lizann Dunegan has also written several books on hiking in Oregon. (Take along)

24. *Lost Treasure Ships of the Oregon Coast* by Theodore Schellhase. Schellhase's 176 page book presents good research on early ships that might have passed by the Oregon Coast. Some may have foundered on the shore; others may have landed there for water or trading with the locals. A few likely drifted there from the Orient on the North Pacific Current (Kuroshio Current extension) and subsequently washed up on the beach. Evidence comes from a variety of sources, all well researched: historical records, ship logs, survivors' accounts, and interestingly the items found by beachcombers over the last two centuries. A large part is devoted to old reports and narratives by the local citizens: beachcombers, Native Americans, historians – and treasure seekers. If you are interested in digging further into the subject, this volume gives you a head start, with more than 150 references, some a century old, including books and newspaper articles. (Read when you get home.)

25. *Lifting Oregon Out of the Mud – Building the Oregon Coast Highway*, by Joe R. Blakely. A short but interesting review on the building of the coast highway, the road that tied the Oregon Coast together. This is the highway you have been driving. It has chapters covering funding, construction, and building the iconic bridges and many historic black-and-white photographs from the era 90 years ago when it was happening. There really was a lot of mud. (Read when you get home.)

26. *Making Wawa* by George Lang. In 200 pages, the author investigates all the possible sources and influences of Chinuk Wawa, the early lingua franca of the Pacific Northwest. It makes for fascinating reading. (Read when you get home. Except for on the Grande Ronde Reservation, you won't find the language spoken anywhere.)

27. *National Audubon Society Field Guide to the Pacific Northwest* by Peter Alden and seven co-authors. This pocket book is a beautifully illustrated guide covering plant and animal life in the forests, deserts, and waters of Oregon and Washington. Some 950 animals

and plants are described, each with a small color illustration. As you will suspect from this publisher, bird species are particularly well represented: 28 pages are devoted to the waterfowl you may see in the estuaries and along the coast. A well-drawn relief map is found inside the back cover. (Take along, especially if you are a birder.)

28. *A Natural History of Western Trees* by Donald Culross Peattie. At 751 pages, this volume tells us just about everything we wanted to know about the trees in the western United States when it was published in 1950. The copyright was renewed some twenty years later by Noel Peattie and a nice introduction added for a later printing in 1991, but there is no indication that the text was updated either time. The book is beautifully, even romantically, written and interesting to read, but it focuses more on the timber industry and the many uses of the trees than on their biology or environmental significance. For instance, the chapter of the Douglas-fir (modern spelling indicating it is not a true fir of the Abies genus) is fifteen pages long, covering mainly the "common" Douglas fir. Two of the pages are devoted to the bigcone Douglas-fir subspecies of Southern California. No mention is made of the ecological importance of either tree or the uses made by the local Native Americans. By contrast, *Northwest Trees* devotes only seven pages to the Douglas-fir and the subspecies but includes good discussions of both these subjects. For tree identification, the Audubon field guide covers it in a third of a page with a good color photograph. (Read at home.)

29. *Northwest Trees* by Stephen F. Arno and Ramona P. Hammerly. Although published in black-and white, this volume contains several truly phenomenal ink drawings of each tree. As it covers the entire Pacific Northwest – Oregon, Washington, Idaho, western Montana, and southern British Columbia – many more trees are included than in the *Trees to Know* book described below. *Northwest Trees* is the updated 30th anniversary edition (2007) of the 1977 classic. The book covers 28 Pacific Northwest conifers along with 24 broad-leafed trees. (Take along, particularly if you are traveling through other parts of the magnificent Pacific Northwest.)

30. *Oregon Camping* by Tom Stienstra: The Complete Guide to Tent and RV Camping. Tom Stienstra, outdoor writer emeritus for The San Francisco Chronicle, has written a fine book that is both a how-to-camp manual and an Oregon campground guide. It begins with an excellent 57-page lesson on camping, from what to wear to dealing with grizzly bear attacks. Fortunately, the Oregon coast no longer has grizzly bears; even black bears are a rare sight, and these pose more of a nuisance than a threat. A 64-page section covers 132 campgrounds and RV parks along the coast and in the nearby Coast Range and Klamath Mountains. You may be traveling the coast, but it is important to be aware of the campgrounds a little farther inland, where one can avoid the cold and overcast summer coastal weather, and camp in the sun. They are usually less crowded but may have more mosquitoes. Each campground has a description, directions, and reservation information. Tom makes a special point about adequate sun protection; he has recently published an article in the San Francisco Chronicle about his battle with melanoma, which he blames on his time in the sun. If you are planning to camp anywhere in the West, Tom has likely written a book about the area you are to visit, so it is worth checking. (If you are camping, this is an essential book to take along.)

31. *Oregon Coast* by Rick Schafer, Jack McGowan, and Jan McGowan. This 95-page paperback is a stunning pictorial tour of the Oregon Coast by a skilled photographer. A few of the images open up to the full 9.5 by 19 inch dimension of the open book. It is the first book in the "Magnificent Places" series, and shows well why the Oregon coast deserves to be the first in the series. Descriptive paragraphs "take readers on an exploration of the diverse and dynamic elements that make up this natural wonder." (Memories)

32. *Oregon Coastal Atlas:* www.coastalatlas.net/. This online atlas provides a wealth of information related to your Oregon Coast excursion. (Access as you travel on your laptop, tablet, or mobile phone.)

33. *Oregon Coast & Coast Range: 100 Hikes/Travel Guide, 4ᵗʰ edition*

by William L. Sullivan. This is a splendid guide to hikes along the Oregon Coast, Coast Range, Klamath Mountains, and even the Willamette Valley. In addition to 51 Oregon coastal hikes, some 42 hikes in the nearby mountains and valleys are included. Most of the featured hikes have two or three versions: an easy hike of less than three miles, an intermediate hike of three to six miles, and occasionally a longer, difficult hike that may be up to 40 miles in length with extreme elevation gain. Thirty-five special scenic highlights are briefly described and illustrated in color. Some frequently-encountered shore birds and wildflowers are also illustrated. The book includes descriptions of more than forty coastal inns and quaint hotels of the sort that may not be included in the AAA Guide. Fifty-one "more hikes" are described briefly along with 57 campgrounds. (Take along if you are a hiker.)

34. *Oregon Coast Birding Trail* website: http://www.oregoncoast-birding.com/. This splendid 48 page website contributes a paragraph on each of 173 bird viewing sites along the Oregon Coast and in adjacent Del Norte County, California. Each paragraph includes driving directions and bird species you are likely to encounter there – both shorebirds and various land birds you might see along the access trails. Maps are included. You will need Adobe Acrobat Reader to view the website. A spreadsheet tabulates 136 bird species that are commonly seen in one season or another and another 113 species occasionally or rarely seen. The website is not illustrated, so taking along the Audubon guide or *Birds of Oregon* will be helpful for bird identification. (Birders can access online as they travel; printing it in advance might be helpful as the file is quite large.)

35. *Oregon Coastal Access Guide* by Kenn Oberrecht. This volume is mile-by-mile guide to local history and scenic and recreational attractions, covering the entire coast from to Astoria to Brookings. Fifty-eight "Must Stop Sites" are described, county by county. Twenty-seven coastal golf courses are listed by town and briefly described in the text. One hundred local festivals and events are listed by date, including such marvels *as Oregon Divisional Chainsaw*

Sculpting Contest in Reedsport, *Blessing of the Fleet* in Garibaldi and several county fairs. An eleven-page section on the history of the Oregon coast sets the scene. (Take along, especially if you have time to partake in the local fairs and festivals.)

36. *The Orphan Tsunami of 1700* by Brian J. Atwater *et al*, USGS Professional Paper 1707. This 16-page pamphlet written in English by American and Japanese scientists details the strange tidal wave that struck Japan in the year 1700 and its apparent source in a massive earthquake along the Cascade subduction zone. This pamphlet is a popularized version of *The Orphan Tsunami of 1700* listed below. (Interesting reading at home.)

37. *The Oregon Encyclopedia*. This online encyclopedia published by the Oregon Historical Society has information about virtually everything in Oregon – places, people, history, and events. Access at oregonencyclopedia.org.

38. *Oregon: End of the Trail*. Published in 1940 by a local branch of the WPA, this thick book is a history lesson on tourism in the state and on the fascinating histories of some of the towns – even towns that aren't there anymore. You won't be able to find it in bookstores; I got a copy to read via inter-library loan. (If you are a history buff, check it out.)

39. *Oregon Geology* by Elizabeth and William Orr. This fine volume presents the geology of Oregon in easily understandable terms. It includes chapters on the Oregon Coast Range and the Klamath Mountains, which provide the watershed for most of the coastal rivers as well as the sediment load. The first chapter includes a well-illustrated explanation of the plate tectonic history of coastal Oregon. The volume includes 37 pages on the geology and tectonic history of the Klamath Mountains of southwestern Oregon and Northwestern California, and 35 pages on the Coast Range and continental margin. (Read before you leave home.)

40. *Oregon River Maps & Fishing Guide* by Frank Amato. This oversize magazine-style publication covers 36 of the most important fishing rivers in Oregon, including several coastal streams. For the

fisherman, it is really an essential guide, as it provides excellent maps of each river and estuary along with boating access points on each. Fish species, catching seasons, and tips for catching them are provided as well. (Take along if you are planning to fish.)

41. *Oregon Road Trips – Oregon Coast Edition* by Mike and Kristy Westby. In this new 200-page book, the authors take you on a nine-day, 360-mile journey down the coast from Astoria in the north to Brookings in the south. They have picked lodging, restaurants, museums, and things to see, and they have chosen well in each category. If you have only a week, you can easily skip a couple of towns or cut the journey short on one end or the other. (Take along)

42. *Oregon South Coast Canoe, Kayak, and Standup Paddle Guide* by Ron Wardman and Tom Baake. A detailed guide to the activities in the book title, covering the South Coast of Oregon from the Florence area to the Smith River, just south of the California state line. Estuaries, lower rivers, and coastal lakes are all covered, including maps and put-in points. Such a useful book makes me hope that the authors are continuing their thorough investigations on the central and northern Oregon Coast. (Take along if you have a watercraft.)

44. *Oregon TourBook* by AAA Publishing. Like all AAA tourbooks, this thin volume provides brief but detailed and accurate information on hotels, restaurants, attractions, and activities organized by town. As it is focused on the entire state, each coastal town receives only a few entries, but the motel and restaurant recommendations have been checked out by AAA and may not be featured elsewhere in these books. (Take along for reliable motel and restaurant listings.)

45. *The Orphan Tsunami of 1700* by Brian Atwater, et al. This is a USGS professional paper by American and Japanese scientists covering in detail the "orphan" tsunami in Japan that was not understood at the time and the West Coast evidence of the earthquake that caused it. From old records describing damage on the Japanese coast it has been estimated that the earthquake must have had a magnitude in the range of 8.7 to 9.2, comparable to the 2011 Tohoku earthquake

in Japan and the 1964 Alaska earthquake – both of similar origin. (Interesting reading for geologists and oceanographers, but somewhat technical and 134 pages long.)

46. *Mile by Mile: Your Mile by Mile Guide to Hwy 101.* https://www.oregoncoasttravel.net/276/oregon_coast/Oregon-Coast-History.htm. This remarkable website has introductory information on each of 54 towns and villages on and off Hwy 101, followed by a comprehensive list of websites for places to stay, places to eat, things to do or see, and other information in and around the town. It is far more inclusive than the AAA and other guides, but offers no quality ratings. For instance, there are 60 websites listed for the town of Florence on the central coast. The website is undated, so you will need to check details on some of the individual entries.

47. *Plants of the Pacific Northwest Coast* by Jim Pojar and Andy MacKinnon. This comprehensive 528-page reference book, written in 1994 and updated in 2014, provides detailed descriptions and illustrations of some 460 plants – from trees to wildflowers to mosses and ferns. Although it was written to cover the coast all the way from Anchorage to Florence, most of the species of the Southern Oregon coast are represented as well. The book devotes a single page to most trees, with two or three color photographs and a nice distribution map, compared to a quarter of a page in the Audubon guide with a single color photograph, and three to seven pages in *Northwest Trees*, with its excellent black and white sketches. Only 11 conifers are covered, compared to 28 in *Northwest Trees* and 23 in the Audubon guide, but to be fair each of those covers a larger territory. The print is extraordinarily small and it pays inordinate attention to Native American uses at the expense of descriptive and ecological information. You probably can't read it in the car. (Take along if you are fascinated by the local botany.)

48. *Pioneer History of Coos and Curry Counties, Oregon: Heroic Deeds and Thrilling Adventures of the Early Settlers,* compiled by Orvil Dodge. This 640-page tome was published 1898 by the Pioneer and

Historical Association of Coos County, Oregon. Its typed pages contain a wealth of historical information on the two counties that you will find nowhere else, except where Dodge's book was used as a source. Dodge was able to personally interview many of the early pioneers. Interestingly, as the work is a compilation of written and verbal accounts of many Oregon residents, what might have been a references section has been replace by a 103-page biographical appendix of the hundreds of contributors and other early residents. Many were born in the counties in the late 1800s; many others were born in other Oregon counties, other states, or even foreign countries in the early nineteenth century. The paragraph-length biographies contain some great passages, from which I quote: "In coming across the plains he was almost scalped by the Indians, but reinforcements arrived in time to save him"; "He crossed the plains in 1854, driving five yoke of cattle, when only 13 years old."; "In 1854 he went to Oregon City to buy a yoke of oxen. In coming back he had to swim the oxen across the Umpqua, and ride on one of them. When he came to Coos Bay the oxen were compelled to swim while some Indians took Mr. Nay across in a canoe." However, you have to search for these fascinating snippets of history, as most of the information is conventional biographical data. The real wealth of the book lies in the 28 text chapters focused on the towns and early events that shaped them. (The book resides in the Harvard University library but a photocopy is available online at http://www.orww.org/Coquelle_Trails/References/Dodge_1898.pdf. You can read it on your laptop at the motel, but be aware that it takes a long time to download.)

It should, however, be kept in mind that Dodge was a compiler, not a researcher. It doesn't appear that he was able to fact-check all of the narratives he recorded, especially of early events, nor did he thoroughly investigate other accounts, which might have been possible at the time but is no longer. Some of his contributors were not kind to the Native American population of the two counties, and he made no effort either to record the Native American history or to justify their response to the invasion of their lands by European Americans. It is strictly a White Man's history of the area. But we must be grateful to Orvil Dodge for what he contributed to our store of knowledge more than a century ago. (Good evening reading.)

49. *The Prehistory of the Northwest Coast* by R.G. Matson and Gary Coupland. The authors focus on the development of the native cultures in the area extending from Crescent City, California, to Yakutat Bay, Alaska, and they cover the subject thoroughly. You will find information here that is not readily available anywhere else. If you really want to dig in, they include over 300 references. Because of the historic information available, the focus tends to be on British Columbia. (This scholarly book is quite expensive: you might consider borrowing it from a library if you are researching the subject.)

50. Rivers of Oregon by Tim Palmer. The book is largely a pictorial journey of rivers across the state, from the Coast Range to the Wallowa Mountains of eastern Oregon. From the dust jacket: "In his small canoe, armed with a notebook and camera, Tim Palmer stalks riverine light, flow, and foliage the way a good predator stalks its prey." Twenty three coastal rivers and creeks are presented, all accompanied by stunningly beautiful color photographs. These are rivers that feed the estuaries and nurture their anadromous fish populations. (Read if you like rivers, especially if you are a kayaker.)

51. Roadside Geology of Oregon by Marli B. Miller. Although this is a statewide treatise, the rocks and geologic history of the Coast Range along the northern coast and the more rugged Klamath Mountains along the southern coast are discussed in some detail. (Take along if you are interested in the geological history of the coastal rock outcrops.)

52. *Shrubs to Know in Pacific Northwest Forests* by Edward C. Jensen. This thin volume devotes a full page to each of the 75 shrubs you are most likely to encounter, and includes five color photographs and a distribution map for each. Bush form, leaves, flowers, and fruit are all pictured. He tells you which fruits are OK to eat, how the indigenous peoples used them, and how each shrub fits

into the habitat as food or cover. A twenty-page introduction serves as a short course on shrubs, their function, and how they got where you find them. The book serves as a companion volume to *Trees to know in Oregon* by Jensen and co-author Charles R. Ross. Well done. (If you are interested in the botany of the coastal forests, this is a good book to take along.)

53. *Trail Guide: Central Coast Ranger District – Oregon Dunes National Recreation Area & Hebo Ranger District*, author anonymous but put together by the Siuslaw National Forest. This thin volume describes 57 hiking trails, all within Siuslaw National Forest, along the coast and in the Coast Range. Trail length, access point, and elevation gain are all given – quarter mile to 15 miles and flat to 3100 feet. Each trail is described; picnic and restroom facilities at the parking lot are noted. Nearby trails that are not within the national forest boundaries are also shown on page-size maps but not otherwise covered. Trail conditions are not addressed, but the Forest Service endeavors to keep them in good shape for all users. (Hikers should take this one along.)

54. *Trees to know in Oregon* by Edward C. Jensen and Charles R. Ross. All the trees you are likely to see along the estuaries and in the nearby forests are included in this beautifully illustrated book. Each has a map showing its distribution in the Pacific Northwest. The Oregon coastal environment does not have a large assortment of native tree species - 13 conifers and 18 broadleaf varieties are shown. (Take along.)

55. *Shore Wildflowers of California, Oregon, and Washington* by Philip A. Munz. This book covers the wildflowers and flowering shrubs found all along the Pacific coast. Each plant has a color photograph and many have useful ink sketches that illustrate various characteristics of the plant. (Take along for the identification and enjoyment of the wildflowers.)

56. Wetland Carbon Storage by David C. Bushnell. In a published letter to the editors of American Scientist, I explore the carbon storage potential of salt marshes during global warming and sea level

rise. It is but one of the advantages of preserving Oregon's estuarine salt marshes. (Not readily available.)

57. Wikipedia. It can be no secret that additional information on any of the subjects in this book can be accessed online, as I have done. Wikipedia is an excellent source. So be sure to bring your cell phone or tablet.

58. *The Year China Discovered America* by Gavin Menzies. This is a fascinating book, a controversial best seller after it was published in 2002 and 2003. It was written by a retired British naval officer documenting his claim that the Chinese discovered America and much of the rest of the world in the early fifteenth century. That the Chinese Muslim eunuch Zheng He commanded a large flotilla of junks and explored the northern shores of the Indian Ocean around this time is well documented. Menzies, using a wide variety of geographic, linguistic, botanical, and other evidence including ancient maps, extends He's voyages to include all the continents of the world including Antarctica and the west coast of the United States, particularly northern California. Historians since the publication have convincingly picked apart much of the data Menzies used for his book and consider it to be "junk history". Nevertheless, it makes for interesting reading. I take no position on the book's veracity. (Read after you return home.)

References

Adams, Michael W., et al, 2011, Chetco: The Story of the River and its People. The Chetco Valley Historical Society, Brookings, Oregon, 476p.

Alden, Peter, and Dennis Paulson, 1998, National Audubon Society Field Guide to the Pacific Northwest. Alfred A. Knopf, Inc., New York, 448p.

Amato, Frank, 2004, Oregon River Maps & fishing Guide. Frank Amato Publications, Portland, Oregon, 48p.

American Guide Series, 1940, Oregon: End of the Trail. Compiled by Workers of the Writer's Program of the Work Projects Administration in the State of Oregon, Published by the Oregon board of control, 541p. plus map inserts.

American Automobile Association, 2016, Oregon TourBook. AAA Publishing, Heathrow, Florida, 192p.

Arno, Stephen F., and Ramona P. Hammerly, 2007, Northwest Trees. The Mountaineers Books, Seattle, 246p.

Atwater, Brian F., Satoko Musumi-Rokkaku, Kenji Satake, Yoshinobu Tsuji, Kazue Ueda, and David K. Yamaguchi, 2015, The Orphan Tsunami of 1700, 2nd Edition. USGS Professional Paper 1707, 134p.

Blakey, Nancy, 2018, By the Shore. Sasquatch Books, Seattle, 233p.

Blakely, Joe R., 2006, Lifting Oregon Out of the mud – Building the Oregon Coast Highway. CraneDance Publications, 104p.

Bishop, Ellen Morris, 2003, In Search of Ancient Oregon. Timber Press, Portland, OR, 288p.

Bishop, Ellen Morris, 2004, Hiking Oregon's Geology, 2nd ed. The Mountaineer Books, Seattle, mbooks@mountaineerbooks.org, 270p.

Bushnell, David C., 2021, Wetland carbon storage. American Scientist letter to the editors with reply by Dr. Ariana Sutton-Grier, 1p.

Cohen, Fiona, 2017, Curious Kids Nature Guide: Explore the

Amazing Outdoors of the Pacific Northwest. Little Bigfoot, an imprint of Sasquatch Books, Seattle, 86p.

Dodge, Orvil, 1898. Pioneer History of Coos and Curry Counties, Oregon, compiled by Orvil Dodge. Published by the Pioneer and Historical Association of Coos County, OR, 640p. Online at: http://www.orww.org/Coquelle_Trails/References/Dodge_1898.pdf

Doughton, Sandi, 2013/2014, Full-Rip 9.0: The next big Earthquake in the Pacific Northwest. Sasquatch Books, Seattle, Sasquatch Books, 273p.

Dunegan, Lizann, 2009, Insider's Guide to the Oregon Coast, 4th ed. Insiders' Guide, Guildford, Connecticut, 222p.

Fleagle, Judy, and Richard Knox Smith, 2011, Crossings: McCullough's Coastal Bridges. Pacific Publishing, Florence, Oregon, 224p.

Fromm, James R., Early Sailing Ships Trading on the Northwest Coast of America 1788-1837. http://3rd1000.com/history3/Early%20Ships/Early%20Ships%20of%20the%20Pacific%20Northwest.htm

Gunther, Erna, 1972, Indian Life on the Northwest Coast of North America, as Seen by the Early Explorers during the Last Decades of the Eighteenth Century. University of Chicago Press, Chicago, 277p.

Henderson, Bonnie, 2015, Day Hiking Oregon Coast. The Mountaineer Books, Seattle, 287p.

Iselin, Josie, 2019, The Curious World of Seaweed. Heyday, Berkeley, California, 251p.

Jensen, Edward C., Shrubs to Know in Pacific Northwest Forests. Oregon State University Extension Service, Corvallis, Oregon, 145p.

Jensen, Edward C., and Charles R. Ross, 2005, Trees to Know in Oregon. Oregon State University Extension Service, Corvallis, Oregon, 151p.

Jewell, Judy, and W.C. McRae, 2018, Coastal Oregon, 7th ed.

Hachette Book Group, Berkeley, California, 248p.

Lang, George, 2008, Making Wawa: The Genesis of Chinook Jargon. UBC Press, Vancouver, Canada, 198p.

Lewis, David G., 2017, Massacre at the Chetko Villages, 1853. https://ndnhistoryresearch.com/2017/04/20/massacre-at-the-chetko-villages-1853/

Lewis, Paul M., 1977, Beautiful Oregon Coast. Beautiful America Publishing Company, Beaverton, Oregon, 72p.

Marshall, David B, Matthew G. Hunter, and Alan L. Contreras, Birds of Oregon, a General Reference. OSU Press, Corvallis, Oregon, 704p.

Matson, R.G., and Gary Coupland, 2009, The Prehistory of the Northwest Coast. Left Coast Press, Walnut Creek, California, 364p.

McCracken, T., and Robert B. Blodgett, 2002, Holy Rollers: Murder and Madness in Oregon's Love Cult. Caxton Press, Caldwell, Idaho, 294p.

Menzies, Gavin, 2002 and 2003, 1421, the Year China Discovered America. Transworld Publishers and HarperCollins publishers, 552p.

Miller, Marli B., 2014, Roadside Geology of Oregon, 2nd ed. Mountain Press Publishing Company, Missoula Montana, 387p.

Munz, Philip A., 2003, Introduction to Shore Wildflowers of California, Oregon, and Washington. University of California Press, Berkeley and Los Angeles, 234p.

Nordahl, Trygve O., 2000, History of Fishing on the Siuslaw. Siuslaw Pioneer Museum, Florence, Oregon, 24p.

Oberrecht, Kenn, 2008, Oregon Coastal Access Guide, 2nd ed. Oregon State University Press, Corvallis, Oregon, 342p.

Oregon Coastal Atlas. CoastalAtlas@lists.oregonstate.edu. Oregon Department of Fish and Wildlife, Research and Development Section, 1979, Natural Resources of Coos Bay Estuary, Estuary Inventory Report, Vol. 2, No. 6, 93p.

Oregon Department of Fish and Wildlife, Research and

Development Section, 1979, Natural Resources of Coquille
    Estuary, Estuary Inventory Report, Vol. 2, No. 7, 53p.
Orr, Elizabeth L. and William N., 2012, Oregon Geology, 6th ed.
    Oregon State University Press, Corvallis, Oregon, 304p.
Oregon Coast Birding Trail Website: http://www.oregoncoastbird-
    ing.com/. The website is sponsored by the National Forest
    Foundation, the U.S. Fish and Wildlife Service, and the Oregon
    Coast Visitors Association, 48p.
The Oregon Encyclopedia: Oregonencyclopedia.org. A project of the
    Oregon Historical Society, available online.
Ostertag, George and Rhonda, 2013, Camping Oregon: A
    Comprehensive guide to Public Tent and RV Campgrounds.
    Falcon guides, Guilford, CT and Helena, MT, 442p.
Palmer, Tim, 2016, Rivers of Oregon. Oregon State University Press,
    Corvallis, Oregon, 162p.
Pardee, J.T., 1934, Beach Placers of the Oregon Coast. United States
    Department of the Interior, Circular 8, 42p.
Peattie, Donald Culross, 1953, A Natural History of Western Trees.
    Crown Publishers, New York, 751p.
Pojar, Jim, and Andy MacKinnon, 2014, Plants of the Pacific
    Northwest. B.C Minister of Forests, Partners Publishing and
    Lone Pine Publishing, Auburn, Washington, 528p.
Rickets, Edward F., and Jack Calvin, 1960, Between Pacific Tides,
    3d ed., revised by Joel Hedgpeth. Stanford University Press,
    Stanford, California, 502p.
Sargent, Alice Applegate, 1921, A Sketch of the Rogue River Valley
    and Southern Oregon History. The Quarterly of the Oregon
    Historical Society, Vol. XXII, No.1, p. 1-11.
Schafer, Rick, Jack McGowan, and Jan McGowan, undated, Oregon
    Coast. Graphic Arts Center Publishing Company, Portland,
    Oregon, 96p.
Schellhase, Theodore, 2009, Lost Treasure Ships of the Oregon
    Coast. Schiffer Publishing Ltd., Atglen, PA, 176p.
Sherriff, Lucy, 2021, Climate Solutions: The scientists fighting to

save the ocean's most important carbon capture system, Washington Post evening edition, July 5, 2021.

Siuslaw National Forest, 2009, Trail Guide: Central Coast Ranger District – Oregon dunes National Recreation Area & Hebo Ranger District. Discover Your Northwest, Seattle, Washington, 59p.

Stienstra, Tom, 2018, Oregon Camping: The Complete Guide to RV and Tent Camping, 5th edition. Moonguides, a Hachette Book Group Company, New York, 423p.

Sullivan, William L., 2018, Oregon Coast & Coast Range: 100 hikes / Travel Guide. Navillus Press, Eugene, Oregon, 270 p.

Sverdrup-Thygeson, Ann, 2018, Buzz, Sting, Bite. Simon & Schuster, 300p.

Tekiela, Stan, 2001, Birds of Oregon Field Guide. Adventure Publications, Inc., Cambridge, Minnesota, 307p.

Ward Tonsfeldt, PhD, 2008, Celebrating the Siuslaw, a Century of Growth. Discover Your Northwest, Seattle, 242p.

Wardman, Ron, and Tom Baake, Oregon South Coast Canoe, Kayak, and Stand-Up Paddle Guide, 2019. Westways Press, Coos Bay, Oregon, 143p.

Westby, Mike and Kristy, 2019, Oregon Road Trips – Oregon Coast Edition. Mike and Kristy Westby, 203p.

About the Author

David Bushnell is a retired earth scientist who, after growing up on the Oregon Coast, earned degrees in geology and oceanography at nearby Oregon State University. These led to a long career as a world-wide exploration geologist, punctuated by intervals as a college instructor in oceanography, geology, and mineralogy.

ABOOKS

ALIVE Book Publishing and ALIVE Publishing Group
are imprints of Advanced Publishing LLC,
3200 A Danville Blvd., Suite 204, Alamo, California 94507

Telephone: 925.837.7303
alivebookpublishing.com

www.ingramcontent.com/pod-product-compliance
Lightning Source LLC
Chambersburg PA
CBHW020523270326
41927CB00006B/427